It may seem obvious that the Great War, with its immense cost in terms of lives lost and injuries of body and mind incurred, must have had a significant impact on the religious faith of the British people. There is much anecdotal evidence to support that perception, but how typical of the wider population of combatants and civilians were those stories? In *Faith in Conflict*, Stuart Bell examines a wide range of published and archival sources to explore how the war affected the beliefs of the churchgoers of wartime Britain, as well as the majority who rarely attended church, but who believed in God and in the afterlife. The language which they heard from the pulpits and the hymns that they sang expressed a variety of responses.

Undergirding everything was a firm belief that God was on the side of Britain – a nation divinely chosen to ensure the triumph of right over military might. *Faith in Conflict* explores how ordinary soldiers pondered how an all-powerful God could allow such carnage and shows that the well-known First World War fatalism was the least problematic response to the apparent randomness of falling shells. The language of the 'God of Battles' and 'Lord of Hosts' is analysed to show how confidence in divine support was founded on a belief that Britain was, like the Israel of the Old Testament, fighting with God's support.

Two particular features of wartime faith are identified: the first is the practice of praying for the dead, which very soon after the start of the war, became almost universal across the Church of England; the second is the idea of a suffering God, which was promoted by the famous chaplain Geoffrey Studdert Kennedy (also known as 'Woodbine Willie'). He argued that rather than a 'passionless potentate', the only understanding of God which made moral sense in the midst of the fighting was a 'comrade God' who wept and shared in his children's suffering.

Stuart Bell shows how the language of chivalry and martyrdom was used to express both the country's confidence in the righteousness of the cause and the belief that those who died in what was a Holy War were assured of eternal salvation. The memoirs of five soldiers – representative of a wide spectrum of faith – are examined; finally, he explores the reasons for the very limited influence of the war on religious practice.

Stuart Bell is an Honorary Research Fellow of St John's College, Durham University and a minister of the Methodist Church. He gained his first degree in Computer Science in the days of punched cards and paper tape, after which he lectured in that subject for seven years. Training at Fitzwilliam College and Wesley House in Cambridge for the Methodist Ministry followed, and he has since served churches in Brighton, Horsham, Southampton and Nottingham. His dissertation for his Oxford MTh examined the influence of the Great War on one group of Anglicans, while his PhD thesis (on which this book is based) looked more widely at the war's impact on the faith of ordinary people in Britain. Stuart Bell has written widely about religion during and after the Great War, and his particular interests include the theology of the famous chaplain Geoffrey Studdert Kennedy (also known as 'Woodbine Willie') and also Arthur Winnington Ingram – the wartime Bishop of London who has been maligned by many writers in the last 50 years.

FAITH IN CONFLICT

The Impact of the Great War on the Faith of the People of Britain

Stuart Bell

Helion & Company Limited

Helion & Company Limited
26 Willow Road
Solihull
West Midlands
B91 1UE
England
Tel. 0121 705 3393
Fax 0121 711 4075
Email: info@helion.co.uk
Website: www.helion.co.uk
Twitter: @helionbooks
Visit our blog http://blog.helion.co.uk/

Published by Helion & Company 2017
Designed and typeset by Mach 3 Solutions Ltd (www.mach3solutions.co.uk)
Cover designed by Paul Hewitt, Battlefield Design (www.battlefield-design.co.uk)
Printed by Lightning Source Limited, Milton Keynes, Buckinghamshire

Cover: Arthur Winnington-Ingram, Bishop of London, addresses troops in France.

ISBN 978-1-911512-67-7

British Library Cataloguing-in-Publication Data.
A catalogue record for this book is available from the British Library.

Contents

List of Illustrations

List of Abbreviations

AV	The 'Authorised Version' of the Bible (1611)
BEF	British Expeditionary Force
BL	British Library, London
BRO	Birmingham City Archives
BTF	*Baptist Times and Freeman*
BW	*British Weekly*
CWP	*Christian World Pulpit*
CUP	Cambridge University Press
DDT	*Derby Daily Telegraph*
DRO	Derbyshire Archives
DSO	Distinguished Service Order
MR	*Methodist Recorder*
NEP	*Nottingham Evening Post*
NRO	Nottinghamshire Archives
OUP	Oxford University Press
PML	*Primitive Methodist Leader*
RAMC	Royal Army Medical Corps
SAB	Author's personal archive
SDM	*Southwell Diocesan Messenger*
UM	United Methodist
VC	Victoria Cross
YMCA	Young Men's Christian Association

Glossary of Ecclesiastical and Military terms

In both the Church and the Army, there is an exception to almost every 'rule'; these notes are intended to explain concisely the terminology of both cultures for those to whom they may be unfamiliar.

Church Denominations

The **Church of England** was the state Church in England and Wales, established by law from the 16th century when Henry VIII rejected the authority of the Pope. The Welsh Church Act of 1914 disestablished the Church of England in Wales, the measure taking effect in 1920. The **Anglican Communion** is the grouping of the Anglican Churches from across the world. At the time of the Great War, the Church of England had many overseas dioceses that during the 20th century became autonomous Anglican Churches. Within the Church of England, the term **Anglo Catholic** was commonly used to describe those clergy and churches which emphasised the Catholic heritage of the Church of England. They were also called 'high-church', as opposed to 'low-church' **Evangelicals** who stressed the significance of the Protestant Reformation and who criticised many high-church practices.

The **Church of Scotland** is, in contrast to the Church of England, Presbyterian in nature (that is, each local church is governed by a group of **elders**), the Anglican Church in Scotland being the Scottish Episcopal Church.

Dissent is a term that was used to describe those who dissented from the laws and worship of the Church of England. Commonly the "old Dissent," primarily Congregationalists, Presbyterians and Baptists who formed dissenting churches in the late 16th and 17th centuries, are distinguished from the "new Dissent", comprising mainly the Methodist movements formed in the 18th and 19th centuries. Subsequently, the terms **Nonconformist** and, from the 20th century, **Free Churches** were increasingly used.

The **Methodist** movement, which became the Methodist Church, was founded by brothers John and Charles Wesley in the 18th century, the original body being termed the **Wesleyans**. Initially, their aim as ordained Anglican priests was to invigorate the Church of England, but they increasingly became alienated from that Church and operated in isolation and sometimes with strong opposition from it. In the late

18th and 19th centuries, several new Methodist movements started, either as breakaway organisations such as the **Methodist New Connexion**, often in reaction to the dominant role of ordained ministers in Wesleyanism, or as new evangelistic groups, such as the **Primitive Methodists.** By the end of the 19th century, all the movements had become Churches, each with their own structure. In 1907 the **United Methodist Church** (UMC) brought together almost all of the Methodist bodies other than the Wesleyans and Primitives. The UMC, Wesleyans and Primitives united in 1932. In the middle of the 19th century, in many areas the total strength of Nonconformist Churches matched or even exceeded that of the Church of England, especially in the industrial towns of the north and some rural counties.

The **Roman Catholic** Church is the largest Church in Western Europe. At the start of the 20th century, Catholicism was accepted in Britain, but still viewed with some suspicion and was somewhat marginalised within British society.

Church structures and Clergy titles

In the Church of England, while **Bishops** have oversight of a diocese (or, in the case of suffragan bishops, oversight of part of a diocese), **Deans** are responsible for, and have authority over, the cathedral of a diocese. They will be assisted by **Canons**, several of whom may be 'residential', sharing in the leading of worship in the Cathedral. All the priests within a diocese are under the discipline of their bishop. **Rectors, vicars** and **perpetual curates** were the Anglican priests responsible for individual parishes, the main original distinction between the titles being the amount of 'tithes' – the local tax levied on the parish – which they received, curates often receiving only a miserly salary. Tithes were abolished in 1836 and the distinction between rectors and vicars has now gone, curates now generally acting as assistants being trained by a vicar or rector in a parish. Nonconformist Churches generally use the term **ministers** to refer to their ordained leaders. In Methodism, **superintendent ministers** had oversight of a **circuit** of typically 10 to 30 churches, served by a number of ministers. Circuits were grouped in **districts** that had little authority, oversight of each Methodist denomination being primarily exercised by the annual **Conference**, under the leadership of the **President** elected for that year.

Army Units and Officers

In World War 1, the British Army comprised a number of **armies**; eventually there were five fighting on the Western Front. Each was commanded by a **General** and was generally formed from two or more **corps**, each of up to around 60,000 men, led by a **Lieutenant General.** Each corps comprised two or more **divisions**, commanded by a Major General, and each infantry Division was formed from three **brigades**, each comprising three or four **battalions**, led by **Brigadier Generals** and **Lieutenant Colonels** respectively. The Division was the smallest unit that included the full range of arms.

Each battalion of around 800-1000 men at full strength comprised four **companies**, each commanded by a **Captain**. Companies were further divided into up to four **platoons**, led by a **Lieutenant**, and then each platoon into up to four **sections** of 10-12 men, usually commanded by a **Lance Corporal**.

Regiments were composed of a number of battalions – commonly two regular and two reserve battalions at the outbreak of the war – but eventually as many as 15 to 20. Battalions were numbered within a regiment so that, for example, the first battalion of the 5th North Staffordshire regiment would be described as the '1/5th North Staffords'. Battalions from the same regiment rarely fought together; rather each would be part of a division composed of battalions from various regiments.

To take the example of Thomas Higgins, whose experiences and reaction to the war will be considered in chapter 8: He was a Lance Corporal, and so in charge of a section of 10-12 men. That section was part of 11 Platoon, within Company C of the 5th North Staffordshire Regiment. On 1 July 1916, the 1/5th North Staffords were part of the 137th Brigade, which also included the 1/6th North Staffords and the 1/5th and 1/6th South Staffords battalions. The 137th Brigade was one of 3 that with a pioneer battalion formed the 46th (North Midland) Division, and that division was one of two which formed the VII Corps, forming the Third Army under the command of Sir Edmund Allenby.

The development of the British Army

There were eventually four distinct elements to the British Army in the latter years of the conflict. First was the **pre-war army**, of which some 156,000 men formed the British Expeditionary Force (BEF) that responded to Germany's invasion of Belgium. The second army was the **Territorial Force** (TF), some quarter of a million volunteers who while keeping their regular employment had signed up for four years with a commitment to regular drills and training and an annual summer camp. Officers and men in the TF were, from early August 1914, encouraged to enlist for overseas service. While recruitment rates varied greatly, by November 1914 some TF units were ready to be deployed in France and Belgium, reinforcing a BEF experiencing high casualty rates. The size of the German army made it inevitable that far more men would be required and so 7 August 1914 saw the first of Kitchener's 'call to arms' for 100,000 men in the recruitment for the third component – his 'New Armies'. Many more hundreds of thousands would be needed and by December 1915 around 2,500,000 men had **voluntarily enlisted** in the army or TF. Finally, in an attempt to balance the needs of the Army and civilian activities such as industry and agriculture, from February 1916 **conscription** doubled the total number of those who served to well over five million – eight times the total of the British army, Territorials and Reserves before the war.

Acknowledgements

I wish to record my thanks to:

Dr John Bourne for his assistance with the glossary of military terms;
the staff of the Nottinghamshire and the Derbyshire Archives for their unfailingly helpful and cheerful service;
the Trustees of Gladstone's Library and the Editorial Board of *Midland History* for their financial support of some of the research discussed in this book;
the Methodist Church at both Connexional and District level for its significant contribution to six years of tuition fees;
my wife, Judith, for her acceptance of the role of 'PhD widow' over that long period;
my PhD supervisor, Canon Professor Michael Snape, for his inspiration, challenge and encouragement.

With the permission of the Publishers, Chapter 6 is a revised version of 'The Theology of Woodbine Willie in Context' in *British Army Chaplains in the First World War* eds. M. Snape and E. Madigan (Farnham: Ashgate, 2013), pp. 95-110, copyright © 2013.

All images in this book are taken from the author's archive.

Material from the memoirs and poems of Jack Titterton is published by the kind permission of the Titterton family.

Introduction

This book is intended to offer an answer to the question, 'How did the First World War affect the religious faith of the people of Britain?' Even if one has recognised that the 'futility and mud' characterisation of the conflict, as promoted by some of the war-poets and repeated by television's *Blackadder Goes Forth*, misrepresented the views of the British people in 1914-18, the sheer scale of human suffering must, one might well think, have had a significant deleterious influence on religious belief.[1] Certainly, my personal experience is that, a century after the conflict, many people assume that that simply must have been the case. Popular books on the First World War have sometimes supported that view. For example, Peter Fiennes' *To War With God: The Army Chaplain who Lost his Faith* had a sub-title that totally misrepresented the story of 'Monty' Guilford, perhaps because it chimed with common perceptions. It also accepted much of the traditional rhetoric about ineffective and cowardly upper-class officers and took at face value well-worn critiques of the role of the Church of England and its chaplains in the conflict.[2] More significantly, it has not been only the popular publications that have supported this 'common sense' view, but also some scholarly writing. One of the earliest academic works specifically discussing religious faith during the Great War was a chapter by Michael Snape and Stephen Parker, published in 2001.[3] After quoting a story of Private Frank Richards about an ordinand who had signed up but had later become infamous for his foul language and excessive drinking,

1 For examinations of and challenges to the mythology of futility and mud, see B. Bond, *The Unquiet Western Front: Britain's Role in Literature and History* (Cambridge: CUP, 2002); G. Corrigan, *Mud, Blood and Poppycock* (London: Cassell, 2004); D. Todman, *The Great War: Myth and Memory* (London: Cassell, 2005). Set on the Western Front in 1917, the last episode of *Blackadder*, 'Goodbyeee', first broadcast on 2 November 1989, portrayed the leading characters going 'over the top' to their deaths in no man's land.

2 P. Fiennes, *To War With God: The Army Chaplain who Lost his Faith*, (Edinburgh: Mainstream Publishing, 2011).

3 M.F. Snape and S.G. Parker, 'Keeping faith and coping: belief, popular religiosity and the British people' in P. Liddle and J. Bourne (eds), *The Great World War, 1914–45: Volume 2* (London: Collins, 2001), pp. 397–420.

they commented, 'such deterioration of faith was no doubt widespread.'[4] Was that the case? Was there a widespread loss of faith during the First World War?

Undoubtedly, some people, especially soldiers exposed to the horrors of warfare, lost their faith and a few individual diaries state as much. On the last page of his narrative of the first day of the Battle of the Somme, Martin Middlebrook quoted Private C. Bartram: 'From that moment all my religion died. All my teaching and beliefs in God had left me, never to return.'[5] Ernest Raymond served as a chaplain during the conflict, returning to Brighton as a curate when demobilized. In the succeeding years he began to examine his own faith, concluding that 'while not *firmly* doubting the dogmas and miracles, I could not longer say in the words of Newman's hymn, "Firmly I believe and truly."'[6] We should note that Raymond offered no specific reason for his loss of faith. Sometimes, changes in a soldier's religious practice may be taken to indicate of a change of belief. For example, Sapper Jack Martin was the son of a Methodist minister and had played the harmonium for his father's services.[7] After the war, his own son said that his father described himself as a Nonconformist, but not 'aligned to any church in particular.' He respected Armistice Day, but 'did not go to church then.'[8] Another Great War chaplain, Kenneth Best, left parish duties in 1920, being a housemaster at Cheltenham College for 20 years before becoming a chaplain again in the Second World War.[9] His biographer described him as becoming an agnostic in later years, although, as so often, the reasons for his loss of faith are not clear. However, ordinary soldiers and civilians, the vast majority of whom, as we shall see, rarely commented on their own beliefs, were highly unlikely to record explicitly any loss of faith. We search in vain for dramatic expressions of lost faith, although the Derbyshire soldier-poet Jack Titterton, whose poem which used a ruined church as a metaphor for a ruined faith and which we shall consider in chapter 8, was more explicit than most of his comrades. Others became disillusioned by organized religion, while still clinging on to faith. In his memoirs written in the 1970s, Ronald Skirth, who had served as a Corporal in the Royal Field Artillery, recounted being demoted to the rank of Bombadier for objecting to a gun being aimed at a church.[10] Later, he wrote in his chapter entitled 'The Road to Disillusion',

4 Ibid., p. 408.
5 M. Middlebrook, *The First Day on the Somme, 1 July 1916* (London: Penguin Books, 1984), p. 316.
6 E. Raymond, *The Story of My Days: An Autobiography 1888–1922* (London: Cassell, 1968), p. 170. The hymn-writer referred to is John Henry Newman, an Anglican cleric and one of the leaders of the Anglo-Catholic Oxford Movement before being received into the Roman Catholic Church in 1845.
7 R. Van Emden (ed.) *Sapper Martin: The Secret Great War Diary of Jack Martin* (London: Bloomsbury, 2009), p. 3.
8 Ibid., pp. 3 and 7.
9 K. Best and G. Roynon (eds.), *A Chaplain at Gallipoli: The Great War Diaries of Kenneth Best* (London: Simon & Schuster, 2011), pp. 12f.
10 R. Skirth and D. Barrett (ed.), *The Reluctant Tommy* (London: Pan Books, 2010), pp. 58f.

> At nineteen I found my standards of conduct obsolete, my ideals shattered. I had lost all faith in institutional religion. My Church had authorized me to break the sixth commandment in the name of patriotism. 'Blessed are the Peacemakers'? Not in 1917. Blessed are the War Winners. … I still believed in God, though I was assailed by doubts. I prayed daily. … If he loved us, if He were omnipotent He could put a stop to it to-day. But then, I thought, perhaps he isn't omnipotent. Eventually I worked it out, – at least for myself. God was all right. … the reason for all this was the wickedness in ourselves and not the indifference of God.[11]

Subsequently, believing that he had been spared by God, Skirth decided that, whilst still obeying orders, he would do all he could to avoid taking another human life, writing to that effect in a letter which he knew would be read by the officers of his unit. However, engagements with significant theological issues such as divine omnipotence were few and far between. Far more often, matters of belief were never mentioned and so any assessment of the scale of the loss of faith remains challenging.

It will become clear in this book that religious belief should not be equated with church-going. Far more people had a simple faith in the existence of God and in life after death than ever attended Church, other than for rites of passage and, perhaps, at Christmas or Easter. However, a quantitative analysis of wartime religious practice is obviously relevant. Clive Field specifically addressed two measures, church attendance and church membership or adherence during the conflict.[12] He reckoned that at least one million regular church-goers enlisted, together with a similar number of occasional worshippers and adherents.[13] Many social factors disrupted church attendance and the widely-reported modest increases in attendance in the opening months of the war were soon reversed. Across the Protestant denominations, there was a general decline in church-going, continuing pre-war trends, although it is impossible to be certain about either the scale of the decline or the significance of loss of faith as a cause. Church membership, however, was carefully recorded. Even so, comparing figures is made difficult by the differing definitions of 'membership' across the denominations. Field showed that membership in the Church of England and the larger and older Free Churches declined during the war, but revived briefly in the 1920s. However, the Nonconformist denominations lost around a million Sunday school scholars and very many adherents. A generation previously, Currie, Gilbert and Horsley had come to similar conclusions about church membership, detailing falls for both Nonconformists and Episcopalians from 1914 and 1915 respectively.[14] These

11 Ibid., pp. 82f.

12 C. Field, 'Keeping the Spiritual Home Fires Burning: Religious Belonging in Britain during the First World War' in *War and Society*, Vol. 33, No. 4 (October 2014), pp. 244-68.

13 Ibid., p. 248.

14 R. Currie, A. Gilbert and L. Horsley, *Churches and Church-goers: Patterns of Church Growth in the British Isles since 1700* (Oxford: OUP, 1977), p. 31. Figures for Scottish Presbyterians show no wartime decline.

trends were slowly reversed after the end of the conflict, membership for both groups reaching pre-war levels by 1925.[15] As Field put it, 'the war was, if anything, a setback for organized irreligion as much as for organized religion', by which he meant that the conflict had a greater impact on those on the 'fringes' of church life or those who believed but rarely attended worship than on the core membership.[16] He concluded that, 'the disruption caused by the war to the everyday life of organized religion probably accounts for the decrease, rather more than loss of faith.'[17] Adrian Gregory, who rightly pointed out that 'religion was far more important to individuals in wartime Britain than is generally believed', noted that the proportion of new-born infants who were baptised reached an historic peak in the 1920s, 'and while this was probably more indicative of respectability, sociability and "folk religion" than deep religious commitment, it is nevertheless hard to reconcile with a deep disgust at orthodoxy on the part of the population at large.'[18]

Certainly, such statistical analyses call into question suggestions of a 'widespread' loss of faith during the First World War. That provisional conclusion leads to a series of supplementary questions which the research discussed here sought to address: Why did the immense human cost of the war not, apparently, have a significant impact on the numbers of British people who were Church members and worshipped regularly? What effect did the conflict have on their faith? In particular, what were their responses to the classical question of theodicy – why an all-powerful God of love permits evil – and how did they reconcile their faith with the unprecedented events of 1914-18?

Most importantly, the aim in writing this book was to focus on the ordinary people of Britain. Many of the most widely-read and widely-quoted works on religion and the First World War have been primarily concerned with the church leaders and their actions and utterances. A handful of clerics predominate.[19] But, given the gender imbalance of typical congregations, what did the proverbial 'woman in the pew' think? What was her minister saying to her from the pulpit? Which hymns was she singing? How was the content of worship affected by the conflict? How was the religious faith of that majority of British people who did believe in God but rarely attended church affected by the First World War? These are the questions that this book seeks to address.

The volume of material on the war and people's religious practice and belief is immense. Every county archive will contain relevant sources; the volume of books published during the conflict was legendary, and, given the significant place of religion in Britain a century ago, it is unsurprising that newspapers, national and local,

15 Ibid.
16 Field, 'Keeping the Spiritual Home Fires Burning', p. 267.
17 Ibid., p. 244.
18 A. Gregory, *The Last Great War: British Society and the First World War* (Cambridge: CUP, 2008), pp. 183f.
19 e.g. the Archbishops of Canterbury and York, the Bishops of London and Oxford, the Dean of Durham (Hensley Henson) and academics such as Henry Scott Holland.

offer a vast range of relevant news and comment. Consequently, the first chapter discusses the boundaries defining this study and then considers some key characteristics of British society's engagement with matters of faith in the broadest sense during the conflict.

The tone of the responses of the Churches and their leaders throughout the conflict was set in the first few weeks of the war. In chapter 2, those responses are discussed and, in particular, compared with pre-war attitudes. The language of a 'Holy War' is shown to have been employed from the first Sunday of the war, and Britain's self-perception as the 'new Israel' and a nation particularly favoured by God is explored. This leads into a discussion, in chapter 3, of the use of two titles for God, 'God of battles' and 'Lord of Hosts', which were increasingly employed to affirm the spiritual nature of a military conflict in which God was on Britain's side. Popular responses to the two theological issues which the losses caused by the Great War must clearly have raised, those of divine omnipotence and divine providence, are then considered in chapter 4 and the wide variety of attempted solutions to the problems are described. Those losses soon led to an emphasis across British society on the concept of redemptive sacrifice, which became a dominant trope in the conflict. Similarly, in a very short time, prayers for the dead became widely accepted. Those themes, together with that of the memorialisation of the war, are examined in chapter 5.

While the standard responses to questions of omnipotence and providence sufficed for many, and assurances that the eternal destiny of those who had fallen in the conflict were assured to some extent mitigated the suffering of the bereaved, for one chaplain, Geoffrey Studdert Kennedy, they were quite inadequate. For him, only a God who himself shared in and was affected by human suffering was worthy of devotion and worship. In chapter 6, his advocacy of a passible God, arguably the most significant theological development to emerge from the Great War, is discussed. Although the ecumenical co-operation which characterised the massive wartime expansion in armed forces chaplaincy provision raised practical and ecclesiological issues, many saw in that experience a model for better relationships between in the Churches – and even reason to work towards the union or reunion of different denominations – in post-war Britain. In chapter 7, the extent of and limits to ecumenical activity both in the theatres of war and on the home front are discussed. Consideration is then given to post-war developments and, in particular, to the Lambeth conference of Anglican bishops in 1920, a meeting that engendered much optimism but which, it will be argued, had little lasting impact on the British churches.

Finally, the nature of the 'diffusive Christianity' that was characteristic of the majority of both civilians and combatants in the Great War is considered by examining the diaries or letters of five soldiers. While two were quite explicit about the nature of their faith, that of the remaining three, beyond belief in the existence of God and in life after death, was far from clear. However, in their unarticulated and unsophisticated faith they were far more representative of the British people of the time than were either the minority who were committed church-goers or the far smaller number who had rejected Christian belief entirely.

1

Setting the Scene

The volume of source material regarding the First World War is immense. In addition to the usual primary sources of newspapers and periodicals, diaries and letters, the conflict elicited a huge increase in the publication of books engaging with the issues raised by the war, a phenomenon which has been repeated in recent times as the centenary has been commemorated. Moreover, the war affected every community and every aspect of society, thus increasing further the range of relevant sources. To make manageable the research task, various boundaries, both ecclesiastical and geographical, have been set, which will be considered in this chapter. This is followed by a discussion of the various sources used in the research, with a particular focus on the strengths and weaknesses of the very different types of material published over the last hundred years. While the volume of extant material relevant to the cultural, social and religious history of the conflict is indeed great, the soldiers and civilians of the First World War seem to have been reluctant to engage with the issue of how it might have affected their faith, or, indeed, that of others. In many cases, it appears that people avoided engaging with that question. This phenomenon, which had an impact on every area of research, will be considered. Finally, two key elements of wartime faith, first the diffusive Christianity which was practised by the majority of the British population and second the ubiquity of hymnody across British society, both of which are highly significant for this study, will be discussed.

Boundaries

Necessarily, some boundaries have been set and some issues left un-explored. First, the focus is almost entirely on the Protestant Churches of Britain.[1] In the early years of the 20th century, British Catholicism functioned largely in isolation from the other denominations. As we shall see, ecumenical activity very rarely included the Roman

1 The exception is the inclusion of the views and experiences of a few Roman Catholic officers, soldiers and chaplains, some of whom were Irish rather than British.

Catholic Church and at a local level that Church generally had a low profile, being far less likely to have its services, activities or pronouncements reported in the press. Furthermore, the supra-national nature of the Church meant that its engagement with issues of faith, theology and international relations raised by the conflict was of a different nature from that of the autonomous British denominations.[2]

Second, no attempt has been made to consider two specific aspects of religious practice during the war. The rise of Spiritualism, which is well-covered in the literature, largely took place outside the Churches and although some church-goers became involved in Spiritualist activities, there is no evidence of a significant influence on the mainstream denominations, other than in the assimilation of elements of the language of spiritualism.[3] Similarly, the development of conscientious objection in response to the introduction of conscription in 1916 has been well-documented.[4] Indeed, it is arguable that in recent times, because the attitudes of the conscientious objectors to war are far more palatable to many contemporary Christians than are those of the men of the Churches who volunteered for military service in 1914-16, conscientious objection has received a disproportionate amount of attention. Such a focus can obscure the reality that a clear majority of people in all the main denominations fully supported Britain's engagement in the war in 1914, the exceptions being the Churches of Christ and the Society of Friends (Quakers). Even then, a third of Quaker men of military age voluntarily enlisted for combatant service.[5] Therefore, while conscientious objection will be encountered in the broader narrative of this study, no attempt has been made to consider it in detail.

A Local Focus

Despite the increasing digitisation of source material, exemplified by the British Newspaper Archive, it was clearly impracticable to contemplate a nationwide

2 Albert Marrin summarized the formal responses to the conflict of the Roman Catholic Church and British reaction to its neutral stance in his *The Last Crusade: The Church of England in the First World War* (Durham, NC: Duke University Press, 1974), pp. 223-5. Notably, Cardinal Bourne, Archbishop of Westminster, visited the British Fleet at Scapa Flow in August 1916 – see T. Johnstone and J. Hagerty, *The Cross on the Sword: Catholic Chaplains in The Forces* (London: Geoffrey Chapman, 1996), pp. 65f.

3 See G. Byrne, *Modern Spiritualism and the Church of England, 1850–1939* (Woodbridge: Boydell Press, 2010). See also J. Hazelgrove, 'Spiritualism after the Great War' in *Twentieth Century British History*, Vol. 10, No. 4 (London, 1999), pp. 404-430, which also summarises wartime Spiritualism. However, note the questioning of Hazelgrove's endorsement of Jay Winter's claims about the prevalence of Spiritualism among soldiers in M. Snape, *God and the British Soldier: Religion and the British Army in the First and Second World Wars* (Oxford: Routledge, 2005), pp. 38f.

4 See, for example, J. Rae, *Conscience and Politics: the British government and the conscientious objector to military service, 1916-1919* (London: OUP, 1970).

5 T. Kennedy, *British Quakerism, 1860–1920* (London: OUP, 2001), p. 313.

examination of the influence of the conflict on people's faith, given that very little of the content of local county archives are accessible other than through exhaustive personal searches.[6] Therefore, at the heart of this study are the results of such a search of the county archives of Derbyshire and Nottinghamshire, an area which at that time was co-terminus with the Anglican Diocese of Southwell, for all material pertaining to the activities of the Churches and peoples' expression of faith and religious practice during the First World War.[7] In virtually every part of England, material relating to the Church of England will dominate the records of church worship, activities and concerns in local archives.[8] Consequently, the nature of the diocese being studied has a significant impact on any conclusions that may be drawn and the great merit of the Diocese of Southwell for a study such as this is its sheer ordinariness. Not only geographically but also theologically it was 'middle England', being dominated by neither Anglo-Catholicism nor staunch evangelicalism. While by 1929, the English Church Union could claim that 18 churches in the Nottingham area were celebrating the Diamond Jubilee of that organisation with special Masses, Michael Austin, *the* historian of the Diocese, concluded that within the area, ritualism was not divisive and the high church clergy were co-operative.[9] The evidence of this study confirms that analysis. In his survey of the pre-war Diocese, Austin identified as local concerns many of the issues, social, political and ecclesial, which are familiar to historians of the period.[10] Furthermore, in its Bishop, Edwyn Hoskyns, the Diocese had a leader who did not play a major role in the Church controversies of the day and who did not try to exert strong theological influence over his own priests or parishes. The Southwell Diocese encompassed one large city, one large town and the rapidly-growing Derbyshire and Nottinghamshire coalfields. It included hundreds of rural villages from the Derbyshire Peak District, in places less than 20 miles from Manchester, to the broad expanse of the lower Trent valley in which the Diocese's minster at Southwell was located. Having been formed in 1884 by amalgamating the archdeaconry of Nottingham in the Lincoln Diocese with that of Derby in the Lichfield Diocese, it was itself divided in 1927 by the creation of the Diocese of Derby. By 1914, there were four archdeaconries within the Diocese, with a population

6 Albert Marrin concluded that a diocese-by-diocese or parish-by-parish analysis of attitudes over the country would be 'neither possible nor, perhaps, desirable in a single lifetime.' Marrin, *The Last Crusade*, p. x.

7 The relevant county archives include also those for the cities of Nottingham and Derby and their respective Anglican dioceses.

8 The cause of this is not only the relative sizes of the denominations, but also the publication of parish magazines and printed orders of service, which was far less common in Nonconformity.

9 M. Austin, *Under the Heavy Clouds: The Church of England in Derbyshire and Nottinghamshire 1911-15* (Whitchurch: Merton Priory Press, 2004), p. 40.

10 Ibid., pp. 9-69.

approaching 1.5 million, around five per cent of the total for England.[11] Southwell's ordinariness and lack of controversialists distinguished it from longer-established and more influential dioceses such as London, Oxford or Winchester. It can, therefore, reasonably be claimed that it was representative of Church of England life during the First World War. To test that assertion and to provide a comparison with the wartime experiences of the churches of Nottinghamshire and Derbyshire, a thorough examination was made of the material in the Birmingham city archives relating to the churches in that area. While more limited in geographical scope, the study was sufficient to identify the effect of the local concentration of Anglo-Catholic parishes in that city which, as will be seen, influenced both ecumenical activity and the language of sacrifice. Apart from those two matters, there was little to differentiate the wartime responses of the two dioceses.

Primary Sources: handle with care!

Two volumes published during the war or its immediate aftermath have been seminal in previous enquiries and have also contributed to this study: *The Church in the Furnace* was edited by Frederick MacNutt and published in 1917, its aim being to make available the writing of Army chaplains on their experiences of the war and the issues which, for them, it raised. It illustrated clearly the wide variety of responses that the conflict elicited. For Llewellyn Gwynne, Chaplain General, it was an opportunity to repeat, even in September 1917, the high rhetoric and purple prose that expressed the hope that victory might bring closer the Kingdom of God:

> our Chaplains, who are part and parcel of this fighting machine, and, according to the highest military authorities, a real asset to our fighting forces, have studied the stages of development and the inner working of this engine of war. This knowledge has given them dreams and visions of a great spiritual fighting machine, which, if realised, may overcome the spiritual foes of humanity – and allow the Kingdom of God to operate on the earth.[12]

MacNutt himself, considering *The Moral Equivalent of War*, was more willing to describe the reality of the war, of men 'almost invisible in the white bandages which swathe their tortured bodies'.[13] Yet he could still write of 'the pure romance of a high purpose, shot through and through with the glory of devotion, not less real because

11 *The Southwell Diocesan Calendar, Clergy List and General Almanac, 1914* (Nottingham: Southwell Diocese, 1914).

12 L. Gwynne, Preface in F. MacNutt (ed.), *The Church in the Furnace*, (London: Macmillan, 1917), p. xx.

13 F. MacNutt, 'The Moral Equivalent of War' in MacNutt (ed.), *Church in the Furnace*, pp. 10f.

almost subconscious and unable to express itself except in deeds.'[14] The contrast with F.R. Barry's view was stark: 'Every speck of glamour or romance has disappeared from warfare long ago; it is just an orgy of monotony.'[15] In his contribution to *The Church in the Furnace* on the faith of the soldiers to whom he ministered, Geoffrey Studdert Kennedy was, like Barry, brutally honest. He quoted an Anglo-Catholic friend's observation, 'In reality the private soldier does not think. He is either simply and splendidly religious or else purely indifferent.'[16] Studdert Kennedy then went on to qualify that view a little: 'It is not accurate to say that he does not think at all. His thought is there, but it is subconscious and chaotic.'[17] Much of that thought will be examined in subsequent chapters, as will Studdert Kennedy's advocacy of a suffering God that first appeared in that volume. Alongside those significant chapters in *Church in the Furnace* were many others that illustrated some chaplains' inability to engage with anything beyond ecclesiastical minutiae. For example, F.W. Worsley assured the reader that, 'The Church has made excellent provision for the treatment of the whole Faith in her selection of Epistles and Gospels for the Sundays,' and observed that, 'It is unfortunate that our Office alone omits the Epiclesis.'[18] When the *Expository Times* informally reviewed *The Church in the Furnace* at some length, it ignored everything but the calls for Prayer Book reform, supporting the chaplains' case.[19] Taken as a whole, the book expressed the shock of the contributing chaplains about the disconnectedness of the Church of England from working-class men, most of whom had had little contact with the Church and little understanding of the Christian faith. That chasm was not new, but had widened throughout the years of the Industrial Revolution. It was the encounter of clergy acting as temporary chaplains with such men that made them recognise the reality of the situation.[20]

Published two years later, *The Army and Religion* report, described as 'An Enquiry and its Bearing upon the Religious Life of the Nation', reported on nearly 300 responses, 'resting on the evidence of many hundred witnesses', to a questionnaire about the state of religion in the army.[21] It was funded entirely by the Y.M.C.A. and edited by the Scottish theologian and Presbyterian minister D.S. Cairns under the guidance of a committee representing a wide range of Protestant denominations and churchmanship. Clearly, the relatively limited scale of the size of the sample, the process by

14 Ibid., p. 18.
15 F.R. Barry, 'Faith in the Light of War' in MacNutt (ed.), *Church in the Furnace*, p. 36.
16 G.A. Studdert Kennedy, 'The Religious Difficulties of a Private Soldier' in MacNutt (ed.), *Church in the Furnace*, p. 375.
17 Ibid., p. 377.
18 F.W. Worsley, 'Beliefs Emphasised by the War' in MacNutt (ed.), *Church in the Furnace*, pp. 74 and 86.
19 'Notes of Recent Exposition', *The Expository Times*, 1918, issue 29, pp. 245-8.
20 For simplicity, throughout this study the term 'clergy' is used, unless indicated otherwise, to refer to ordained ministers of all the Christian denominations.
21 D.S. Cairns (ed.), *The Army and Religion* (London: Macmillan, 1919), p. vi.

which responses were transmitted to the committee, primarily through chaplains and Y.M.C.A. workers, and the recognition of the committee's role in 'shaping' the report all mitigated against it being a quantitative assessment of the faith or religious practice of the wartime army.[22] Moreover, Cairns used the report to advance his own agenda for the post-war Church. As Michael Snape has argued, 'the nub of the report was a manifesto for far-reaching change in the post-war church, a manifesto that included the reinterpretation of Christian doctrine, the "Christianizing" of the social order, the democratization of church government and an emphatic commitment to the cause of international peace.'[23] Nevertheless, the reports of individual soldiers' attitudes to faith and religion offer a narrative to be set alongside other sources.

Inevitably, all such sources mediated through interested third parties were vulnerable to editorial scrutiny and amendment. For example, when clergy reported in their parish magazines on letters received from the 'boys' of the parish at the Front, they were predisposed to strike a positive note, omitting any bad news – if, indeed, the correspondent had not done so already. Similarly, the inserts widely published in parish magazines, such as *The Sign*, *The Kingdom*, *The Church Leader* and *The Church Standard* were almost invariably positive and patriotic in tone, reporting enthusiastically on the commitment of men of the Church to the war effort and the work of chaplains.[24] Most chaplains' accounts of their work focussed on the success of what they were doing, the Anglo-Catholics affirming the willingness of the men to receive Holy Communion and the evangelicals enumerating the number of 'decisions' made by soldiers.[25] As we shall see, across the breadth of contemporary sources, hagiography of 'Tommy' was widespread and the self-evident disconnection of the fighting men from the Church was the cause of concern about the past failure of the Church to engage with the working classes. Church newspapers rarely considered issues of faith that the war might have been thought to raise. Rather, reflecting the constituencies that they served, even those publications that had urged greater efforts to avoid hostilities prior to 4 August 1914 soon became supportive of Britain's engagement in the conflict. Only a few individuals challenged such support, bringing accusations upon themselves of being unpatriotic. Denominational magazines such as the *Wesleyan Methodist Magazine* and the *Aldersgate Magazine* occasionally carried more reflective articles, offering theological perspectives on relevant issues. However, such material was almost invariably written by well-known denominational figures. National newspapers reported the pronouncements of national figures of Church and State, not least on those many occasions when the various parties in the Church of England engaged

22 Ibid., p. vii.

23 M.F. Snape (ed.), *The Back Parts of War: The YMCA Memoirs and Letters of Barclay Baron, 1915-1919* (Woodbridge: Boydell Press, 2009), pp. 87-9.

24 Examples at NRO, PR 16,795/7; NRO, PR 29,042; NRO, PR 8847/12; NRO, PR 9147/2.

25 For example, see 'Letter from Fr. Fitzgerald' in *C.R. The Chronicle of the Community of the Resurrection*, no. 49 (Lady Day 1915), pp. 19f.

in acrimonious public debate. Such utterances provide a context for the attempt of this study to examine the influence of the war on the faith of those who would never have their letters published in *The Times*. A far more productive source has been the local and regional newspapers of the period. Here are to be found reports of local events, personal accounts from soldiers at the Front and the opinions of individuals on various relevant issues. During the course of the research reflected in this study, the British Newspaper Archive increased its coverage to around 100 newspapers published during the period of the conflict.[26] While this represents only a minority of titles, the number is sufficiently large to give confidence that they are reasonably representative of the local and regional press of the time. Unexpectedly, the archive shows how widely local news stories were propagated across Britain – whether as part of a syndication system or as the consequence of crude plagiarism is not clear.

Both nationally and locally, published sermons offer one answer to the question about what congregations were hearing from the pulpit. While in the vast majority of cases we cannot ascertain how the sermons were received, there is little evidence that hearers were not in agreement with what they were told about, for example, the moral validity of Britain's engagement in the conflict. Since the aim of the research was to ascertain how the First World War affected people's faith, it was clear that a key source would be personal diaries, letters and memoirs. In addition to the diary of Thomas Pickbourne and the memoirs of the Jack Titterton, found in the Nottinghamshire and Derbyshire archives respectively, a search was made of over one hundred of the published diaries, memoirs and collections of letters from the period. Each of those genres has its strengths and weaknesses. It must be recognized that letters sent home from the Front, in addition to having to pass the censor's eye, were also widely self-censored so as to spare the family in England from the horrors of warfare.[27] Memoirs are always subject to the influence of the failings of human memory, the temptation to tell people what they want to hear and the vulnerability of witnesses to the confusion of their views at the time with their reflections many years later. The attitudes to the conflict of the 1960s and 1970s that, as we have noted, influenced the scholarship of that period, could not but have affected how some former soldiers recalled their experiences. Similarly, some of the publications representative of the ambivalent attitudes towards the conflict of the late 1920s and 1930s, the very time when many of the war poets' works were so eagerly received, must be treated with caution. Consequently, every attempt has been made to base the research primarily on contemporaneous diaries and, with a measure of caution, letters. Similarly, publications in the years 1914-19 have been taken as far more reliable indicators of wartime attitudes than later work.

26 www.britishnewspaperarchive.co.uk

27 Officers were often permitted to self-censor their own letters. The primary concern was references to geographical locations or the movement or military successes of particular units.

Silent Witnesses

Just occasionally, one encounters a combatant diarist or letter-writer who was able and willing to reflect how his experiences affected his faith. One of them was Lt. Col. E.W. Hermon, a veteran of the South African War who had been educated at Eton and Christ Church, Oxford. In two years he wrote 600 letters to his wife and on 19 October 1915, while serving on the Front Line around four miles south of Bethune, he reflected on his gruelling experiences and his faith:

> Well, I got back at 3 a.m. this morning alright after a very unpleasant night. Clearing a battlefield is not an amusement I can recommend except that it has the effect of making one perfectly callous to everything connected with life and death. I cannot believe that this is the end of life. After what I saw last night I am convinced that the soul of man must be so to speak 'detachable'. It is impossible that if there is a Divine will ruling all life, I cannot believe that that is the finish. The soul must leave the body and go elsewhere. I saw it last night as clearly as if it were written in capital letters. I buried 41 poor fellows including a subaltern officer. … I don't know how to express what I said earlier on except that I am convinced beyond shadow of doubt that there is a future life. Not that I ever doubted it for a moment, but it has been one of those things that without actually knowing one has believed in but I somehow feel now that it's a snip.[28]

However, Hermon was decidedly atypical of his fellow officers. Despite the intention of this study to focus primarily on diaries and letters written by 'ordinary' people during the conflict, a major issue soon became apparent; the silence on matters of faith of most witnesses of the Great War. To some extent, this phenomenon can be seen as a particular manifestation of that unwillingness of soldiers to share their experiences of fighting with those 'at home'. A further factor was the traditional reluctance of the British to talk about matters of faith at all. As his recent biographer has written of Donald Hankey, the soldier best known for his two volumes of essays about his wartime experiences, *A Student in Arms*, 'Religion was not even discussed at home. It was something you did rather than talked about.'[29] As for the practice of religion, because for so many people it was unremarkable, it was literally not remarked upon. For example, it was not until almost the conclusion of Georgina Lee's wartime diaries that she wrote in January 1919, addressing her young son, Harry, 'Your little extempore prayer every night is so sweet.'[30] Clearly

28 A. Nason (ed.), *For Love and Courage: The Letters of Lieutenant Colonel E.W. Hermon from the Western Front 1914–1917* (London: Preface Publishing, 2009), pp. 117f.

29 D. Hankey, *A Student in Arms* (London: Melrose, 1916); D. Hankey, *A Student in Arms Second Series* (London: Melrose, 1917); R. Davies, *'A Student in Arms': Donald Hankey and Edwardian Society at War* (Farnham: Ashgate, 2013), p. 20.

30 G. Roynon (ed.), *Home Fires Burning: The Great War Diaries of Georgina Lee* (Stroud: The History Press, 2006), p. 288.

for the previous four years such daily bedtime prayers had not been thought worthy of mention. The inability of ordinary lay people with a limited education to engage with any implications that the war might be thought to have for their Christian faith is hardly surprising and the majority made no attempt at all. In her diary, a Derbyshire farmer's wife and church treasurer, Maria Gyte, recorded in September 1914: 'Mr. Sherlock called and had tea and we had a long conversation about his sermon last Sunday. I told him he had spoken rather strongly about the young men of Sheldon not being patriotic.'[31] However, that was the only time that she attempted to engage with any ethical or religious matters in her extensive diary. Thomas Livingstone, a Glaswegian shipping clerk, kept a detailed diary throughout the conflict. He was clearly a regular if not frequent church-goer and recorded visits from church members and the change of ministers: 'A female representative from the Kirk up tonight. We have a new minister. How nice.'[32] Of any relationship between his faith and the war, not a word was written.

The approach of Captain Thomas Nash, who served with the 16th Battalion of the Manchester Regiment, was to append to his purely narrative diary an element of philosophical or religious comment by prefacing every chapter with an appropriate verse.[33] Thus, for example, the account of his departure from England was preceded by this verse:

> A piquet frozen on duty,
> A mother starved for her brood,
> Socrates drinking the hemlock,
> And Jesus on the rood;
> And thousands of other who nameless,
> The path of duty trod –
> Some call it consecration,
> And others call it God.[34]

Chapter 9 of Nash's diary recounted his experiences in the trenches near Verdun in early 1916. It was headed by four short verses, ending,

> He fell: The rest marched on to victory;
> The hard fought day was won –
> Ah God, my little son:

31 G. Phizackerley (ed.), *The Diaries of Maria Gyte of Sheldon, Derbyshire 1913-1920* (Cromford: Scarthin Books, 1999), p. 30.
32 T.C. Livingstone and R. Scott (ed.), *Tommy's War: A First World War Diary 1913-18* (London: Harper, 2008), p. 256.
33 T.A.M. Nash (ed.), *The Diary of an Unprofessional Soldier* (Chippenham: Picton, 1992).
34 Ibid. p. 7. The verse is the fourth of *Each In His Own Tongue* by William Herbert Carruth (1859-1924), first published in 1914.

He is not dead, my son: There is no death.
His strong and tireless soul
Marches to some great goal.[35]

The chapter concluded with these verses:

Requiescant
The anguish and the pain have passed,
And peace has come to them at last;
But in their stern looks linger still
The iron purpose and the will.

Dear Christ, who reigns't above the flood
Of human tears and human blood,
A weary road these men have trod;
O house them in the house of God.[36]

The editor indicated that the author had commenced the transcription of his diary in the Autumn of 1917. It would appear that all the verses which Nash added to his narrative had been published by the summer of 1918, the last one probably being Siegfried Sassoon's *Trench Duty*.[37] *The Diary of an Unprofessional Soldier* thus presents one officer's attempt to offer a philosophical and religious reflection on his wartime experiences, quite distinct from his transcribed narrative. His use of others' verses enabled Nash to do so without explicitly stating his own views about his experience of war, thus maintaining something of the conventional diarists' objectivity.

A more surprising 'silent witness' was, perhaps, the Revd. Andrew Clark, vicar of Great Leighs in Essex throughout the conflict. Between August 1914 and December 1919, Clark wrote a detailed diary of life in the village. In total, it ran to around three million words. However, neither in the published edited edition nor in a wide sampling of the original manuscripts is there to be found anything that might be termed 'theological reflection' on the war.[38] As his editor pointed out, Clark did not even mention at the time the death of his wife, so determined was he to produce a dispassionate account of

35 Ibid. p. 59. The verse is part of an apparently anonymous poem published in the *Windsor Magazine*, Vol. 42, 1915, p. 465.
36 Ibid. p. 69. The verses are from a poem by F.G. Scott, published in G.H. Clarke (ed.) *A Treasury of War Poetry* (Boston: Houghton & Muffin, 1917).
37 *Trench Duty* was first published in *Counter Attack and Other Poems* (London: Heinemann, 1918). Despite thorough searching, it has not proved possible to identify two of the poetic extracts which Nash used.
38 J. Munson (ed.), *Echoes of the Great War: The Diary of the Reverend Andrew Clark 1914–1919* (Oxford: OUP, 1985); Mss. diary: Bodleian, MSS. Eng. hist. e. 88-177c.

the course of the war and its impact on Great Leighs.[39] He did record a recruiting sermon preached by another clergyman, a recruiting speech invoking God, a Congregational minister's view of the war and an elderly woman's 'theological difficulty' about why God did not strike down the German airmen who flew so very near heaven. However, of any theological difficulties that he himself might have had, there is no record.[40] Andrew Clark was far from alone in his disinclination to engage with the ethics of the conflict or any challenge to faith that it might be thought to pose. To take but one example, while P.B. ('Tubby') Clayton's popular *Tales of Talbot House* is full of moving and sometimes dramatic stories of the 'Everyman's Club' for soldiers set up behind the lines in Poperinghe, Belgium, there is not a trace of any reflection about the war.[41] One cause of clerical non-engagement with the influence of the conflict on faith and theology may well have been that many were ill-equipped to attempt such a task. Bishops would habitually ordain Oxford or Cambridge graduates with, at best, only a basic theological education. Despite the development of Anglican theological colleges in the nineteenth century, it was not until after the First World War that ordinands were required to have attended such a college. Moreover, those colleges, formed partially in response to the increasing secularization of the ancient universities, commonly focused on the 'handing down' of Biblical criticism and Patristic and orthodox theological teaching – literally 'indoctrination'.[42] Parish clergy were often, therefore, unable to reflect theologically on war and, moreover, were not expected to do so. The same was no doubt true of similarly-trained chaplains. In his 1922 book *Disenchantment*, C.E. Montague, the main leader-writer for the *Manchester Guardian* who had served for much of the war as a press officer, included in his critique of Anglican chaplains this comment:

> What, indeed, could the average army chaplain have done, with his little budget of nice traits and limitations? How had we ever armed and equipped him? When you are given an infant earth to fashion out of a whirling ball of flaming metals and gases, then good humour, some taste for adventure, distinction at cricket, a jolly way with the men, and an imperfect digestion of thirty-nine partly masticated articles may not carry you far.[43]

This lack of theological education may well account for both the very limited clerical response to Studdert Kennedy's advocacy of divine passibility discussed in chapter 6

39 Munson (ed.), *Echoes of the Great War*, p. xii.
40 Ibid., pp. 11, 14, 245 and 95.
41 P.D. Clayton, *Tales of Talbot House* (London: Chatto & Windus, 1919).
42 See M.D. Chapman, 'Living the Truth: Cuddesdon in the History of Theological Education' in M.D. Chapman (ed.) *Ambassadors of Christ: Commemorating 150 Years of Theological Education in Cuddesdon 1854–2004* (Aldershot: Ashgate, 2004), pp. 1-22.
43 C.E. Montague, *Disenchantment* (London: Chatto & Windis, 1922), p. 79. The 'thirty-nine ... articles [of religion]' are historic statements of the doctrines and practices of the Church of England.

and also the prominence of Nonconformist preachers, whose denominations often stressed the need for academic rigour in the theological training of their ministers, in the analysis of sermons engaging with questions of providence and omnipotence in chapter 4.

Finally, it should be noted that there was limited theological reflection from those very people of whom it might have been expected, the academic theologians. Writing in October 1915, the editor of the *Hibbert Journal*, the Unitarian minister L.P. Jacks, suggested that 'a theological holiday, partial at all events, has actually been imposed upon Europe.'[44] He reported an enormous reduction in the numbers of theological books being published. One cause, he suggested, was the cessation of the supply of new German theology and diminished respect for the old. More significantly, the war had challenged people's understanding of human nature. 'Men will hesitate in the propositions they make about God', he wrote, and 'we don't quite know what to think, what to say. … Man, meanwhile, is neither as wise nor as good as he thought he was.' What effect, he wondered, would this 'holiday' have on the post-war direction of theology? As we shall see, Jacks' cautious introspection was not uniformly replicated across the Churches, although his analysis may offer one explanation for the 'silence' of some witnesses.[45] Certainly, there was very little theological and ethical reflection comparable with that associated in more recent times with, for example, the Falklands War or the invasion of Iraq.[46]

Diffusive Faith and Folk Religion

Critically important for this study's attempt to assess the influence of the First World War on the faith of the people of Britain is an understanding of the nature of that faith. Until the formation of the Mass-Observation (MO) research organisation in 1937 and the rise of opinion polls, assessing what Britons believed was highly problematic. This is well illustrated by Michael Snape's *God and the British Soldier*, in which there is a clear contrast between the authority with which attitudes to religion in the Second World War could be reported and the inevitable caution about anything that might be asserted about the earlier conflict. For example, he quoted an MO survey in 1943:

44 The Editor [L.P. Jacks], 'A Theological Holiday – and After', *The Hibbert Journal*, Vol. XIV, No. 1 (October 1915), pp. 1-14.

45 A month earlier, Jacks had caused controversy when he had argued that the war had brought "a peace of mind such as she has not possessed for generations' and had helped to overcome social divisions. 'The Peacefulness of Being at War' in *The New Republic*, 11 September 1915, pp. 152-154.

46 See, for example, C. Williamson, 'The Church of England and the Falklands War' in Parker and Lawson (eds), *God and War*, pp. 165-186; P. Lee, 'Military Intervention in the Cold War Era' in Parker and Lawson (eds), *God and War*, pp. 187-205; E. Filby, *God and Mrs. Thatcher: The Battle for Britain's Soul* (London: Biteback Publishing, 2015).

> among all the samples studied, never more than a tiny proportion of 1–4% say they have *lost* their faith. In general the effect of war has been to confirm pre-existing attitudes, to strengthen faith where it existed before; but also to confirm and strengthen attitudes of scepticism, agnosticism and indifference.[47]

There exists no comparable material relating to the First World War. Many writers have written of a 'spectrum' to describe the wide variation in faith across the population, although how one might locate a particular individual within such a spectrum is inevitably somewhat subjective.[48] It is easier to measure religious practice, although that itself is a complex task. Clive Field sought to quantify 'religious belonging' in Edwardian Britain by comparing and evaluating various contemporary measures of religious observance alongside previous attempts at similar assessments.[49] He concluded that while around one quarter of adults worshipped on any given Sunday and two-fifths at least monthly, around a half had some connection with the churches and rites of passage reached almost the entire population, with only one per cent professing no faith at all. Approximating from the first two figures suggests that around two-thirds of the population worshipped only rarely or infrequently, yet virtually all of them said that they had a Christian faith. Given the predominance of women among committed church-goers – approximately 60 percent in most surveys – around 70 percent of men could therefore be categorised as 'believing but not (often) attending.' Field cited conflicting evidence on the correlation between social class and church attendance.

In 1903, Edward Talbot, then Bishop of Rochester, in one of his Charges to his diocese addressed the failure of the Church to reach the working classes.[50] He suggested that the power of Christ worked in two ways: the 'embodied' and the 'diffusive', represented in the Gospels 'by the net gathering in the company of believers, and the leaven hidden in the lump.' The two forces should, he said, be mutually contributive. While not dismissive of diffusive Christianity, he warned that it was often 'capricious, shallow and unbalanced' and 'washy and thin' in its teaching. However, his hearers should not condemn or despair, but understand and hope. In coining the term 'diffusive Christianity' he was, of course, describing that clear majority of Edwardian Britons who believed in God but rarely attended church. Subsequently, the concept has been further explored by, among others, Jeffrey Cox and Michael Snape.[51] For

47 Snape, *God and the British Soldier*, p. 201, quoting MO, FR 1572.

48 See R. Schweitzer, 'The Cross and the Trenches: Religious Faith and Doubt Among Some British Soldiers on the Western Front', *War and Society*, vol. 16, no. 2 (October 1998), pp. 36f. and R. Schweitzer, *The Cross and the Trenches: Religious Faith and Doubt Among British and American Great War Soldiers* (Westport: Praeger, 2003)., pp. 195 ff.

49 C. Field, '"The Faith Society"? Quantifying Religious Belonging in Edwardian Britain, 1901–1914', *Journal of Religious History*, Vol. 37, No. 1 (March 2013), pp. 39-63.

50 G. Stephenson, *Edward Stuart Talbot, 1844–1934* (London: SPCK, 1936), pp. 157-9.

51 J. Cox, *The English Churches in a Secular Society: Lambeth, 1870–1930* (Oxford: OUP, 1982), pp. 90-128; Snape, *God and the British Soldier*, pp. 19-58.

Cox, it informed his interpretation of the attitudes of the working-class people of Lambeth at the turn of the twentieth century who resisted the equating of true religion with church-going and resented being called 'pagan'.[52] Snape pointed out that diffusive Christianity pervaded all levels of British society and, as Callum Brown had observed, 'what made Britain Christian' was not church-going but 'the way in which Christianity infused public culture' and shaped individuals' identities.[53] Despite the persistent temptation for clerics and their congregations to apply the 'pagan' epithet to non-church-goers, to describe the majority of the Edwardian population in this way would be quite misleading. Despite their lack of religious knowledge – a topic commonly raised by the chaplains – those 20 million or more people did believe in God and the vast majority of them also believed, however incoherently or unorthodoxly, in life after death. The recognition of this 'diffusive Christianity' is key to understanding the influence of the First World War on personal faith and also the influence of faith on attitudes to the conflict and to its immense cost. Moreover, it affected greatly the work of Anglican chaplains, who were expected to minister not only to the church-going minority, but to the masses of 'diffusive Christians'.

In his study of popular religion in Lambeth, Cox sketched out the nature of the folk religion of the diffusive Christians of 1870-1930. Despite contemporary claims to the contrary, he wrote, 'The argument that the poor believe in the Trinity "in their own way" should be discounted altogether.'[54] Rather than being unorthodox or Unitarian on the nature of Christ, most people were, he suggested, 'pre-orthodox'. In keeping with chaplains' assessments that the soldiers had simply not understood the theological teaching of the Church, Cox suggested that, rather than rejecting such teaching, what most working class men and women believed was 'simply the most that a millennium of indoctrination had achieved in implanting Christian ideas in the popular mind.'[55] It was something more than simple theism, though not much more. Cox concluded that in late 19th century Lambeth, there was little of the magic and superstition of 18th century rural England: 'Semi-pagan superstition had subsided into "luck".'[56] As had Cox, in her seminal work on Southwark in a similar period, Sarah Williams rejected the analyses of late Victorian clerics about the nature of such 'popular' or 'folk' religion.[57] She noted also that as late as the 1960s and 70s, scholars had simplistically equated religion with traditional church practice.[58] Williams also criticised Cox for isolating the 'Christian end' of the spectrum of diffusive Christianity, by which

52 Cox, *The English Churches*, pp. 91f.
53 Snape, *God and the British Soldier*, p. 22.
54 Cox, *The English Churches*, p. 94.
55 Ibid.
56 Ibid., p. 95.
57 S.C. Williams, *Religious Belief and Popular Culture in Southwark c.1880–1939* (Oxford: Clareendon Press, 1999).
58 Ibid., p. 2.

one assumes she meant the 'orthodox end'.[59] Certainly, we should be cautious about treating folk or popular religion and what might be termed ecclesiastical religion as two quite distinct entities.[60] As there was a continuous spectrum of frequency of church attendance, so there was a similar (but not necessarily correlated) spectrum of religious belief. Williams' conclusions about superstition in urban folk religion were quite different from Cox's: 'Like the South Lindsey villager, the south London costermonger used charms and enacted rituals to harness the super-empirical realm in order to serve the present and to assist, as Lovett argued, "in bringing about the desires of the wearer or to ward off all that may be hurtful or unfortunate."'[61] However, she, too, emphasised the importance of 'luck' and actions believed to improve one's own luck. We shall see later how these examples of folk religion manifested themselves in the attitudes and practices of soldiers.

The ubiquity of hymnody

As will become clear in subsequent chapters, hymns had a prominent place in wartime Britain. For Anglican clergy constrained to use prayers only as permitted by their bishops, appropriate hymns allowed them to respond pastorally to the current situation and to express theologically their attitudes to the war. Unsurprisingly, *O God, our help in ages past* was most frequently selected for services marking significant events or dates during the war. Hymn-writers, both established and novice, wrote many hymns, most commonly to assert the righteousness of and the Divine support for Britain's cause. Many diaries record communal hymn-singing, some organised by chaplains and some quite spontaneous. Furthermore, hymn-tunes formed part of every band's repertoire. For example, Capt. Rowland Fielding reported that at every guard-mounting when out of the line, as the old guard marched away, the band would play *Abide with Me*. 'It is a pathetic tune, I think, and always makes a lump come into my throat.'[62] Moreover, innumerable 'songs of the trenches' were irreverent and humorous parodies of popular hymns.

The key to these varied uses of hymns was, of course, their ubiquity in Edwardian society. For the officers, the majority of whom at the outbreak of war had been educated in public schools in which Christian worship was a daily experience, repetition had burned popular hymns into their memories. As far as the men of the army of August 1914 and subsequent volunteers and conscripts were concerned, while the practice of organised religion had been in gentle decline since the closing quarter of

59 Ibid., p. 5.

60 This is one of the key arguments in Eamon Duffy's analysis of medieval religious faith in *Stripping the Altars* (London: Yale University Press, 1992).

61 Williams, *Religious Belief*, p. 84, quoting E. Lovett, *Magic in Modern London* (Croydon: Folk-Lore Society, 1925), p, 65.

62 R. Fielding and J. Waller (ed.), *War Letters to a Wife* (Staplehurst: Spellmount, 2001), p. 182.

the 19th century, nevertheless, as was noted above, in England around 40 percent of the adult population in 1914 worshipped at least once a month. Moreover, even the non-church-going men had been educated and brought up in a late Victorian and Edwardian England in which the language of belief had remained hugely influential. At least 80 percent of the adult population of 1914 had attended Sunday schools in their childhood, invariably singing hymns.[63] Furthermore, the role of the Church of England in the English education system continued to be significant. It has been estimated that in 1880, voluntary schools (the overwhelming majority of which were Church of England) were educating around 2 million children, while the school boards, set up by the 1870 Education Act to provide rates-supported elementary education for England and Wales, were educating about 750,000 scholars. In 1895, the numbers educated in Church of England voluntary schools still exceeded those in board schools.[64] Moreover, in the latter group, the vast majority of local school boards required 'religious observances' including hymns, prayers and Bible readings, as part of the daily life of the schools. For all but a very small number of combatants, therefore, their school days would have included such acts of worship. In pre-war Southwark, even those who rarely attended church 'sent their children to Sunday school with dogged determination, sang hymns in one another's homes, prayed in private, and continued to separate the Sabbath from the rest of the week by a series of rituals and observances.'[65] Williams observed that hymns were 'closely interwoven' with the fabric of both family life and community activities. She concurred with S.S. Tamke's conclusion about Victorian society that hymns learned in childhood had made a deep and lasting impression, the lyrics remembered into adulthood.[66] As one contributor to *The Army and Religion* put it, many men were 'deeply ignorant of Christian doctrine while being remarkably well versed in Christian hymnody.'[67] It is unsurprising, then, that hymnody provided a popular and accessible means for soldiers and civilians alike to express their religious feelings about the war.

We turn now to an examination of the initial responses of the Churches, their leaders and members to the outbreak of the First World War.

63 Field, '"The Faith Society"?', p. 58.

64 S.J. Brown, *Providence and Empire, 1815-1914* (Harlow: Routledge, 2008), pp. 413-5; J. Hull, 'School Worship (England and Wales)' in Paul Bradshaw (ed.), *New SCM Dictionary of Liturgy and Worship* (London: SCM, 2002), p. 424.

65 Williams, *Religious Belief*, p. 7.

66 Ibid., p. 149, quoting S.S. Tamke, *Make a Joyful Noise unto the Lord: Hymns as a Reflection of Victorian Social Attitudes* (Ohio: Ohio University Press, 1978), p. 78.

67 Cairns (ed.), *The Army and Religion*, p. 116.

2

A Holy War and a Favoured Nation

The Outbreak of War

As the title of one of the more widely-discussed books published to mark the centenary of the outbreak of the Great War suggests, a case can be made that Europe 'sleepwalked' into the conflict and that the outbreak of hostilities involving all the major European powers took most of them by surprise.[1] Certainly, in the summer of 1914, Britain was much more concerned by 'the Irish Question', growing industrial unrest and the campaign for women's suffrage. Even at the beginning of August, the imminent outbreak of war did not silence that campaign. George Bell, the biographer of Randall Davidson, Archbishop of Canterbury, quoted Mrs. Davidson's diary entry for 2 August 1914: 'At 3 *Westminster Abbey, Randall preached* – TEXT "OUR FATHER". Just as he began – cries arose from transept seats "Votes for women". The Suffragettes had chained themselves to the seats!'[2] Yet, although this may not have been appreciated at the time, how the Churches and their leaders responded to the declaration of a state of war on 4 August 1914 was crucially important in establishing the nature of their engagement with all the theological and ecclesiological issues that the conflict would raise over the succeeding four years. The patterns established in August 1914 would, as we shall see, change little in that period. When Davidson resumed his sermon after the suffragette protestors had been removed, it was with the affirmation, 'This thing which is now astir in Europe is not the work of God but the work of the devil.'[3] Even then, he thought it 'just conceivable that for us in England, the storm-cloud will roll by unbroken.' On the same day, John Percival, Bishop of Hereford, wrote to Canon Bannister, 'Do you think we could get the Mayor to call a meeting of citizens to urge the Government to adhere to the policy of neutrality and

1 C. Clark, *The Sleepwalkers: How Europe went to War in 1914* (London: Penguin, 2013).
2 G.K.A. Bell, *Randall Davidson, Archbishop of Canterbury* (London: OUP, 1952), p. 735.
3 Bell, *Randall Davidson*, p. 735. *The Times*, 3 August 1914, p. 8 reproduced the sermon with some textual variation from Mrs. Davidson's quotation.

efforts for peace? I have joined a Committee of protest against the mischievous utterances of our jingo press.'[4] Both he and Bishop Hicks of Lincoln had been active in various pre-war peace movements, including the Neutrality Committee that had had Ramsay MacDonald among its leaders.[5] Nevertheless, within a week of the declaration of war, Percival wrote a long letter to *The Times*, concluding that, 'Under these circumstances I am brought to the conclusion that in obedience to our treaty obligations, and in support of Belgium's just claim, our country had no choice but to take up the sword if honourable dealing was to have any chance of surviving in international affairs.'[6]

It was Germany's invasion of 'brave little Belgium' which had totally undermined the peace-time anti-war movements. In consequence, there was hardly any debate about the morality and ethics of Britain's declaration of war on Germany and precious little analysis of what, for example, the doctrine of the 'Just War' might say about a conflict which had taken the whole nation by surprise. Few contemporary biographers suggest that their subjects stopped for more than the briefest moment to consider the theological implications of the situation in which the country found itself. Among the 'few' was Cosmo Lang, Archbishop of York, who recorded in his own notes,

> I was harried with anxiety as to the rightfulness of the Church in any way supporting war; and I well remember the real torture of mind when I tried to think out the problem in September while in retreat at Cuddesdon.[7] But I was driven to the conclusion, right or wrong, that the War was righteous, that we were bound in honour to enter it, and that the Church could not rightly oppose it. Even now, with all the disappointment which has come, I am still convinced that no other course was possible.[8]

The different responses to the war of the Church of England's leaders were largely a matter of degree – for example in the certainty with which views were expressed or the nature of the language used – rather than of significantly divergent opinion on major issues. Of Charles Gore, Bishop of Oxford and the leading Anglo-Catholic of his generation, his biographer wrote, 'The war broke on Gore with a horror of great darkness. … But he was firmly convinced that no other course lay open to the country

4 W. Temple, *Life of Bishop Percival* (London: Macmillan, 1921), p. 356.

5 G. R. Evans, *Edward Hicks – Pacifist Bishop at War* (Oxford: Lion Books, 2014), pp. 179-196. The subtitle of the book seriously misrepresents Hicks' views, more accurately described by Evans as 'very sceptical of the justification of the grandiose imperialism of a British Empire at the height of its dominant position in world affairs', ibid., p. 180.

6 Temple, *Life of Bishop Percival*, pp. 357f. and *The Times*, 12 August 1914, p. 7.

7 An Anglican theological college in the village of that name, located six miles east of Oxford.

8 J.G. Lockhart, *Cosmo Gordon Lang* (London: Hodder & Stoughton, 1949), p. 246. Lockhart did not record the date of the comment.

than to participate. The war was a judgment of God, and all its consequences must be endured to the bitter end until human insolence had been laid low.'[9]

Gore's view that the war was a judgment of God was not uncommon in the opening months of the conflict. In a sermon published in the *Baptist Times and Freeman* on 28 August 1914, the Revd. A. J. Nixon likened the 'war cloud' to the cloud over Noah.

> But may not this war be a judgment of God upon our times, even as the Flood in the times of Noah? Is God now thundering the message we would not heed in the still, small voice? ... It is painfully evident to all that the present is a time when God has brought a cloud upon the earth: 'This also cometh from the Lord of hosts, who is terrible in judgment.'[10]

President of the 1915 Primitive Methodist Conference, J.D. Thompson declared, 'this is not a normal time. It is a day of the Lord, a *Dies Ire*, a day of wrath and judgment.'[11] Like many others, he was not precise in defining the target of that judgment; Germany or all the protagonists. A rather more subtle argument was offered by A.E. Garvie, the Congregationalist principal of New College in London, when in a 1916 sermon he argued that, 'We may speak of the war as God's judgment on sin in the sense that it is the inevitable consequence of the sins of the nations in their relationships with one another; but we must not speak of it as though it were an arbitrary punishment inflicted by God.'[12] Certainly, use of the language of judgment like Garvie's was not very different from the argument that the conflict was simply the consequence of God giving free will to the nations. From the start, others advocated that analysis, the *Methodist Recorder* on 6 August 1914 commenting, 'It is no use speaking of what is come as a judgment of God. Men are simply eating of the fruit of their own ways.'[13] In May 1916, Victor Richardson wrote to his friend, Edward Brittain, 'Again, I don't think many people – apart from the very Low Church party of our own English Church ... – really think that this War is a punishment for those who have suffered in it and through it.'[14] Gore was, of course, no member of the Low Church party. However, it does appear that support for the idea that God had sent the war as an act of judgment on Britain and Germany alike declined as the war progressed. Victor Richardson's comment implies one reason for that; it was unacceptable to suggest

9 G. L. Prestige, *The Life of Charles Gore – A Great Englishman* (London: Heinemann, 1935), p. 369.
10 *BTF*, 28 August 1914, p. 670.
11 *PML*, 17 June 1915, p. 375.
12 *CWP*, 22 March 1916, p. 179.
13 *MR*, 6 August 1914, p. 3.
14 Letter dated 31 May 1916. A. Bishop and M. Bostridge (eds), *Letters from a Lost Generation* (London: Virago, 2008), p. 257. Edward was the brother of Vera Brittain, famous for her *Testament of Youth* (London: Gollancz, 1933), in which Victor and Edward are prominent.

that the rapidly-growing losses were a consequence of divine action. Increasingly, the people of Britain simply blamed the war solely on German militarism and the Kaiser, who had been allowed to cause such carnage by God's gift of free will. In his 1915 visitation, Edward Talbot, bishop of Winchester, told his clergy that they had found that the war 'was right and therefore necessary. ... The question was decided for us upon a simple issue of national honesty and honour towards a weak and defenceless people.'[15]

Across the breadth of English Protestantism there was in general a correlation between the ecclesiological proximity of a denomination to the established Church and the strength of its support for the war. For example, the Wesleyan Methodists were determined to demonstrate that their patriotism and support for the conflict were at least a match for the Church of England. Conversely, the less deferential and more politically-radical Primitive Methodists – from which would later come many conscientious objectors – were far less homogeneous in their attitudes. On 6 August 1914, a front-page article in the *Primitive Methodist Leader*, 'The Madness of Europe' by Arthur Guttery, (presumably written before Britain's declaration of war) stated,

> Civilisation stands on the brink of ruin. A wave of madness has swept over Europe, and Britain is invited to plunge into a fury that is insane. We are urged to wreck our country, endanger our Empire and to abandon all dreams of social progress. ... The Christian Churches must plead for peace and the neutrality which makes peace possible if they are not to be craven in the hour of crisis. ... The duty of England is clear; it is to strive for peace, to localise the conflict, and to refuse to share an international infamy.[16]

A week later, four correspondents vehemently criticised the article, one wondering if Mr. Guttery had 'lost his mental balance', another asserting that 'Peace cannot be purchased at the cost of faithlessness to obligations and of national dishonour' and a third asking rhetorically, 'Are we to have peace at any price and allow a maniac to dominate this country and the whole of Europe?'[17] However, by then Guttery had modified his own views somewhat, writing under the heading, 'The Duty of the Empire',

> We would preserve our neutrality as a gracious asset if we could. We have no hatred of the German people, for we pity their thraldom to a monarch who, moved by panic or passion, has become a danger to Europe; but much as we hate war, and much as we protest against the diplomacy that has led to it, we are

15 E.S. Talbot, *The War and the Duty of the Church* (London: Macmillan, 1915), p. 2.
16 *PML*, 6 August 1914, pp. 553f.
17 *PML*, 13 August 1914, pp. 575 & 578. Two letters defending the original article were published in *PML*, 20 August 1914, p. 598.

> compelled by the logic of pitiless events to believe that the defeat of the Kaiser's ambition is the first step towards securing the peace and progress of mankind.[18]

In the *Baptist Times and Freeman* on 14 August there was published a formal letter to the ministers and members of churches in the Baptist Union, signed by its leaders, calling upon the churches 'to be instant in prayer for the restoration of peace' and to 'pray that the sword may soon be sheathed'.[19] A week later, a sermon preached by the prominent Baptist minister John Clifford was reported: 'I hate war with the whole force of my being,' he said. 'Yet when I looked at the situation and weighed the evidence, I could not believe that our Government had taken a wrong step ... the only thing I can say is that we are forced into it.'[20] By September, the newspaper was publishing a sermon entitled 'A Righteous War' which stated, 'We have never gone into conflict with a clearer conscience or better reasons ... we have in France, Belgium and Britain the forces of freedom and progressive life ... Our land has stood for the right.'[21] In the following month there was published one of the few letters in the religious press to challenge the Churches' support for the conflict. Hilda Macalpine wrote to

> protest against this justification of war by the representatives of a Christian Church ... To me the saddest feature of this war has been the way in which the leaders of the Churches have justified it and urged the Christian young men in their Churches to take part in it, together with the way in which almost the whole religious Press has devoted its pages to advocating the prosecution of this 'righteous war.'[22]

She was very much in the minority, though her description of the support of the religious press was apposite, reflecting as it did the attitude, however reluctantly reached, of the vast majority of the leaders of almost all the main Christian denominations. In Scotland, the Commission of the Assembly of the United Free Church, meeting a week after the outbreak of the war, unanimously adopted a resolution asserting that Britain's engagement in the conflict was 'just and necessary'.[23]

That reaction was reflected locally in the East Midlands. The vicar's letter in the September 1914 issue of the parish magazine of Elmton-cum-Creswell, two villages ten miles north of Mansfield, Nottinghamshire, opened with a quotation:

18 *PML*, 13 August 1914, p. 577.
19 *BTF*, 14 August 1914, p. 647.
20 *BTF*, 21 August 1914, p. 656.
21 *BTF*, 11 September 1914, p. 692.
22 *BTF*, 9 October 1914, p. 756.
23 *Aberdeen Journal*, 13 August 1914, p. 6.

> In my judgment every Christian man may give his whole-hearted loyalty to his King and country in this war and yet honestly believe that in doing so he is not disloyal to the Kingdom of God. I dare to say we can carry out this cause without shame or misgiving in the presence of Him Who is the Judge of the whole earth and ask Him to bless it.[24]

The words were those of the Prime Minister, Herbert Asquith, who, said the vicar, the Revd. W. Bathurst Soole, had striven 'earnestly and persistently' with Sir Edward Grey to the very last moment, 'for they are worthy of our best and noblest traditions of our race.' For Asquith, it was not simply that there was a spiritual or religious dimension to the conflict; rather there was a moral imperative for Christian men to engage in the war. Narratives affirming Grey's attempts as Foreign Secretary to avert the conflict recurred repeatedly in both sermons and newspaper articles in the first weeks of August. In the September 1914 issue of the *Southwell Diocesan Messenger*, distributed across the diocese to clergy and churches and widely quoted in local newspapers, the Bishop of Southwell, Edwyn Hoskyns, asserted that, 'the moment has arrived when we must carefully consider how to co-operate with God on over-ruling this evil for good.' An anonymous article on 'The War', almost certainly written by the editor and Rector of Shardlow, Robert Farmer, affirmed that, 'A united people, feeling the justice of their cause, may in quiet, humble confidence plead before the Throne on High.' In the parish magazine of St. Peter's, East Bridgford, the Rector declared in a long letter, 'A hundred years ago, Napoleon threatened the freedom of Europe. Britain saved it and we must do so now.' In the same month, the Vicar of Daybrook appealed to the young men of the parish who had not already enlisted 'to come forward to help in the defence of our King and country.' The Vicar of Everton told his people, 'We are confident, we entrench ourselves behind the righteousness of our cause.' However, reflecting a widely-expressed concern about the moral condition of British society, he added, 'but it is doubtful whether the state of our national life justifies such confidence.' Similar views were expressed by the ministers of All Saints, Nottingham, St. Oswald's, Ashbourne, and, no doubt, innumerable others whose declarations were never recorded, nor thought in any way remarkable.[25] There is no evidence of dissentient local clerical viewpoints. The Elmton-cum-Creswell parish magazine also included the transcript of a sermon preached by the vicar on 9 August in which he had declared,

> Our word to France and Russia is a word that cannot be broken. The appeal of brave little Belgium was an appeal which could not be ignored. … *'Our hands*

24 DRO, D 3283 A/PI 16/5.

25 *SDM*, NRO, DR 1/1/12/14/27; NRO, PR 6538; NRO, PR 19, 762/3; NRO, PR 29, 042; NRO, PR 29, 042; DRO, D0662.

> *are pure; for peace, for peace we have striven.'* ... and we can now with a clear conscience claim the succour of Almighty God in this great fight.[26]

The clergy of the Church of England in particular made a significant contribution to the nationalistic fervour of the opening months of the conflict. While their recruiting sermons might only have been heard in second-hand summaries by many of the young men at whom they were aimed, once they had enlisted, local clerics had a public role in the process by which reservists were assembled to march off for training and, later, for embarkation. Charles Beresford has described in detail the coming together in early August of the companies of the 6th Battalion of the Sherwood Foresters in south-east Derbyshire, after which,

> On Saturday the whole Battalion attended a special service in Chesterfield Parish Church ... it was a solemn and patriotic occasion ... Archdeacon Crosse, himself an old Volunteer, told them that they had been called to arms for a cause that was just and right. 'Remember you are Englishmen, and a good Englishman is a God's man.'[27]

Such services, some in churches, others in town squares, confirmed both for those departing and for family members remaining the moral validity of Britain's engagement in the conflict and divine approval for the fevered nationalism that was sweeping the nation. Subsequent to the initial invasion of Belgium, the destruction of the ancient library at Louvain and innumerable accounts of German soldiers brutalising Belgian civilians had the effect of silencing any residual resistance to Britain's engagement in the conflict. The stream of Belgian refugees and their presence throughout the war in the towns and cities of Britain, often supported by church-organised charitable work, served as a constant reminder of why Britain was fighting and as an implicit – and sometimes explicit – warning about the consequences of a German invasion of Britain, however unlikely from a military perspective that might have been.

Pause for thought?

There is little evidence from this period, locally or nationally, of any widespread engagement with the New Testament as part of the process by which individual ministers and Church bodies came to form a judgment about Britain's involvement in the war. As we shall see in the next chapter, recourse was frequently made to narratives of the battles of the Israelites in the Old Testament as a source of Biblical inspiration. Participation in a conflict which from the start was characterized as one between good and evil, a Godly nation and a godless nation, right and military might, ceased

26 DRO, D 3283 A/PI 16/5.
27 C. Beresford, *The Bath at War* (Bakewell: Country Books / Ashridge Press, 2007), p. 17.

to be controversial for the vast majority of church leaders within a very short time. However, among the unprecedented volume of books, pamphlets and leaflets that were published, some did seek to engage with the more challenging Gospel texts and there were a few volumes that critically examined the war in the light of Christian theology and tradition. Perhaps the best of these was *The War and the Kingdom of God*, edited by George Bell, Chaplain to the Archbishop of Canterbury. The editor's introduction expressed the dilemma faced by the contributors when he wrote, 'All the writers in this book are at one in their belief that on 4 August, 1914, England was morally bound to go to war'[28] but it also recognised that, 'War seems to be and is incompatible with that Kingdom [of God].'[29] Within that volume, H.L. Goudge's essay on *Christianity and War* did take seriously the moral teaching of Jesus recorded in the Gospels and examined it in some detail. The fundamental issue that he addressed was to whom and to what human institutions the ethical instructions of Jesus to his first century followers applied. The development of his argument typified the predominant response to such questions:

> Certainly His teaching is in its broad principles final and universal. … But His teaching was not given directly to the world; it was given to a special body of men upon whom a special Divine vocation rested. … If He says, 'Resist not him that is evil' (Matt. 5:39) the police and the army ought alike to disappear.[30].

He argued that pacifism was bound to an 'individualistic' concept of religion and failed to take account of the role of the Church in society. Even if Jesus' teaching on non-resistance should apply to the Church, 'it does not apply to "the children of this world" or to the corporate action of "the kingdoms of this world".'[31] He contrasted the situation in first century Palestine under the total domination of Rome with a contemporary Europe of numerous independent states, arguing that the Jesus could not envisage the current context when preaching. Goudge resisted the temptation to suggest that the coming of the Kingdom of God might be brought closer by a military victory and the whole essay is remarkable for the absence of any direct reference to Germany and the atrocities, both real and mythological, of which Germany had been accused and which had led to calls for a more aggressive military response. In his method of reconciling the teaching of Jesus in the Sermon on the Mount with the Churches' near-unanimous support for engagement in the conflict, he was typical of scores of other commentators. Some took Jesus' injunction against resisting evil and asked somewhat rhetorically if any Englishman could follow that teaching if his home

28 H.L. Goudge (and others), G.K.A. Bell, (ed.) *The War and the Kingdom of God*, (London: Longmans, Green & Co., 1915), p. 4.
29 Bell (ed.), *The War and the Kingdom*, p. 6.
30 H.L. Goudge, 'Christianity and War' in Bell (ed.) *The War and the Kingdom*, pp. 20f.
31 Ibid., p. 28.

had been invaded by marauding Germans who were about to outrage his wife and his daughter. That narrative and the self-evident conclusion to be drawn about the righteousness of Britain's cause against Germany was repeated frequently in press articles, letters and sermons.

A Holy War

The identification of the Great War as a 'holy war' by various Church leaders has been critically reported by many scholars. However, few of them appear to have sought to understand why it was thought entirely appropriate to describe it in that way. Neither has the widespread nature of its use been documented. On the very first Sunday of the conflict, the Bishop of Salisbury preached to a congregation of 5000 attending a solemn service of intercession in the Cathedral. As the *Western Gazette* reported, 'There in the Temple of the God of Peace he laid his hand on his heart and said before God that there was no doubt on our side it was a just war, it was a righteous war; and if carried out in the spirit of our Christianity it was a holy war.'[32]

It was also seen as a holy war because of its portrayal as a fundamental struggle between good and evil, a characterisation that was bolstered by every report of the atrocities committed by German forces in Belgium. For example, the *British Weekly* on 10 September 1914 carried an account of a sermon preached by the Revd. Samuel Parkes Cadman in Marylebone Presbyterian Church on the previous Sunday:

> The congregation listened with strained attention and in absolute silence, except at one point, when the preacher's reference to two little Belgian girls of ten and twelve who had been outraged by German soldiers called forth a storm of indignation. 'It is a holy war' he declared emphatically.[33]

Such rhetoric had become commonplace and was widely reported in the first few months of the conflict, for example at a church parade for Reservists in Chelmsford, at a 'war meeting' at St. Keverne in Cornwall, in a Bishop's message quoted in a parish magazine in Coventry and in the leader column of *The Manchester Courier*.[34] Moreover, there is no evidence that usage of the term 'holy war' diminished during the period of the war. In the East Midlands, the Bishop of Southwell referred to a 'holy war' in the

32 *Western Gazette*, 14 August 1914, p. 5.

33 *BW*, 10 September 2014, p. 580. Parkes Cadman was a Wesleyan Methodist Minister who from 1901 served the Central Congregational Church in Brooklyn, New York. The reported sermon was presumably preached during one of his annual visits to the UK. Biographical information from http://www.dawleyheritage.co.uk/unpublished-articles/111/samuel-parkes-bio, retrieved 8 March 2015.

34 *Chelmsford Chronicle*, 25 September 1914, p. 7; *The Cornishman*, 10 September 1914, p. 5; *Coventry Evening Telegraph*, 5 September 1914, p. 2; *The Manchester Courier and Lancashire General Advertiser*, 4 September 1914, p. 4.

Diocesan Messenger in 1916 and again in 1918: 'I have never feared to speak of this war as a holy war for our Allies, and of our men as crusaders.'[35] Local newspapers across the country reported similar affirmations by innumerable ministers.[36] In 1920, a local clergyman in Derby, addressing the congregation at a memorial service, asserted, 'It would certainly be a sad calamity if it should ever be forgotten that the war was a holy war. It was God's battle that men went out to fight.'[37] The use of the language was not confined to the clergy; among others the Labour MP Will Crooks affirmed the war as 'holy' in 1915, as did Viscount Haldane and Prince Arthur of Connaught.[38] Rudyard Kipling wrote a poem with that title in 1917, a laudatory piece about John Bunyan, who in his allegorical story *Holy War* telling of a battle between good and evil had – so Kipling believed – foreseen the war that Britain was now waging against the forces of the Devil.[39] Sapper Caleb Fletcher, serving 'in a small town in France quite close to the Belgian border' wrote home to Derby in June 1915, recounting the Bishop of London's addresses to the troops at Easter, describing the conflict 'as a "Holy War", a war which we should consider ourselves specially chosen to continue until "Right" had conquered "Might".' Later in the letter, he mused, 'Perhaps you will be able to understand my thoughts the first time I viewed all this terrible life of suffering. I could not help wondering where there could possibly be a God to allow such things to occur. And then one remembered that this is a "holy war".' That episcopal visit to the Front in Holy Week 1915 was widely reported in the press and described in soldiers' letters home.[40] In his memoirs, Sir Morgan Crofton, who served with the 2nd Life Guards, described a 'short and impressive' service conducted by Winnington-Ingram and reported a total of 60 services (all with congregations over 1000) and 22 hospital visits, ward by ward.[41] We cannot, of course, assess the impact on the ordinary soldier in France or the typical church or chapel-goer in Britain of the sustained use of such language. Sapper Fletcher quoted the Bishop's words two months after he had heard them and so they had clearly been well remembered. Furthermore, it expressed just what the nation, soldiers and civilians alike, wanted to hear; we are engaged in a just war, fighting for God and right as well as King and country.

35 *SDM*, January 1916, NRO, DR 1/1/12/14/29; *SDM*, January 1918, reported in *DDT*, 7 January 1918, p. 4.

36 e.g. *DDT*, 19 August 1915, p. 2; *Newcastle Journal*, 6 Feb. 1915, p. 10; *Western Daily Press*, 18 May 1915, p. 3; *Coventry Evening Telegraph*, 7 September 1914, p. 2.

37 *DDT*, 9 March 1920, p. 2.

38 *DDT*, 19 August 1915, p.2; *Newcastle Journal*, 6 February 1916; *Western Daily Press*, 18 May 1915, p. 3.

39 Published in *Aberdeen Journal*, 8 December 1917, p. 2.

40 M. Austin, *Almost Like a Dream – A Parish at War* (Whitchurch: Merton Priory Press, 1999), pp.17f. and 14. See also G.V. Smith, *The Bishop of London's Visit to the Front* (London: Longmans, 1915).

41 G. Roynon (ed.), *Ypres Diary 1914–1915; The Memoirs of Sir Morgan Crofton* (Stroud: The History Press, 2010), pp. 204 and 214.

It has been the use of this rhetoric by the Bishop of London which has been so prominent in critical narratives of the Church of England's support for the conflict. For example, on three occasions over sixteen years, Duncan Forrester drew attention to the Bishop's use of the term. His final account read thus:

> The Bishop of London called on every able-bodied man to fight for God and country, and wrote to the *Guardian* in 1915, proclaiming that it was the Church's duty 'to mobilise the nation for a holy war'.[42]

Forrester's source was Alan Wilkinson, who, to say the least, did not have a very high opinion of the Bishop.[43] What Wilkinson did not relate – and therefore of which Forrester would be unaware – is the reason for the brevity of Winnington-Ingram's original article. He had been asked by the *Guardian's* editor to give his advice in a sentence and, as he wrote in the next issue but one, 'in a sentence it is impossible to justify or explain or modify, and I certainly never meant the sentence to have the solitary prominence it was given, as I understood it to be one of many words of advice from others to be given at the same time.'[44] While Henry Scott Holland, Regius Professor of Divinity at Oxford, wrote to the *Guardian* to criticize the language, the correspondence does not seem to have attracted the level of contemporary interest which one might expect from its prominence in scholarly and more popular literature of the last 40 years, much of it using Wilkinson as the source.[45]

To turn to Albert Marrin's *The Last Crusade* is to encounter a more neutral assessment of the Bishop of London's influence:

> The fact that holy war rhetoric was taken up by preachers soon after Winnington-Ingram's declaration neither proves that he inspired their enthusiasm nor that they 'borrowed' the idea from him. What does seem likely is that he, together with several others whose activities are documented less adequately, acted as

42 D. Forrester, *Beliefs, Values and Policies: Conviction Politics in a Secular Age* (Oxford: Clarendon, 1989), p. 66; D. Forrester, 'The Scope of Public Theology', *Studies in Christian Ethics* vol. 17, no. 5, 2004, pp. 5-19; D. Forrester, *Apocalypse Now: Reflections on Faith in a Time of Terror* (Farnham: Ashgate, 2005), p. 2. A distinction must be drawn between contemporary references to the *Guardian*, a weekly Church newspaper published from 1846 to 1951, and modern references to *The Guardian*, formerly the *Manchester Guardian*, a daily national newspaper.

43 See, for example, A. Wilkinson, *The Church of England and the First World War* (London: SCM, 1978), p. 2.

44 A.F. Winnington-Ingram, Letters to the Editor: 'The Bishop of London and a Holy War', *Guardian*, 24 June 1915, p. 577.

45 H. Scott Holland, Letters to the Editor: 'The Bishop of London and a "Holy War"', *Guardian*, 27 June 1915, p. 563.

> a catalyst, clarifying at a crisis in the war hitherto vague ill-defined ideas and verbalising their feelings.[46]

Marrin listed five other bishops who used similar language. As we have seen, Winnington-Ingram was not the first to speak of the conflict as a 'holy war' and much of the criticism of him has been based on an anachronistic expectation that men born in Victoria's reign might have reflected late 20th century Christian attitudes to nationalism and conflict. Inherent in the rhetoric of engagement in a 'holy war' are a number of claims about the nature of the conflict. Implicit is the assertion that the war was not simply a military conflict between two Christian (or nominally-Christian) nations caused by conflicting geo-political interests, but rather one between good and evil – as exemplified by Randall Davidson's sermon on 2 August 1914. The battle was not simply for Britain and her allies, but for God himself.

It must also be recognized that the rhetoric of God being 'on our side' was as much a feature of Germanic declarations as British ones. As on 1 August 1914, Europe stood on the brink of conflict, British newspapers quoted a speech of the Kaiser:

> This is a dark hour for Germany. The sword is being forced into her hands. If at the last hour our opponents do not see eye to eye with us, I hope, with God's help, we shall so wield it that when all is over we can sheath it with honour … And now I leave you to God. Pray to Him to help our gallant army.[47]

This was fully understood in Britain, the reaction generally being one of sarcastic incredulity since it was inconceivable that God could be aiding Britain's enemy. On 7 August 1914 in the *Western Times*, a pseudonymous and somewhat discursive summary of 'Mid Devon News', claiming that Germany believed that she had already secured the God of Battles for her side, offered this verse: 'We Germans in Providence always confide, / And feel whatever is done, / The Lord will ever be on the side / Of William the Second to None.'[48] Later that month, a correspondent in Holland referred in the *Aberdeen Journal* to the 'holy-war doctrines of the Kaiser.'[49] We shall examine the significance of the 'God of Battles' rhetoric in the next chapter. The declaration of Russia that she, too, was engaged in a holy war was widely reported and the characterisation in popular culture of the conflict as one between Godly and Godless nations (until, of course, the fall of the Tsar) was reinforced by the publication of images such as those of thousands of Russian soldiers receiving Holy Communion from their chaplains, just like the postcards printed of British soldiers at prayer, some published by the *Daily Mail.*

46 Marrin, *The Last Crusade*, p. 139.
47 e.g. *Manchester Evening News*, 1 August 1914, p. 4.
48 *Western Times*, 7 August 1914, p. 10.
49 *Aberdeen Journal*, 28 August 1914, p. 3.

A Favoured Nation

The identification of the First World War as a 'holy war' does seem problematic from a contemporary perspective. However, when that conflict is properly recognised as effectively marking the end of the Victorian era in England (the formative years of her wartime military, ecclesiastical and political leaders having coincided with the height of Victorian self-confidence), then such a title is more easily understood. As we shall see, Britain's claim that God was on her side and the rhetoric of the 'holy war' were founded on the assumption that the success of the British Empire could not have been but divinely-ordained. Moreover, the 19th century expansion of the Empire and the missionary endeavours that accompanied it were inextricable. Britain saw her task as extending the Empire not for her own benefit but to bring to less privileged (and, implicitly, inferior) races the benefits of good government, impartial judicial systems and productive economic structures. The motto of David Livingstone, perhaps the most famous British missionary of the nineteenth century, was 'Christianity, commerce and civilization.'[50] Addressing Cambridge University in 1857, in urging that others should join and develop his work, he declared, 'I go back to Africa to try to make an open path for commerce and Christianity.'[51] After Livingstone's death, that motto would be carved on the statue dedicated to him at Victoria Falls. Integral to such altruism, expressed though the ideals of service and duty, was an imperial evangelicalism, bringing the Christian faith to benighted souls – often characterised as 'heathen' or 'gentiles'.

On the Sunday after the start of the war, a Wesleyan minister informed his congregation in Bedford that 'God had his own purposes to fulfill, and that he was on our side, and victory would be ours.'[52] Typically, on 9 August 1914, Bathurst Soole preached in Creswell parish church, looking back to the previous Sunday, on which his focus had been the prophet Ahab's hesitation on the eve of war.[53] Throughout the conflict, verses describing the battles in which Israel had conquered her opponents provided rich pickings for preachers stressing Britain's unique relationship with God. Thomas Pickbourne, a Methodist lay preacher who lived in Nottingham in the latter years of the conflict, wrote in his diary on Good Friday, 1918,

> We are fighting not for gain, political or national, but for truth, righteousness and justice. … As I believe in God & justice and in the righteous govt. of the

50 M. Osborne and S. Kingsley Kent, *Africans and Britons in the Age of Empires, 1660–1980* (Abingdon: Routledge, 2015), p. 48. See also A.W. Porter, *Religion versus Empire? British Protestant missionaries and overseas expansion, 1700-1914* (Manchester: Manchester University Press, 2004).

51 S. Neill, *A History of Christian Missions (revised edition)* (Harmondsworth: Penguin Books, 1986), p. 267.

52 *Bedfordshire Times and Independent*, 14 August 1914, p. 6.

53 DRO, D 3283 A/PI 16/5.

> world! As I believe in the fact that in the days of Israel's national peril when Hezekiah was on the throne and God stepped in to save the nation, so now I believe that he will step in to save The World from a new Sennacherib & a grosser tyranny.[54]

Britain was the new Israel, with God indubitably on her side, just as he had been when Israel had waged war with her enemies. She had been divinely-chosen by God to carry out his work in defeating a Germany whose leaders had rejected God. In short, Britain was especially favoured by God. Across the nation, this view was repeated in innumerable church sermons. An insight into this early form of national exceptionalism, showing it to pre-date both the war and, indeed, the years immediately prior to the conflict, is offered by the collections of hymns published in 1887 and 1897 to celebrate Queen Victoria's Golden and Diamond Jubilees. While offering by the standards of modern hymnody an undistinguished amalgam of doggerel and near-xenophobia, they stress the divinely-chosen and anointed role of the British sovereign as head of God's most-favoured country. For example, Edward Bickersteth, Bishop of Exeter, had written in 1887, 'God of our fatherland, / Stretch forth Thy glorious hand / And shield our isle! / Beautiful, brave and free, / As her own guardian sea, / May she for ever be / Under thy smile!' John Ellerton, author of *The day thou gavest, Lord, is ended*, offered for a children's service a hymn which, after recognising that not only English children but also 'dusky Indian' and 'strong Australian' cry 'God save the Queen', expressed Britain's divinely-given role with the couplet, 'God, Who in her maiden weakness / Called her to her mighty task.' In 1897, a hymn by S. J. Stone offered to God 'Praise for the sweet compassion / Which makes the wide world own / That Love's divinest fashion / Is set from England's throne.'

In the middle of the war, John Paterson-Smyth, Archdeacon of Montreal, asserted,

> In the mysterious calling and election of God, Britain is the elect nation of the world to-day. We say it in all wonder and humility. For it is not we, but God who has done it. We know not why. Just as we don't know why one man is born in a princely home and another, no worse than he, is born in a slum— so we don't know why a little island in the Atlantic mists, which might well be but a fishing station or one of the little appendages of some foreign despot, should be the proudest empire of the world or why it should bask in the light of Christianity for fifteen centuries while poor Africa and India are in the darkness of heathendom. We know not. That is the mystery of God's election.[55]

54 NRO, DD 2560/1/6.
55 J. Paterson-Smyth, *God and The War* (London, 1916), p. 13.

Lt. Harry Lawson, formerly headmaster of Buxton College, epitomised the conflation of Christianity and British identity when he wrote to his former pupils from France in July 1917:

> I've got one thing in particular to say to you all ... It's a Christian thing, and it's a British thing. It's what the Bible teaches- It's what the Christian martyrs suffered in persecution for. It soon found a route in England and began ... to spread abroad and become the heritage of the Empire. It's the story of the Crusaders, of the Reformation, of the downfall of the power of Spain, of our colonisation, of the destruction of Napoleon's might, of the abolition of slavery, and of the coming awakening of Germany. The thing is this: playing the game for the game's sake.[56]

Peter Parker, in his examination of the influence of the ethos of the public schools on the First World War, described that ethos as, 'a gentlemanly tradition of loyalty, honour, chivalry, Christianity, patriotism, sportsmanship and leadership.'[57] Moreover, as Christopher Moore-Bick pointed out, such an ethos found widespread expression in Victorian and Edwardian society, influencing those whose education was far more humble, a factor that would be of particular importance as the war progressed and officers had to be recruited from 'non-traditional' backgrounds.[58] The conflation of patriotism, Christianity and 'playing the game' influenced every stratum of society.

Together, belief in Britain's divinely-favoured nation status and total confidence that she was engaged in a 'holy war' were critically important, first in reconciling engagement in the conflict with Christian faith and second in providing the basis for a narrative of righteousness that would reduce the impact of the experience of war on the personal faith of a large number of Britons. On these foundations would be built a structure of theological discourse which would enable the country to assert that status as the 'new Israel', to explain God's action (or apparent inaction) in the conflict, and to interpret the sacrifices of the fallen and maimed as redemptive acts.

Conclusion

It is clear that by September 1914, the vast majority of both Church leaders and ordinary church-goers were fully supportive of Britain's declaration of war, believed to have been forced upon it by Germany's invasion of 'brave little Belgium'. Similarly, the rhetoric of a 'holy war' was employed from the start of a conflict which was viewed by

56 L. Houseman (ed.) *War Letters of Fallen Englishmen* (London: Gollancz, 1930) reprinted with Foreword by J. Winter (Philadelphia: Pine Street Books, 2002), p. 169.

57 P. Parker, *The Old Lie – The Great War and the Public School Ethos* (London: Bloomsbury, 1987), p. 17.

58 C. Moore-Bick, *Playing the Game: The British Junior Infantry Officer on the Western Front 1914-18* (Solihull: Helion, 2011), p. 236.

most Britons as being a spiritual battle of 'right' against 'might' as much as a geopolitical one. Fundamental to Britain's confidence that God was on her side was her self-perception as being a nation especially chosen and divinely-favoured. We shall now examine how that view, which enabled Britain to see herself as the 'new Israel', was confidently expressed in the language of the 'God of Battles' and the 'Lord of Hosts'.

3

God of Battles – Lord of Hosts

Introduction

In an evaluation of how Britain responded in religious and spiritual terms to the Great War, the language which was employed is often just as revealing – if not more so – than explicit theological pronouncements. In particular, the use of different titles or names for God emphasising particular divine attributes made clear which of those characteristics were most important for those engaged in preaching, praying or singing hymns. As was noted in the Introduction, in the case of sermons, written prayers and hymns, those hearing, reciting or singing them may not have chosen the language or composed each phrase, but by selecting particular biblical texts, prayers or hymns, those leading worship were affirming their content. Similarly, the printing in a newspaper of a particular hymn is an indicator of, at the very least, the views of the editor. It is not unreasonable to assume that in most cases, preachers and editors alike would have been responding to the popular mood and offering material to match their hearers' or readers' beliefs and attitudes, even if they themselves might not have been able to articulate those thoughts. What is certain is that the rhetoric discussed in this and the previous chapter was widely-expressed, widely-read and widely-heard during the Great War, perhaps on a greater scale than previous work has indicated.

From a contemporary perspective, two names for God, 'God of battles' and 'Lord of hosts' are notable because, although both were widely used during the conflict, they have largely fallen out of the modern Christian vocabulary. Indeed, the former has disappeared as the Churches' attitudes to warfare have changed, especially since the Second World War. As we shall see, those phrases offered further means of expressing the special relationship that was believed to exist between the forces of the Empire and the God who had enabled that Empire to cover a quarter of the globe. In evoking stories of great historic military triumphs, they encouraged the hope and the faith that the God who had given the Israelites victory over their oppressors would do the same for Britain and her allies. While, as the war progressed, the rhetoric of sacrifice and suffering (to which we shall turn in chapter 5) became increasingly prominent, the 'God of battles' and 'Lord of hosts' discourse persisted. This chapter will trace the origins of these titles, explore their usage and the meaning attached to them and show how the changing context – not least the growing casualty lists – affected the way in which these terms were used.

Before the Great War

O God of battles! steel my soldiers' hearts;
Possess them not with fear; take from them now
The sense of reckoning, if the opposed numbers
Pluck their hearts from them. Not to-day, O Lord,
O, not to-day, think not upon the fault
My father made in compassing the crown!

Henry V, Act IV, Scene 1.

The year was 1415 and the setting of the scene imagined by William Shakespeare was the eve of the Battle of Agincourt. Henry V, who would later lead his troops into battle and participate in the hand-to-hand fighting, was praying that his forces would not be daunted by the numerically-superior French army, and was invoking God's help – the help of the God of battles – in the fighting which was to come. Five hundred years later, as northern France was again the scene of battle, that same rhetoric was repeatedly used to express confidence that the God who over many centuries had given the people of Israel military victories would do the same for Britain. It is clear that the discourse of the God of battles was not one which had remained dormant from the time Shakespeare wrote *Henry V* – probably in 1599 – until it re-entered public discourse on 4 August 1914. Its immediate and widespread use precludes that possibility and examples of its expression before the Great War abound. For example, during the Crimean War, there was published a sermon by a Wesleyan Methodist minister with the title, *The Besiegers' Prayer; or, A Christian Nation's Appeal to the God of Battles for Success in the Righteous War.*[1] The text of the sermon was taken from Psalm 60:9-12 and references in those verses to the siege of a fortified city were, in the preacher's words, 'adapted to express our own solitude under the present circumstances of the nation, and therefore appropriate as a foundation for our present meditations.' It equated the fortified city of the Psalm with Sebastopol, 'the fall of which is considered essential to the success of the allied cause.' Psalm 60:12 was seen as a perfect expression of confidence in God's power, as applicable to Crimea as it had been to the Psalmist: 'Through God we shall do valiantly: for he it is that shall tread down our enemies.' (AV).[2] Such adaptation of Old Testament stories of divine support and intervention for the armies of Israel would become commonplace in the Great War and was a key characteristic

1 J. Carrol, *The Besiegers' Prayer; or, A Christian Nation's Appeal to the God of Battles for Success in the Righteous War* (Toronto: The Guardian Office, 1855), p. 4.
2 Authorised Version

of the 'God of battles' discourse, which had featured also in both the American Civil War and the South African wars.[3]

Not only was there an established rhetoric of Britain's past military glories, invoking Henry V, the Battle of Waterloo and other conflicts, but such language was waiting to be drawn upon from the existing hymnody of the time. For example, in the dominant hymnbook of the period, *Hymns Ancient and Modern*, the hymn 'Stand up, stand up for Jesus' included this verse:

> Stand up, stand up for Jesus, the solemn watchword hear;
> If while ye sleep He suffers, away with shame and fear;
> Where'er ye meet with evil, within you or without,
> Charge for the God of battles, and put the foe to rout.

Written in Philadelphia in 1858 during an evangelical revival, the hymn's original focus was clearly on spiritual warfare, but, like so many other similar compositions, it was unselfconsciously used to express attitudes to a conflict which was seen to be both spiritual and military.[4] When the hugely-popular hymnbook *Songs of Praise* was published in 1926, its editor, Percy Dearmer, found no place for the hymn. However, the enlarged edition of 1932 included that particular verse (unlike most other hymnbooks), but with 'God of battles' altered to 'God of freedom'. In the companion volume, *Songs of Praise Discussed*, Dearmer apparently saw no need to explain or justify the change, but simply noted it.[5] We observed in chapter 1 the pervasive influence of hymns and hymn-singing in pre-war and wartime British society and that influence continued after the conflict.

Whereas Shakespeare had provided the first of the two divine descriptors, the second had clear Biblical origins. For example, variants on the names, 'God of hosts', 'Lord of hosts' or 'Lord God of hosts' occur over 50 times in the book of Isaiah alone, 13 times in the Psalms and repeatedly across many other books of the Old Testament. In the vast majority of cases in which 'Lord God of hosts' is used – primarily in first Isaiah – the contexts are indicative of a God who brings destruction, either on the people of Israel or on their enemies.[6] For example, 'Therefore thus saith the Lord

3 See, for example, J.D. Borthwick, *Poems and Songs on the South African War* (Montreal, 1901), Reprinted: (London, 2013), p. 91.

4 R. Watson and K. Trickett (eds.), *Companion to Hymns and Psalms* (Peterborough: Epworth, 1988), p. 409. See also S. Bell, 'Malign or Maligned? – Arthur Winnington-Ingram, Bishop of London, in the First World War' in *Journal for the History of Modern Theology / Zeitschrift für Neuere Theologiegeschichte*, vol. 20, no. 1 (Nov. 2013), pp. 117-133 for a detailed discussion of the conflation of the military and spiritual aspects of the conflict.

5 P. Dearmer, *Songs of Praise Discussed* (London: OUP, 1933), p. 343.

6 'First Isaiah' denotes the first 39 chapters of the book, which, unlike later ones, do relate to the prophet of that name.

GOD of hosts, O my people that dwellest in Zion, be not afraid of the Assyrian: he shall smite thee with a rod, and shall lift up his staff against thee, after the manner of Egypt.' (Isaiah 10:24). In Jeremiah 46:10, we find,

> For this *is* the day of the Lord God of hosts, a day of vengeance, that he may avenge him of his adversaries: and the sword shall devour, and it shall be satiate and made drunk with their blood: for the Lord God of hosts hath a sacrifice in the north country by the river Euphrates.

The more commonly-used 'Lord of hosts' is not so consistently associated with destruction and judgment and in 1 and 2 Samuel is used primarily as a simple title for God. However, in first Isaiah, it is associated with divine 'wrath', 'zeal' and 'scourging'.[7] While the word 'hosts' is commonly taken to refer to heavenly hosts, as in its traditional use in the Eucharistic worship of most Christian denominations, 'Holy, holy, holy, Lord God of hosts', in more general use, 'Sabaoth', the Hebrew word for 'hosts', meant 'armies', For the people of Israel in, for example, the time of Isaiah, to have distinguished between their own armies and the hosts of heaven would have been to create a false dichotomy for both were divinely-authorized and divinely-inspired, engaged in God's purposes for his world. The God of the heavenly hosts was the God who enabled the earthly armies to succeed against the oppressors and opponents of the people of Israel. As we shall see, a similar understanding would be widely expressed nearly three millennia later.

Well before the Great War, the language of the 'Lord of hosts' featured in popular hymnody, especially in hymns employing militaristic imagery. For example, the first verse of Charles Wesley's well-known *Soldiers of Christ arise* ended with this affirmation: 'Strong in the Lord of Hosts, / and in his mighty power. / Who in the strength of Jesus trusts / is more than conqueror.' The first part of the hymn, which originally ran to 16 8-line verses, is based on Ephesians 6:10-18. Every reference but one to militaristic imagery in those verses is defensive in nature ('armour', 'loins girt about with truth', 'breastplate', 'feet shod', 'shield of faith' and 'helmet of salvation'), the exception being the 'sword of the Spirit'. However, not all later hymns and adaptations of military metaphors showed the same restraint.

War is Declared

Very soon after war was declared, the language of 'God of battles' and 'Lord of hosts' became commonplace. The Bishop of Sheffield called for support for special services of intercession announced by the Archbishops of York and Canterbury. Referring to previous national crises of the Spanish Armada and the war with Napoleon, he affirmed, 'With faith in a just and merciful God ... we shall make our appeal to the

7 e.g. Isaiah 1:24, 9:7 and 10:26.

God of battles.'[8] Early in 1915, *The Times* published a hymn which made precisely the same historic connections:

> O God, to Whom our fathers prayed,
> When in their darkest hour
> Thy Hand the great Armada stayed,
> And broke Napoleon's power.[9]

At the end of September 1914, the *Christian World Pulpit* published a half-page article headed '700BC and 1914AD.' Starting with the affirmation, 'And it shall come to pass in this day that the Lord shall give thee rest from thy sorrow,' it was primarily a condemnation of the King of Babylon: 'The Lord of hosts hath sworn, ... that I will break the Assyrian in my land, and upon my mountains tread him under foot.'[10] The whole article was simply a quotation of Isaiah 14:3-27, with no comment or explanation apparently thought necessary. Not only were the people of Britain to be equated to the people of Israel, but Germany was the new Babylon and the Kaiser was the new King, the 'Lucifer' (Isa. 14:12). Four years later, the analysis of the *Methodist Recorder* on the signing of the Armistice was that, 'The vengeance of God has overtaken "Babylon the Great, which hath made all the nations to drink of the wine of the wrath of her fornications"' – those words being a paraphrase of the apocalyptic imagery of Revelation 14:8.[11]

In his seminal work, *Christian Attitudes to War*, Roland Bainton traced the history of Christian warfare in the name of the God of hosts. He showed that Clovis, the Frankish King who converted to Catholicism in 496 regarded Jesus as the new 'Yahweh of hosts'. Of the European colonisation of New England, Bainton commented,

> In 1742 Samuel Phillips declared that with regard 'to the Aboriginal natives ... there is no method so likely to subdue, or to humble them, as to march forth in quest of them.' In this we should try to 'engage the Lord of hosts on our side.'[12]

As in the Old Testament, it was believed that a lack of faith in the Lord of hosts would lead to defeat in the battle, but true faith would lead to military success. Less well-known hymns that had been written for earlier conflicts soon came into widespread use. A good example was the hymn commonly printed under the title 'For the Men at the Front' which had originally been written by John Oxenham (a pseudonym for the poet, journalist and novelist William Dunkerley) for the South African War:

8 *Sheffield Evening Telegraph*, 8 August 1914, p. 2.
9 *The Times*, 20 Feb 1915, p. 9.
10 *CWP*, 30 September 1914, p. 215.
11 *MR*, 17 November 1918, p. 3.
12 R.H. Bainton, *Christian Attitudes to War and Peace* (New York: Abingdon Press, 1960), p. 168.

Lord God of Hosts, whose mighty hand
Dominion holds on sea and land,
In Peace and War Thy Will we see
Shaping the larger liberty.
Nations may rise and nations fall,
Thy Changeless Purpose rules them all.[13]

Some five million copies of the hymn had been sold by April 1916 and it was frequently included in orders for intercessory and memorial services.[14] While the SPCK publication, *In Hoc Signo: Hymns of War and Peace*, largely avoided the more violent imagery of the 'God of battles', it drew widely on the language of the Lord or God of hosts. 'O Lord of Hosts, who didst upraise / Strong captains to defend the right' had been written by A.C. Benson (librettist of *Land of Hope and Glory*) in 1899 and it drew widely on the history of the people of Israel's conflicts. In keeping with a volume that struck a relatively sober note when compared with the many aggressively patriotic hymns published with great speed and limited skill in the opening months of the conflict, it concluded,

So let the slayer cease to slay;
The passion healed, the wrath forgiven,
Draw nearer, bid the tumult cease,
Redeemer, Saviour, Prince of Peace!

Another hymn in *In Hoc Signo*, 'O Lord of Hosts! Almighty King! / Behold the sacrifice we bring,' had been written by Oliver Wendell Holmes during the American Civil War. These and many others were ready to be re-presented in a new conflict. In the next four years, innumerable similar hymns would be published in both religious and secular newspapers, sometimes in response to particular developments in the war. Very often, they did little more than equate the battles of the Israelites – specifically the ones in which they had been victorious – with those of Britain and her allies in 1914-18, and in doing so affirm divine endorsement for their military efforts. Across Britain, would-be poets and hymn-writers offered their work for publication in local newspapers. The *Dundee Times* published 'J.B.'s' *Oh! God of battles hear our cry*, which concluded:

God give us strength, then grant us power!
With strength and peace the world to bless,

13 J. Oxenham, *'All's Well' – Some Helpful Verse for These Dark Days of War* (London: Methuen, 1915), p. 13. (In 18 months the book sold 175,000 copies, running to 18 impressions.)

14 e.g. NRO, 5/99/1, *Charles St Wesleyan Chapel, Newark, Order of memorial and intercessory service for those who have fallen and for those on active service, 19/9/1915*. Also NRO, 7/327/6-8, *Hucknall Wesleyan Sunday School Anniversary order*, 1915.

For Britain's power must ever rule
With justice, truth and righteousness.[15]

The Cornishman printed a rousing patriotic song, *Our Country's Call*, with the repeated affirmation, 'To God of Battles leave the rest / And forward undismayed!'[16] An intercessory hymn was published in the *Exeter and Plymouth Gazette* that called on the God of battles to 'look down in pity', guard Britain's forces, soothe the wounded, sustain the widows, poor and fatherless, and grant everlasting peace.[17] The suggested tune was the suitably sombre 'Eventide', traditionally used to accompany *Abide with me.* Other newspapers and journals appropriated existing poetical works to express the mood of the times. Thus, the *Newcastle Journal* printed a 'Hymn before action':

The earth is full of anger,
The seas are dark with wrath,
The Nations in their harness
Go up against our path:
Ere yet we loose the legions–
Ere yet we draw the blade,
Jehovah of the Thunders,
Lord God of Battles, aid![18]

The source of the two verses printed was identified as 'The Seven Seas', a volume of poems published by Rudyard Kipling in 1896. It had been written in response to the failed Jameson Raid in South Africa and published in *The Times.*[19] However, the editor of the *Newcastle Journal* was highly selective in his choice of verses, omitting one that asked for God's mercy for those with a proud heart, rebellious brow, deaf ear or uncaring soul. Another excised stanza had asked that God's wrath should not befall 'those who kneel beside us / At altars not Thine own.' Kipling had also called for divine protection from pride, terror, revenge and 'lawless error' but such sentiments did not match the mood of August 1914 and those verses were omitted.

Use of the rhetoric was not limited to the established Churches: For example, on 27 August 1914, a speaker at a special meeting of the United Free Church of Scotland in Edinburgh, called to 'consider the duty of the Church at this time of national crisis', declared that his hearers should 'make their appeal to the God of battles who was able

15 *Dundee Courier*, 25 August 1914, p. 4.
16 *The Cornishman*, 24 September 1914, p. 3.
17 *Exeter and Plymouth Gazette*, 14 September 1914, p. 2.
18 *Newcastle Journal*, 7 August 1914, p. 4.
19 R.H. MacDonald, *The Language of Empire: Myths and Metaphors of Popular Imperialism, 1880-1918* (Manchester: Manchester University Press, 1994), p. 169. The Jameson Raid was an abortive attack in 1895-6 on the Transvaal led by the British colonialist Leander Starr Jameson. It exacerbated British-Boer animosity, leading to the second Boer War.

to give the victory.'[20] On 5 September, the *Dundee Courier* reported on a great meeting at the Guildhall in the City of London:

> There the Prime Minister of the Mother Parliament of a united Empire and the leader of His Majesty's erstwhile Opposition stood side by side to voice the call of the Motherland to her sons the world over to come and fight for right against the legions of barbarism, treachery, and shame. Beside them was the Archbishop of Canterbury, supporting the appeal in the name of the God of Battles.[21]

However, the detailed 7,000 word report in *The Times* indicates that the Archbishop did not actually speak at the event; the *Dundee Courier's* correspondent apparently being the originator of the 'God of battles' rhetoric as an explanation for the Archbishop's presence.[22] Indeed, we should be cautious about over-stating the use of this discourse; many Church leaders seem never to have employed it in their sermons and writing.

Two Sides, one claim

As is universally recognised, the Great War was one between forces that both claimed and were confident of divine support for their cause. Rarely was this matter discussed at any depth; from a British perspective any view other than that God was on her side did not merit serious consideration. As Conservative leader Andrew Bonar Law addressing an audience in Bootle in December 1914 confidently stated, 'the German Emperor would find that he was mistaken in thinking that the God of battles was on his side.'[23] A common response to the association of such rhetoric with Germany was to criticise her for using such language, while apparently ignoring its use in Britain. For example, the essayist and journalist Arthur Clutton-Brock in one of the *Papers for Wartime* series published by OUP in 1914-15, commented, 'You can talk at the same time about the God of battles and about the survival of the fittest. In Germany the Kaiser talks about the first, and the professors about the second.'[24] In a later paper, the theologian J.H. Moulton sought to draw a distinction between the theology of Germany and Britain and her allies: 'We draw the sword with no less resolution because we draw it with horror and loathing; but we mean Love to have the last word when Belgium, and France, and Serbia, and Poland, and the dominions of the Turk, are all delivered from the god of battles into the hands of the God of Peace.'[25] Perhaps he did not capitalise the reference to 'god of battles' to reflect his belief that that god was not the true God.

20 *Aberdeen Journal*, 27 August 1914, p. 6.
21 *Dundee Courier*, 5 September 1914, p. 3.
22 *The Times*, 5 September 1914, p. 9.
23 *Birmingham Daily Post*, 22 December 1914, p. 8.
24 A. Clutton-Brock, '6. The Cure for War' in *Papers for Wartime* (London: OUP, 1914), p. 6.
25 J.H. Moulton, '31. British and German Scholarship' in *Papers for Wartime*, p. 5.

God of Battles: God of Peace

The problem of the quite different understandings of the nature of God implied by the conjunction of 'God of battles' and 'God of peace' was exemplified by one of those many hymns of limited merit written in the opening months of the war. Printed in October 1914 in *Dawn of Day*, a widely-published insert for parish magazines, was a hymn which started, 'Great God of Battles, God of Peace'.[26] Subsequent descriptors of God's nature such as pity, love, glory and hope offered no solution to that problematic juxtaposition of 'battles' and 'peace'. Exemplifying the self-evident tension between such portrayals of God were two wartime publications of the YMCA: One was 'A Brief Order of Prayer in Time of Battle', a leaflet of prayers, hymns and readings for use in the theatres of war, in which were tabulated suggested Bible readings, one for each day of the week.[27] Six were from the Old Testament while the other, from the letter to the Hebrews, offered a list of Old Testament characters whose faith had enabled them to conquer kingdoms, administer justice, obtain promises and shut the mouths of lions. Typical of the first six are accounts of David fighting and defeating the Philistine Goliath, of Joshua and his army marching round the besieged city of Jericho to bring down its walls, and of the Lord defeating the million-strong army of Zerah the Ethiopian.[28] In the last reading, although it was Asa who drew up Judah's battle lines, the Chronicler was quite clear to whom the victory should be attributed: 'So the Lord defeated the Ethiopians before Asa and before Judah, and the Ethiopians fled.'

In contrast, in one of the many articles and short series published in *Y.M. – The British Empire YMCA Weekly* (later to be re-titled *The Red Triangle*) which addressed issues of popular faith, under the heading 'Questions men are asking at the Front', chaplain E.G. Miles wrote, 'To me it is getting more difficult every day to reconcile the God of love with the God of battles.' Published on 16 June 1916, just two weeks before the Battle of the Somme, he was highly critical of the language of the God of battles:

> A man in whom all the finer instincts have decayed … might be forgiven when he confuses the God of battles and the God of love; but to another man whose senses are awake to moral and spiritual issues there is bound to be a growing difficulty in attempting to reconcile the God of love and the God of battles … Between the two there is an age-long struggle, and they have no point in common.[29]

26 *Dawn of Day*, October 1914, copy at DRO, A/PI 16/16-17.
27 Birmingham Special Collections, YMCA / K / 1 / 1.
28 Hebrews 11:32-40; 1 Samuel 17: 43-51; Joshua 6:2-7; 2 Chronicles 14:2-12.
29 *Y.M. – The British Empire YMCA Weekly*, 16 June 1916, p. 557.

For many Christians, the God of battles discourse was totally incompatible with their faith. Some church leaders avoided using it while others entered into argument over it. In an exchange of letters in *The Times* in February 1915, the Revd. E.B.A. Somerset of Barnsley wrote with heavy sarcasm:

> After reading the letters you have published on this subject, I feel that Dr. Eyre alone of all your correspondents has a true idea of what a clergyman should be and do. Plainly we are called to be modern Samuels, and to hew Teutonic Agags in pieces to the glory of the Lord. Are we not priests, and must we not offer sacrifices? And what sacrifice so acceptable to the God of battles as a holocaust of German blood?[30]

When the 2nd and 4th Burnley Batteries attended morning worship in that town in March 1915, the vicar preached on 'Fight the good fight of the faith' and in a typically patriotic sermon complained that Britain's 'foes deliberately maintained might as right. They had set up the heathen God of Battles and Hate in the place of the God of Love.'[31] It was, said the Revd. B. Winfield, a religious war and a holy war. In her memoirs, Mabel Dearmer, who served and died in a field hospital in Serbia in 1915, wrote of a conversation with her son, Christopher, who could not accept her lack of support for the conflict:

> 'I can't help it, my dear,' I replied; 'I can't hate my enemy.' ... He went unsatisfied, and I envied the proud mother who sends her sons, proud of them, proud of the war that calls them out, proud of the God of battles. But that God is not my God, and my heart was heavy.[32]

A former Quaker, called to defend his objection to military service at a local tribunal in Burnley in September 1916, stated, 'I am not prepared to serve the God of Battles but the God of peace and Righteousness.' Asked by the mayor how many Gods he thought there were, the applicant replied, 'It seems the Christian Church keep changing theirs. They did not used to believe in the God of Battles.'[33] One of the most powerful repudiations of the language and meaning of the 'God of battles' discourse can be found in the work of the virtually unknown Derbyshire soldier-poet Jack Titterton who served as a gunner with the Royal Garrison Artillery from 1916. While still working as a farmer, on 23 November 1914, a time at which the use of this rhetoric was at its peak, he wrote:

30 *The Times*, 24 February 1915, p. 10. Agag was king of the Amelekites with whom Samuel fought – 1 Samuel 15.
31 *Burnley Express*, 17 March 1915, p. 2.
32 M. Dearmer, *Letters from a Field Hospital* (London: Macmillan, 1915), p. 50.
33 *Burnley Express*, 21 September 1918, p. 3.

> Glory to the God of Battles,
> He is God indeed;
> See how all the vassal nations
> In His service bleed.
> Dying on his blood-red altar,
> Slaughtered round His throne,
> Glory to the God of Battles,
> He is God alone.

The fifth and final verse read:

> You may laud Him in your temple,
> Call Him great and good;
> Will he then remit the harvest
> Of your tears and blood?
> Still the awful stream rolls onward,
> Still the heroes fall.
> Glory to the God of Battles,
> He is Lord of All.[34]

We can be reasonably certain that this and his other poems had little influence, for they were never published and appear to have remained undiscovered in the Derbyshire archives for many decades. What is far less clear is how representative Jack Titterton was in his revulsion at such a title for God and the human cost of a conflict undertaken to the accompaniment of such rhetoric. Certainly, no editor of a mainstream newspaper or journal would have risked the opprobrium of the public by publishing such satirical critiques. We shall examine more of Titterton's work in a case study in chapter 8.

More moderate arguments against the language of the 'God of battles' that were published were often themselves challenged: A letter-writer to the *Sheffield Evening Telegraph* in January 1916 argued that the God who gave the injunction, thou shalt not kill,

> is also reported as giving instructions to His people … to go up to battle against their enemies and His, He, their leader, guiding, instructing not to spare but to punish with the sword, describing himself as the God of Battles, giving to them victory when their cause was righteous.[35]

34 DRO, D 4690/1/5/1-3.
35 *Sheffield Evening Telegraph*, 17 January 1916, p. 4.

Two months later, a rector in Newcastle addressed directly the suggestion that the 'God of battles of the tribal god conception represented the view of the older dispensation' and had been supplanted by the New Testament's revelation of God: 'Nothing could be more untrue … if the God of the Prophets be the God of Battles. He is a God who fights against the big bully Assyria … and Who slays Goliath … by David's sling and five small stones.'[36] A letter to the *Hull Daily Mail* published on 19 July 1916 and stressing the power of prayer less than two weeks after the start of the battle of the Somme asserted,

> Readers of the Bible will recollect that when Hezekiah was King of Judah, Senacherib, King of Assyria, invaded Judah, and after destroying many towns, etc, drew near to Jerusalem, the capital, and sent a blasphemous letter to Hezekiah, threatening destruction. This letter was laid by prayer before the God of Battles, who sent his angel to the camp of the Assyrians, and destroyed 180,000 of them in the night.[37]

There was no need for the writer make explicit the contemporary message. It should not, however, be assumed that the discourse of the 'God of battles' was always expressed in such a bellicose manner, urging the Empire's forces into bloodthirsty conflict. For some, the phrase was simply an expression of their understanding of the nature of God. For example, on 2 July 1917, the *Nottingham Evening Post* carried an officer's account of the preparation of the Sherwood Foresters (a regiment based in Derbyshire and Nottinghamshire) for the battle of the Somme a year earlier. Headed 'Did their duty and so they died!' and noting that, 'There are probably few people in Nottingham who did not lose friends or relatives in the fighting,' it reported,

> Presently came the Padre asking permission to say a few short prayers preparatory to proceeding to the trenches. Just two simple prayers, one of which I remember began, 'Lord God of battles'. Then the Lord's Prayer said very humbly, very earnestly, and very reverently by all, and last the voice of the Padre half-drowned by the din of the guns, 'The blessing … Almighty … upon … now and for evermore,' and then the Sherwoods made their peace with their Maker and were ready. Dusk soon fell … Then came the long wait for the appointed hour.[38]

36 *Newcastle Journal*, 4 March 1915, p. 5.
37 *Hull Daily Mail*, 19 July 1916, p. 2.
38 *NEP*, 2 July 1917, p. 1.

Lord of Hosts

Although arguably a less bellicose title for God, 'Lord of hosts' was nevertheless understood by many to have a very similar meaning. Certainly, it reaffirmed the Divine role in ensuring a righteous outcome to the conflict. Like the language of a 'Holy War', it was from the very start of the conflict felt to speak to the current situation. On the first Sunday of the war, worshippers in Biggleswade Parish Church heard a sermon on the text, 'The Lord of Hosts is with us, the God of Jacob is our refuge', being assured that the 'present European crisis' was comparable with the invasion of Judah by the Moabites and Ammonites recounted in 2 Chronicles.[39] The Vicar of Luton similarly told his congregation that 'we may say in all truth that the Lord of Hosts is with us' and that the country was doing God's bidding in fighting for 'hearth and home' and to defend the Empire which God had placed in its trust.[40] An article in *Dawn of Day* published in October 1914, headed 'War and our Duty', declared, 'We are at war! A peace-loving nation, we have been drawn ... into a conflict of which no man can see the end.' The anonymous author referred to St John's vision 'in which the spirits of demons are let loose upon the earth at Armageddon' and concluded, 'The God of Hosts controls all war-issues. Without reliance on Him the weapons of our warfare are untrustworthy.'[41]

While the title was often employed without any indication that its usage needed justification or explanation, in his Presidential Address to the Primitive Methodist Conference in Reading in 1915, John Day Thompson declared,

> 'I find the expression "Lord of Hosts" everywhere in the Scriptures, and I accept it as a right an honest admission of a great truth. I find that the leaders of armies, and the armies themselves, have done noble works which I recognise as God's works. ... I believe that the Spirit of God really calls the soldier to his duties, fits him for them, as he calls me to mine.' So said Frederick Denison Maurice, and I endorse his words.[42]

Since F.D. Maurice was remembered as one of the leading Christian socialists of the 19th century, Thompson's quoting of him would have a particular significance for a denomination that at a local level was far from universally supportive of the conflict and among the membership of which there would later be many conscientious objectors. In a sermon published in 1917, the Revd. W.H. Findlay, a prominent Wesleyan Methodist minister, declared, 'this outbreak of evil and suffering, if it uses up some of the old resources, must needs ... operate mainly in calling out the overwhelming

39 *Biggleswade Chronicle*, 14 August 1914, p. 3.
40 *Luton Times and Advertiser*, 14 August 1914, p. 4.
41 DRO, A/PI 16/16-17 – *Dawn of Day*, October 1914, p. 235.
42 *PML*, 17 June 1915, 'The War in its Religious Aspects', p. 375.

reserves of the *Lord of Hosts*.' We may note both his use of italics in emphasis and the title of the sermon: 'Super-Victory'.[43] Certainly, there is evidence that the title 'Lord of hosts' was seen as being particularly appropriate when God's chastening or cleansing activity was being sought. As the South African War ended, Henry Scott Holland, a Christian Socialist, had published a hymn which he had written,

> JUDGE eternal, throned in splendour,
> Lord of lords and King of kings,
> With Thy living fire of judgment
> Purge this Realm of bitter things:
> Solace all its wide Dominion
> With the healing of Thy wings.[44]

However, when it appeared in the 1909 *Fellowship Hymn-Book* and the 1916 *Congregational Hymnary*, 'Lord of Lords' was changed to 'Lord of hosts', apparently calling upon God to use the power implicit in that title to bring about a cathartic change in Edwardian society or an end to the conflict.[45] Subsequently, in post-war hymn books which printed 'Judge Eternal', 'Lord of hosts' almost invariably became 'Lord of Lords' again.[46] This may be indicative of a disenchantment with that title for God which had become popular during the war. Others used 'God of hosts' in much less aggressive ways, implicitly seeking to distinguish between the power of the heavenly hosts and that of earthly armies. Stephen Gwynn quoted Mabel Dearmer's rough autobiographical draft:

> I knew that if I had been a man I could not have fought, for the way in which I read the words of Christ is that the Kingdom of Heaven is gained by a different method altogether. 'Not by might, nor by power, but by spirit, saith the Lord of Hosts.' It is a method which has not been tried by diplomats.[47]

A chaplain described a picnic for Scottish soldiers passing through Malta:

> All too quickly the shades of night began to fall, and we gathered once more in a large group and sang the Doxology. As I looked up … and caught the swell

43 W.H. Findlay, 'Super-Victory' in B. Mathews (ed.), *Christ and the World at War* (London: James Clark, 1917), pp. 186-7.
44 Published in *The Commonwealth, A Christian Social Magazine*, vol. VII, no. 7 (July 1902).
45 *The Fellowship Hymn-Book* (London, 1909). It was a hymnbook intended for use in Adult Schools, Brotherhoods, 'Pleasant Sunday Afternoons' (P.S.A.) and similar meetings, compiled by representatives from the National Councils of Adult School Unions and P.S.A Brotherhoods.
46 e.g. *Songs of Praise* (1925), *Methodist Hymn Book* (1933),
47 Dearmer, *Letters from a Field Hospital*, p. 48.

> of their song as it blended into a mighty chorus, 'Praise God from Whom all blessings flow', I felt within the surge of a triumphant emotion. These men were bound to win, for theirs was the confidence of David, 'The Lord of Hosts is with us; the God of Jacob is our refuge.'[48]

In a sermon in December 1916 on Isaiah 31:5 – 'As little mother-birds hovering, so will the Lord of Hosts defend Jerusalem' – the Archdeacon of Nottingham, the Revd. W.J. Conybeare, declared 'Such is God in his tender care for us. He is afflicted in all our afflictions.'[49] The Methodist army chaplain Thomas Tiplady wrote of a final service near Achicourt in northern France:

> Lance-corporal Gilbert James was missing too – he whom I had known lose his breakfast to attend a service in a cold, dirty old barn. And many others were absent, whose departure to the land beyond our mortal reach was to us like the putting out of stars. We were leaving the Arras Front, and we sang a hymn for those who had taken our places :
>
> 'O Lord of Hosts, Whose mighty arm
> In safety keeps 'mid war's alarm,
> Protect our comrades at the Front
> Who bear of war the bitter brunt;
> And in the hour of danger spread
> Thy sheltering wings above each head. ...'
>
> I had to find a new voice to start it, for our little harmonium had been destroyed by a shell, and our precentor, Sergeant G.C. Cordery, was lying in a grave beside his Medical Aid Post at Guemappe ... His path was onward and upward, and his place was in the heavenly choir.[50]

It is too easy to allow the sentimental language of Tiplady's narrative, typical not only of him but of countless other writers from the theatres of war, to induce a cynicism in the modern reader which may cause us to doubt the author's sincerity. The use of ephemeral hymns, with crude rhymes such as 'Protect our comrades at the Front / Who bear of war the bitter brunt' (a hymn which he himself had written to be sung to the tune usually associated with *Eternal Father strong to save* – Melita) may also appear

48 A.G. Mackinnon, *Malta, the Nurse of the Mediterranean* (London: Hodder & Stoughton, 1916), p. 201.
49 *The Guardian*, 21 December 1916, p. 1131. Conybeare appears to have quoted from *Rotherham's Emphasized Bible*, 1902.
50 T. Tiplady, *The Soul of the Soldier* (London: Revell, 1918), pp. 75-6.

problematic.[51] However, the professed aim of the book was to paint a picture of the 'soul of the soldier' at the Front, of which in his introduction he wrote,

> and his glory and greatness were so radiant that the mud on him could not be seen. It sank into insignificance, and could not dim the splendour of his character. It was as the spots on the sun.[52]

Such was the language and such were the sentiments of the time. Reports of chaplains' experiences, printed at great length in religious newspapers and then often collected in books which sold in large quantities, were not intended as critical analyses of the chaplains' endeavours, nor of the men for whom they cared. They were intended to encourage and affirm. As such, they were typical of a much broader range of 'uplifting' communications from the theatres of war and Tiplady was one of thousands who wrote in those terms.

Geoffrey Studdert Kennedy was one of many to challenge such a eulogising of Tommy Atkins. Addressing one group of soldiers, he declared, 'Now, when Mr. Bottomley says you are splendid fellows, I am with him all the time. But when he says you are all saints! – well, take a look at one another!'[53] If the express purpose of such books as Tiplady's is recognised, then both the language and the style can be seen to be consistent with that aim, albeit fully deserving of the 'period piece' epithet. Across the vast range of material written by chaplains during the war there is a clear ambiguity shown by their determination to affirm the courage and selflessness of the vast majority of soldiers set alongside their constant concerns about the behaviour of many men, as evidenced by the recurring problem of venereal disease. Inevitably, many would be both exceptionally brave and self-sacrificial, yet also engaged in the immoral activities that so troubled the chaplains. A more significant question than Tiplady's sincerity is raised by the hymn that he quoted and in particular its expression of trust in God's providence, praying for his 'sheltering wings', as those singing gathered at the funeral of a soldier who had not been sheltered by those wings. That is a question to which we shall turn in the next chapter. Another poem by John Oxenham, *All Clear*, published in 1919, looked back at the conflict, seeing in the victory the work of the divine hosts:

> Great hosts of angels hovered o'er the fight
> And heartened those who fought that fight for Right,
> That they prevailed.

51 See *MR*, 3 August 1916, p. 1.
52 Tiplady, *Soul of the Soldier*, pp. vii-viii.
53 D.F. Carey, 'War Padre' in Mozley (ed.), *G.A. Studdert Kennedy by his Friends* (London: Hodder & Stoughton, 1929), p. 131. Horatio Bottomley was editor of the popular patriotic magazine *John Bull* during the war.

> Long, long and bitter was that final strife,
> Till Life was smitten to the verge of death.
> But, by God's mercy, Life won through at last,
> The hosts of Ill were smitten hip and thigh,
> And Earth thanked God for its delivery.
> And so at last the long-closed Door stood wide,
> And none gainsayed it now, and none denied
> Christ's right of entrance with the Sweeter Life
> Which meant an end for ever to all strife.[54]

Here, quite clearly, was a much more subtle use of the imagery of the battle between God's hosts of angels and the 'hosts of ill'. Again it can be seen that the Great War was seen not simply as an earthly military conflict, but also a heavenly and spiritual one between the forces of right and those of wrong. In subsequent verses, similar in style to the vision of John in Revelation, Oxenham painted a picture of the return of Christ,

> As King Omnipotent to reign
> Within the hearts of men;
> As Lord Supreme of Death and Life,
> As peaceful victor in the strife,
> ... To found His kingdom upon earth,
> To give to Life a nobler birth,
> And heal it of its shame.[55]

It was one of Kipling's most popular poems which would set the tone – a tone which can all too easily be misconstrued and misjudged – for more considered responses to the conflict than was more usually associated with the language of the 'Lord of hosts'. Written for Queen Victoria's diamond jubilee in 1897, the first four lines appear to be a conventional re-assertion of the divinely-authorised nature of the British Empire:

> God of our fathers, known of old—
> Lord of our far-flung battle line—
> Beneath whose awful hand we hold
> Dominion over palm and pine—

However, that verse ended with this couplet: 'Lord God of Hosts, be with us yet, / Lest we forget—lest we forget!' and every stanza concluded with that repeated warning,

54 J. Oxenham, *'All Clear!' A Book of Verse Commemorative of the Great Peace* (London: Methuen, 1919), pp. 18-19.
55 Ibid., p. 27.

'Lest we forget—lest we forget.' The poem, which is in reality a prayer, warned of two dangers for the Empire as it celebrated the Jubilee; first that it should go out of existence – 'The tumult and the shouting dies– / The Captains and the Kings depart' – and second that it should lapse from having true Christian faith at its heart:

> If, drunk with sight of power, we loose
> Wild tongues that have not Thee in awe—
> Such boastings as the Gentiles use,
> Or lesser breeds without the Law—

That last line has understandably proved problematic for those who have read in it the very jingoism which *Recessional* was challenging. Writing in 1942, George Orwell, hardly a natural ally of Kipling, sought both to clarify the meaning of that line and to correct any suggestion that *Recessional* is anything other than a critique of nationalistic hubris:

> An interesting instance of the way in which quotations are parroted to and fro without any attempt to look up their context or discover their meaning is the line from 'Recessional', 'Lesser breeds without the Law.' This line is always good for a snigger in pansy-left circles. It is assumed as a matter of course that the 'lesser breeds' are 'natives', and a mental picture is called up of some pukka sahib in a pith helmet kicking a coolie. In its context the sense of the line is almost the exact opposite of this. The phrase 'lesser breeds' refers almost certainly to the Germans, and especially the pan-German writers, who are 'without the Law' in the sense of being lawless, not in the sense of being powerless. The whole poem, conventionally thought of as an orgy of boasting, is a denunciation of power politics, British as well as German.[56]

Orwell went on to identify the Biblical sources which Kipling had used in the poem and he sought to distinguish 'the prophet of British Imperialism in its expansionist phase' with his 'bouncing vulgar vitality' from the Fascism of the 20th century. Stewart Brown identified *Recessional* as part of a wave of 'New Journalism' of the 1890s, in which 'perceptions of the Christian, moral and civilising mission of empire were giving way to darker views of imperialism as an exercise of naked power for the exploitation of colonized peoples.'[57] At the very outbreak of the war, the Revd. H.B. Kendall, a past-President of the Primitive Methodist Conference, had written on the front page of the *Primitive Methodist Leader*, 'Events are indeed conspiring to make

56 G. Orwell, *Review of* T.S. Eliot (ed.) 'A Choice of Kipling's Verse', first published in *Horizon*, February 1942. Reprinted in S. Orwell and I. Angus (eds.), *Essays, Journalism and Letters of George Orwell, vol. II, 1940–43* (London: Harcourt, 1993), pp. 184f.

57 Brown, *Providence and Empire 1815-1914*, p. 378.

us, in the French phrase, 'furiously to think', and all our thinking will surely be on the lines of Kipling's great Recessional hymn.'[58] It became prominent in public worship, for example at a united Free Church service in Birmingham in August 1916 and a Congregational service of remembrance at Derby in October 1917, at which a solo, *Return O God of Hosts*, was sung before a Roll of Honour of 107 names was read.[59] A writer in the *Methodist Recorder* in 1916 reported on attending two services on one Sunday that had both started with *Recessional* and suggested that it 'will be sung at least for a hundred years.'[60] A survey of more than 80 booklets, leaflets and orders of services dating from 1914 to 1921, most of which are located in the Nottinghamshire or Derbyshire archives, shows it to be the third most commonly-used hymn, after *O God our help in ages past* and *For all the saints who from their labours rest. Recessional* had been included in the 1909 *Fellowship Hymn Book*, in the companion to which Frederick Gillman identified it as an expression of 'true patriotism'.[61] It then found its way into many post-war hymn books, as its repeated 'Lest we forget, lest we forget' became an integral part of the memorialisation ceremonies. It remains part of many commemorations of Anzac Day in Australia and New Zealand.

In Later Years

As the war progressed, the rhetoric was accompanied by a growing recognition of its cost. Nevertheless, the 'God of battles' and 'Lord of hosts' discourses were not discarded, but rather were accompanied by more sombre, reflective and penitential utterances. Drawing on the significance of 1915 as the centenary of the battle of Waterloo, a poem, '1815–1915' by Annie Lamont in Dundee started with the recognition, 'There's a bloody plain in Flanders / Where men have fought and died.' It concluded, 'O God of battles lend Thine aid, / And set us free again.'[62] After visiting the trenches in 1916, the Bishop of Birmingham called for the 'uttermost' support for the 'splendid' men, for sacrifice of leisure and gold, and for the readers of the diocesan magazine to 'commend our cause to the God of Battles and then, before 1917 dawns, though peace may not be declared, still the world will know where victory is going to dwell.'[63] Psalm 46, the refrain of which reads, 'The Lord of hosts is with us, the God of Jacob is our refuge', was the text for a sermon 'A hymn of faith in a time of war' preached at Bloomsbury Baptist Chapel by Thomas Phillips early in 1917. He compared the imagery of destruction of the earth, the mountains and the seas in opening verses with 'the experiences of our men on the fields of death when the

58 *PML*, 13 August 1914, p. 569.
59 *Birmingham Gazette*, 1 August 1916, p. 5; DRO, D2608/21/2, *Victoria Street Congregational Church, Sunday 14 October 1917*.
60 *MR*, 22 June 1916, p. 8.
61 F.J. Gillman, *The Story of our Hymns* (London: Swarthmore, 1921), p. 107.
62 (Dundee) *Evening Telegraph*, 18 June 1915, p. 6.
63 *Birmingham Gazette*, 3 February 1916, p. 8.

great shells fall around them.'[64] As with the use of hymns, so with the interpretation of Old Testament texts, wartime practices were consistent with pre-war expositions. For example, Hensley Henson, then Dean of Westminster had a decade before the outbreak of the war preached on the same Psalm in the commemoration of the refounding of the Bishopric of London, 13 centuries earlier: 'as we recall that long and various history ... we can take heart again, and be sure that, come what may, Christianity has nothing to fear.'[65]

As the war progressed, less often was the choice made between the discourse of divinely-validated military action and that of divinely-exemplified personal sacrifice. Rather, those two themes became interwoven in the affirmation of divine endorsement. At the end of 1916, a poem by 'L.S.R.' published in *The Spectator* demonstrated a complex and nuanced use of the familiar rhetoric. The focus was not the battle, but its cost. The poet's concern was that the sacrifice of the fallen would be rendered futile by an unjust peace:

> O GOD of battles, o'er the din of war
> Hear us we pray, the wives of those who lie
> Slain on the ravaged fields of France; who gave
> Themselves for England, freely gave their lives
> To rid the world of lust and cruelty.
> Let not dissension here within our gates
> Weaken our purpose. O take not in vain
> Those men we gave. Let not their children feel
> The shame of any armistice—give strength
> And union, Lord, to those who guide our England,
> Until the stubborn fight is won—until
> Atonement for each drop of blood is made.
> For thus alone may all our sons enjoy
> The Peace their parents won by blood and tears.[66]

Armistice, Peace and Retrospection

When the heat of the battle was over and the armies had been demobilised, Church leaders and theologians had an opportunity to reflect on the experience of a war which had been so staunchly supported by almost all the mainstream Churches. In *The Army and Religion*, D.S. Cairns offered this conclusion about the wartime experience:

64 *BTF*, 2 March 1917, p. 136.
65 H. H. Henson, *Westminster Sermons* (London: James Clark, 1910), pp. 11-23, 20.
66 *The Spectator*, 16 December 1916, p. 13.

> The soldier's God is once more the God of Battles, who clothes Himself with the storm. He is not the judge of righteousness and wrong, not the friend of the fatherless and the widow's protector, not holy, or just, or good ...[67]

Cairns' comment was made in a section on 'Trench Fatalism' which he described as being always theistic, but empty of moral content. For many soldiers, he wrote, God was the 'Lord of Fate and the Master of Life and Death.' While that analysis may well have been correct, it is not readily apparent whether such 'trench fatalism' was a consequence of the war, or rather had simply been a wartime manifestation of one aspect of pre-war popular religion. In a series of lectures on sacrifice and reconciliation published in 1921, the Wesleyan Methodist scholar W.L. Lofthouse looked back at the response of the Church to the outbreak of war in 1914:

> [W]hen the cataclysm took place, few of her spokesmen could do anything save call on the God of battles to show the right and crush the oppressor and the tyrant, as if the Almighty Himself, twenty centuries after He had sent Jesus to commend His love to sinners, had no other alternative.[68]

In a book of sermons on the Apostles' Creed, published in 1921, Geoffrey Studdert Kennedy sought to draw a distinction between belief in the monarchical God of the Old Testament of which 'God of battles' was but one expression and his hope for a new post-war faith, developing from his wartime critique of the worship of – in his frequently-used phrase – a 'passionless potentate'.[69] He wrote that in 'Christian theology of the orthodox sort,' God is 'the God of battles, Who declares War and maintains Peace. Whatever happens is the result of His command ... and sudden death in a thousand forms are the weapons that He wields.' However, he wrote, 'men thought in those days in terms of Providence and Security; we think in terms of Progress and Adventure. They thought in terms of Despotism, and we think in terms of Democracy and Self-Government.'[70] We may note his reference to the 'God of progress' – just the words which would be used by Percy Dearmer in 1932 to replace 'God of battles' in his editing of *Stand up, stand up for Jesus*.

As was often the case, a particularly perceptive observation about the development of the 'God of battles' rhetoric within the Empire came from someone outside it. To illustrate his argument that common worship requires a common agreement on values, Walter Harris, an American Episcopalian minister, wrote in 1928:

67 Cairns (ed.), *The Army and Religion*, p. 163.
68 W.F. Lofthouse, *Altar Cross and Community* (London: Epworth, 1921), p. 300.
69 G.A. Studdert Kennedy, *The Hardest Part* (London: Hodder & Stoughton, 1918), pp. 9-10. For a discussion of his theology of a suffering God, see chapter 6.
70 G.A. Studdert Kennedy, *I Believe; Sermons on the Apostles' Creed* (London: Hodder & Stoughton, 1921), p. 34.

> I recall a service in St. Paul's Cathedral just after the outbreak of war. The preacher bade us worship and trust the God of battles. It was plain that the majority saw in such a God an object worthy of reverence and they worshipped Him. A young American tourist [presumably the writer] standing by was half puzzled at, half contemptuous of, the service. The nationalist hymns, the thunder of the Old Testament lesson, the exhortations of the preacher, the litany and the responses, found no answer in him at that time. There was a temperamental distinction between him and the congregation; they were involved in the passions of nationalism and were already experiencing that upsetting of values which is consequent upon war. He was still immune; for him Germans were still a foreign nation not the enemy; for him there was still no thought of God as a God of battles.[71]

For Harris, the 'God of battles' discourse had come into widespread use because of the changed attitude of Britain towards Germany. Having previously been viewed simply as a foreign country and, therefore, inherently inferior through not being God's chosen nation (as Kipling's *Recessional* had so clearly expressed it), once August 1914 had arrived, Germany had become the enemy. Consequently, to the association of Britain with Israel was added that of Germany with the Assyrians – or any of the other historic oppressors of God's people. Once that similitude had been established, the discourse of the 'God of battles' seemed irresistible to many people.

During the conflict, James Moffat, renowned for producing one of the first colloquial translations of the Bible and at the time Professor of Church History at the United Free Church College in Glasgow, had written an article, *The Influence Of The War Upon The Religious Life And Thought Of Great Britain* – one of the very few attempts at any assessment during the conflict. He had asserted in 1916,

> There might be a return to the Lord of Hosts rather than to the Lord, an exploiting of Christianity in the interests of patriotism of the lower order, which would really spell weakness instead of strength. ... I think we may congratulate ourselves that there has not been any movement in this direction throughout Great Britain. ... I have been struck with the comparative lack of an exaggerated emphasis upon the Old Testament. One almost expected that such a stress would be laid on the Old Testament, for ... men instinctively turn to the prophets and the history of Israel, with a passionate thirst for words corresponding to their day and danger. I do not think this tendency has been nearly so marked as it was, if I can judge from history, during the Indian mutiny or the Crimean war.[72]

71 T.L. Harris, *Christian Public Worship* (New York: Doubleday, 1928), pp. 51f. It should be noted that the publication of this book took place at a time of significant reaction against the war in the USA.

72 J. Moffat, 'The Influence Of The War Upon The Religious Life And Thought Of Great Britain', *The American Journal of Theology*, vol. XX, no. 4 (October 1916), pp. 481-493.

How can we reconcile Lofthouse's critique of the widespread call in 1914 to 'the God of battles to show the right and crush the oppressor and the tyrant' with Moffat's analysis? One obvious explanation is Moffat's perspective. His geo-political location is unlikely to have been significant, since Scottish support for the conflict was not markedly different from that in England. More important may have been his place within the United Free Church of Scotland, given that support for Britain's engagement across the British Free Churches was in general more nuanced and qualified than in the established Church of England. However, it should be noted that by the time of the Great War, the United Free Church was increasingly aligning itself with the Church of Scotland, with which most of its churches would unite in 1929. Most significant was probably Moffat's *locus* as an academic, for what he said may well have been true of the circles in which he moved. There was no 'return to the Lord of Hosts' in the academic papers of the period and few if any academic theologians preached on the 'God of battles'. Furthermore, it is noticeable that most of the war-like hymns written to catch the mood – and arguably to encourage the mood – of the nation, were printed not in the church newspapers or official anthologies of hymns but in popular and populist national and regional newspapers. What James Moffat observed may well have differed from the experience of the proverbial man in the pew. As for his reference to 'the comparative lack of an exaggerated emphasis upon the Old Testament', an analysis of the Biblical texts of the sermons printed in *Christian World Pulpit* during the Great War does not support Moffat's conclusions:

Table 1 Use of Old Testament texts in sermons published in *Christian World Pulpit*

Period	Context	Sermons with OT text	Sample size
July 1900 – June 1901	South African War	36%	280
July 1904 – June 1905		28%	265
July 1913 – June 1914	Immediately pre-WW1	36%	298
July – December 1914	Outbreak of WW1	47%	133
1915	WW1	36%	283
1916	WW1	38%	245
1917	WW1	35%	226
1918	WW1	29%	206
January – June 1919	Immediately post-war	26%	109
July 1940 – June 1941	WW2	36%	345
July 1960 – June 1961		26%	247

Clearly, the use of OT texts in the First World War was comparable with the sample year from the South African War. We may note the very similar figures for the peacetime years of 1904-5, 1919 and 1960-61. Furthermore, there was a significant rise in the use of such texts in the opening months of the conflict and a general slow decline from 1916. We should not assume that the sermons published in *Christian World*

Pulpit were any more than broadly representative of the tens of thousands preached each week across the country. However, while proportions might well vary according to, for example, denomination, the trends identified above are likely to be indicative of the wider experience.

Most of the hymns addressing the 'God of battles' or 'Lord of hosts,' often little more than hastily-written pieces of patriotic doggerel, disappeared as quickly as they had appeared. Others – the more nuanced and less militaristic ones – were revised so as to be more suitable for an immediate post-war era in which the Churches prayed that between them the League of Nations and God would ensure a lasting peace. For example, one of the many hymns that had been written for Queen Victoria's Golden Jubilee was Henry Burton's paean of praise to God:

> O King of Kings, O Lord of hosts, whose throne is lifted high
> Above the nations of the earth, the armies of the sky.
> The spirits of the perfected may give their nobler songs;
> And we, Thy children, worship Thee, to whom all praise belongs.
>
> Thou who didst lead Thy people forth, and make the captive free,
> Hast drawn around our native land the curtain of the sea,
> To make another holy place, where golden lamps should shine,
> And human hearts keep loving watch around the ark divine.
>
> Our bounds of empire Thou hast set in many a distant isle,
> And in the shadow of our throne the desert places smile;
> For in our laws and in our faith 'tis Thine own light they see –
> The truth that brings to captive souls the wider liberty.

The hymn continued for a further three verses, developing the theme of a chosen people, recipients of God's goodness and favour. It had been published in the *(Wesleyan) Methodist Hymn-Book*, in the 'King and Nation' section.[73] Sung frequently during the war as a classic example of the expression of Britain's 'specially-favoured nation' status, in its employment of the 'God of hosts' rhetoric it was more measured in tone than many other hymns. As such, it was not discarded after 1918, but was, rather, modified to serve the new age. One of the first post-war hymn collections was the 1920 Supplement to the *Fellowship Hymn-Book*. The new material comprised 115 hymns, including G.K. Chesterton's *O God of Earth and Altar*, J.R. Lowell's *Once to every man and nation* and F.M. North's *Where cross the crowded ways of life*, all of which would become popular in the inter-war period. Burton's *O King of Kings, O Lord of Hosts* found a place, but in a very different form. Both the second and the third verses, with their confident assertion of Divine favouritism, were removed. Those that remained

73 *(Wesleyan) Methodist Hymn-Book* (London: Wesleyan Methodist Church, 1904).

stressed that all the riches of Britain were God's gift, without explicitly distinguishing it from other parts of God's world and the concluding stanza prayed that the King of Kings and Lord of hosts would be with them in future years, leading them to 'heaven's eternal day'. With the excision of the references to 'bounds of empire' and 'our throne' so much of the national pride implicit in the language of 'Lord of hosts' as the Empire had celebrated Victoria's Golden Jubilee had been discarded, and it had become little more than another name by which to address God.

The Persistence of the Rhetoric

From a contemporary perspective, we might assume that the Great War saw the end of the rhetoric of the 'God of battles'. Had not the loss of so many lives made it so unpalatable as to be unutterable? A new understanding of the relationship between divine omnipotence and human free will was called for and the identification of human war with spiritual conflict, thus validating the appropriation of hymns of spiritual warfare such as *Onward Christian soldiers* and *Soldiers of Christ, arise* would surely not be repeated. However, on 23 October 1942, Field Marshal Montgomery concluded a message to the troops of the Eighth Army at Alamein with these words:

> Therefore, let every officer and man enter the battle with a stout heart, and the determination to do his duty so long as he has breath in his body. AND LET NO MAN SURRENDER SO LONG AS HE IS UNWOUNDED AND CAN FIGHT. Let us pray that 'the Lord mighty in battle' will give us the victory.[74]

If one of the lessons of the First World War was that the rhetoric of the 'God of battles' was irreconcilable with that of a God of love, then we may conclude that the lesson took several decades and the even greater loss of life in the Second World War, to be fully learned.

Conclusion

While the language of the 'God of Battles' and the 'Lord of Hosts' has – apart from the latter's place in Eucharistic liturgies – generally fallen out of use in contemporary British Christianity and can offend modern sensibilities, it was prominent in the discourse of the First World War. However, a distinction must be drawn between the two phrases, which had quite different origins. The former, a title originated by William Shakespeare, was far more belligerent in tone and was avoided by many Church leaders. It did, however, resonate with the unrestrained patriotism of much of the popular press. While less obviously militaristic in emphasis, 'Lord of Hosts' was

74 B.L. Montgomery, *Forward to Victory* (London: Hutchinson, 1946), quoted in Snape, *God and the British Soldier*, p. 74.

commonly employed to assert the association of Britain in its conflict with Germany with the people of Israel of the Old Testament and their battles with the Assyrians and other aggressors. This link was a key element in Britain's claim of the righteousness of her cause, the confident assertion that God was on her side, and the characterisation of the war as a battle between military might and ethical right. However, if Almighty God were indeed on Britain's side, then as time passed and the numbers of deaths and casualties escalated, increasing numbers of people began to wonder why an all-powerful God was allowing such suffering and how belief in divine Providence should be understood in the face of the apparent random-ness of the paths of bullet and shell on the battlefield. In the next chapter, we shall examine the variety of responses to those questions.

4

Omnipotence and Providence

Introduction

When we turn to issues of divine omnipotence and divine providence, we are addressing those theological questions that were most obviously raised by a war that involved such an immense loss of life, physical and mental injury, material destruction and financial cost. The problem of why, if God is all-powerful and all-loving, there is suffering in the world has troubled people of faith in the Judaeo-Christian tradition for millennia, the story of Job being the classic Biblical example of a struggle with this conundrum. During the war, many argued that the question had not changed. Rather, the sheer scale of loss and destruction posed the old question with greater force than ever before. As the Anglican chaplain Russell Barry put it in *The Church in the Furnace*, 'In a sense the war has not produced new problems. It has only heavily underlined the old ones. The 'blank misgivings' with regard to suffering have always been in the minds of thinking men.'[1]

In this chapter, we shall consider the manner in which the question was posed – primarily focusing on the nature of divine omnipotence – and then answered. A closely-related issue is that of divine providence, the understanding of God's activity in the created world. Although this is rarely evidenced in the primary sources which will be considered, a distinction is often made between 'general providence', relating to God's on-going care for the universe, and 'special providence', relating to specific acts of divine intervention, such as miracles. Much has been made in scholarly work of some famous reported wartime miracles, such as the 'Angel of Mons' and the apparent survival of crosses, crucifixes and other religious artifacts in otherwise totally-destroyed churches, villages and towns.[2] There remains little light to be cast on such matters. Rather, we shall examine popular attitudes towards divine providence,

1 Barry, 'Faith in the Light of War', p. 46.
2 See, for example, J. Hayward, *Myths and Legends of the First World War* (Stroud: The History Press, 2010), pp. 47-62 and Wilkinson, *The Church of England*, pp. 149f.

considering both narratives suggesting divine intervention and those lamenting its absence. As has been widely noted, there was much debate about the location of the fine line between religious devotion and superstition about objects associated with divine intervention. Many practices associated with Catholicism or Anglo-Catholicism, such as the use of the rosary or the carrying of crucifixes, came to have a broader appeal. Another frequently-reported characteristic of combatant faith has been fatalism, which we shall consider in relationship to the questions of omnipotence and providence.[3]

Providence, Fatalism and Luck at the Front

Notwithstanding the apparent reluctance of many ordinary soldiers to write about their beliefs and religious practices, some men were willing to express unselfconsciously their faith in diary or letter. For example, Arthur Borton, described by the editor of the family diaries as an 'upper-middle-class "ne'er-do-well"' before the war,[4] wrote from Salonika to his father in April 1916, 'You can probably realise how much it means to me, but I cannot put in words the gratitude I feel to some unseen power, that I should have been allowed to be alive and in my present position at the present time.'[5] The conflict was perhaps the happiest time of Borton's life. He was awarded the VC and the DSO but post-war depression led to alcoholism, dis-inheritance and an early death as a 'broken-down hero'. The language of the 'unseen power' would appear to be typical of the nature of the 'diffusive faith' of many public school-educated officers – Borton having been to Eton – for whom a vague theism was all that remained from the years of compulsory religious activity. A more orthodox faith was expressed by Eric Heaton when he wrote home two days before the battle of the Somme in which he would die. A 'son of the manse' who had been educated at the Methodist Kingswood public school, Heaton wrote:

> My darling Mother and Father. I am writing this on the eve of my first action. ... I cannot tell if it is God's will that I should come through – but if I fall in battle I have no regrets save for my loved ones I leave behind. ... Well, I cannot write more now. You are all in my thoughts as I enter this first battle. May God go with me.[6]

A day later, 2nd Lt. Jack Engall, wrote to his parents,

3 See, for example, Schweitzer, *The Cross and the Trenches* (2003), p. 224.
4 G. Slater (ed.), *My Warrior Sons – The Borton Family Diary, 1914-18* (London: P Davies, 1973), p. 15.
5 Ibid., p. 102.
6 S. Price (ed.), *If you're reading this . . . Last letters from the Front Line* (London: Frontline Books, 2011), p. 134.

> I took my Communion yesterday with dozens of others who are going over tomorrow. … I placed my soul and body in God's keeping, and I am going into battle with His name on my lips, full of confidence and trusting implicitly in Him. I have a strong feeling that I shall come through safely; but nevertheless, should it be God's holy will to call me away I am quite prepared to go; … I could not wish for a finer death; and you, dear Mother and Dad, will know that I died doing my duty to my God, my Country and my King.[7]

He, too, died on the Somme. A convert to Catholicism, Captain Rowland Fielding had been commissioned into the Coldstream Guards but transferred to the 6th Connaught Rangers when efforts were made to employ Catholic officers in the Irish Regiments after the Easter rising. In March 1918, he wrote to his wife, 'We have crammed years of life into a week, during which my usual Providence protected me, though the Battalion – indeed the whole Division – is practically gone.'[8] That the war letters of an Irish academic and former Irish nationalist MP, Thomas Kettle, could be included in Laurence Houseman's *War Letters of Fallen Englishmen*, a title justified by the author by the 'lack of a more comprehensive word', says much about the Anglo-centric attitudes of the time.[9] On 10 August, Kettle wrote to his wife:

> If God spares me I shall accept it as a special mission to preach love and peace for the rest of my life. If he does not, I know now in my heart that for anyone who is dead but has loved enough, there is provided some way of piercing the veils of death and abiding close to those whom he has loved till that end which is the beginning.[10]

A 'Lancashire lad' assured his chaplain, 'I shall be glad when I can see them again. I know there's been a Providence over me. It's my mother's and sweetheart's prayers that have kept me.'[11] Some chaplains also expressed their confidence in divine providence in unequivocal terms. Kenneth Best wrote, 'Never shall I forget my first service under fire. We all felt that God's good Providence watched over us and nobody was hit.'[12] Pat Leonard related how in an air-raid the only bell tent to be destroyed had been an unoccupied one, adding, 'and men still deny the existence of GOD!'[13] After another

7 Houseman (ed.) *War Letters of Fallen Englishmen*, p. 107.

8 Fielding and Waller (ed.), *War Letters to a Wife*, p. 164. So great had its losses been, the battalion was formally disbanded in August 1918.

9 Houseman (ed.) *War Letters of Fallen Englishmen*, p. xxix.

10 Ibid., p. 167.

11 C.S. Wallis, *Fifty Thousand Miles on a Hospital Ship* (London Religious Tract Society, 1917), p. 159.

12 Best and Roynon (eds.), *A Chaplain at Gallipoli*, p. 96.

13 P. Leonard, (eds. J. Leonard and P. Leonard-Johnson) *The Fighting Padre: Letters from the Trenches, 1915–1918, of Pat Leonard, DSO* (Barnsley: Pen and Sword, 2010), p. 73.

narrow escape, he commented, 'But out here a miss is as good as a mile, and the shield of faith is still mighty to save.'[14]

Edwin Campion Vaughan, a Roman Catholic 2nd Lt. brought up in the Midlands, served on the Western Front for eight months in 1917 with the Royal Warwickshire Regiment. In his diary, he reported a visit to Rouen cathedral for Benediction, attendances at Mass, discussions with his padre and attending a local church. One entry described a long talk with 'Sullivan', 'starting with reminiscences of days on Salisbury Plain and ending with religion. This latter topic was always our standby for earnest argument, he being a very sincere C of E and one of the rare few whom I have met who can speak calmly on the RC faith.'[15] For him, God's providence was a reality. Within an account of life on the front line, surrounded by corpses and under frequent enemy bombardment, he wrote:

> I was climbing over the fallen rock, when my foot slipped and I fell into the front line. Even as I fell there was a crack and a chip of rock flew off. A sniper must have had me spotted all the time, and my slip was an act of Providence, though the sniper must have patted himself on the back for securing another victim.[16]

However, for many soldiers, officers and, indeed, chaplains, the question of divine providence was problematic. While David Cairns' ulterior motives in producing *The Army and Religion* that were noted in the Introduction mean that the evidence he presented should be treated with some caution, he was more willing – perhaps because of those motives – than were many chaplains to record the religious doubts of combatants. He reported the comment of a hut worker in France on his contact with soldiers on the Western Front: 'The whole question of God's providence in relation to human life commands their attention.'[17] Two reports were typical and revelatory of the way in which such doubts were expressed:

> From a sergeant in the RAMC, who describes himself as an agnostic: 'Many were profoundly affected by the war. ... How are we to reconcile this frightful thing with an all-loving, all-wise, all-powerful Creator?' I think a biggish proportion of the rank and file are really secretly thinking of such things, but vaguely and without definite expression.

14 Ibid., p. 153.
15 E.C. Vaughan, *Some Desperate Glory; The World War One Diary of a British Officer* (London: F. Warne, 1981), p. 19.
16 Ibid., p. 34.
17 Cairns (ed.), *The Army and Religion*, p. 158.

> From an officer in a West Country regiment. 'As a result of the war there arise doubts as to the existence of God, or, if He exists, doubts as to His power to interfere with the world-order as He apparently does not do so now, when such sufferings and bloodshed would stir the heart of a God.'[18]

Geoffrey Studdert Kennedy summarised the difficulties inherent in attributing one soldier's miraculous escape from death or injury to divine providence while a few feet away another died: '"I believe in God the Father Almighty, and a trench mortar has just blown my pal, who was a good-living lad, to pieces." Why cannot they see Him? Because of the contradiction.'[19] One of the most prolific chaplain-writers was the Wesleyan Methodist, Thomas Tiplady, who both regularly contributed articles to the *Methodist Recorder* and also published two volumes of 'letters on life and thought at the Front … all written in tents and billets within range, or sound, of the guns.'[20] The fact that at times parts of south-east Kent were within 'sound of the guns' does rather undermine Tiplady's apparent intention to stress how near he was to the action at all times. His narrative was one of enthusiasm and affirmation, offering generalisations about millions of men such as, 'Tommy's mind is a fine one and a contented one.'[21] He could liken the sound of guns to the thud of incoming waves although he did not deny 'the frightful cost of war'.[22] One may therefore wonder whether this comment was more an expression of his own deep faith, or indeed of his hopes for one outcome of his ministry, rather than being typical of those to whom he was ministering:

> Sceptics sitting at home in comfortable chairs point to the shell-ploughed fields of the Somme as the burial-place of a fallen Christianity; but that is not the view of the officers and men on the spot. There, amid the evidences of man's cruel hatred and greed, they realize most fully the presence of Christ and the love that made Him die for them. They cannot understand the mystery of God's providence, but they are assured of His presence and love. It is there, too, that they are seen at their noblest.[23]

A New Zealand surgeon, Arthur Martin, happened to be in London in the summer of 1914. Enlisting as soon as was possible, Martin served with the RAMC for eight months. Much of his narrative was concerned with the organization of medical care, the treatment of different wounds and deficiencies in the equipping and preparation of the BEF in general and the RAMC in particular. Within that account, he described a scene during the battle of the Aisne,

18 Ibid., pp. 26-27.
19 Studdert Kennedy, 'The Religious Difficulties of the Private Soldier', p. 379.
20 T. Tiplady, *The Cross at the Front* (London: Revell, 1917), p. 7.
21 Ibid., p. 14.
22 Ibid., pp. 29 and 42.
23 Ibid., p. 154.

> Here was a scene of ghastly horror. On the road lay mangled and bleeding horses, dead men lying in all sorts of convulsed attitudes, upturned wagons, smashed and splintered wood. Add to this the agonised groans of our wounded men, the shrill scream of dying horses, and that impalpable but nevertheless real feeling of standing in the face of the Creator – one can, perhaps, then feebly picture this scene of carnage, of the solemnity of death, and of the pitiless woe of this devastation.[24]

The sense of a divine encounter was common to both Tiplady's and Martin's accounts and each, in different ways, referred to the horrors of war. However, while for the chaplain, in such scenes of carnage officers and men realised the presence of Christ, for the surgeon, the encounter in the horrors of the battlefield – the details of which he did not spare the reader – is with the Creator. A regular church-goer who, like so many others, made little of his attendance at religious services in France and Belgium, Martin did not choose to identify the 'devilish, hellish, bloody, awful, and terrible' nature of the warfare as either a challenge to faith or an encouragement of it.[25] He continued, 'Where could one find here a trace of the glory, pomp, and magnificence of war?'[26] Whereas many chaplains saw signs of the divine presence in the human response to suffering, in acts of bravery and sacrifice, it was in the desolation that Martin felt to be 'standing in the face of the Creator'.

A simplistic ascription to divine providence of an otherwise unaccountable escape from peril was often problematic for even the least theologically-literate soldier. Robert Rider, training for the Methodist ministry when war was declared, wrote as a chaplain who had initially served as a soldier.[27] As a group of officers worshipped, led by Rider, a bomb fell five yards away, causing multiple deaths and serious injury with only the padre escaping entirely. In the conversation that followed, Rider tried to cheer his commanding officer, suggesting that the fact that he had been absent when the bomb fell had been providential.

> 'This tragedy, Colonel, was perhaps not staged by Providence, but it can be used by Providence.' The officer replied, 'I suppose, Padre, I'm a lucky dog, but I really cannot see how God can have anything to do with it. A 'stolen respite' is scarcely

24 A.A. Martin, *A Surgeon in Khaki: Through France and Flanders in World War I* (London: Arnold, 1916), re-printed with an introduction by G. Harper ((Lincoln, NE: University of Nebraska Press, 2011), p. 87.

25 Ibid., p. 88.

26 Ibid., p. 87.

27 A.C. Robinson and P.E.H. Hair (eds.), R.J. Rider, *Reflections on the Battlefield – from infantryman to chaplain 1914–1919* (Liverpool: Liverpool University Press, 2001). The narratives are memoirs, mostly written in the 1930s and '40s, 'almost certainly drawing on a war diary' (p. 1). This has understandably led to the editors at some points querying Rider's identification of the dates at which various views were expressed.

providential. Even if it were, I reckon He's made a d*** poor selection to single me out for the distinction.'[28]

Nevertheless, such explanations were commonplace. Writing to his parents in July 1915, Lt. Gerald Grenfell of the Rifle Brigade reported on his servant's narrow escape when, while he was making tea for Grenfell, 'a "crump" crumped most effectively the dugout in which he reposes 18 hours out of the 24. I have forbidden him to mention his "providential escape" to me again, under pain of being returned to duty.'[29] As for the traditional assertion that God, through his providential action, determines when someone is to die, Russell Barry wrote of the words in the burial service, 'We are even ordered to give God "hearty thanks" because it hath "pleased Him to deliver this our brother out of the misery of this sinful world." I utterly refuse to believe that statement.'[30]

Letters, diaries and chaplains' reports indicate three different ways of explaining why some men were killed and many more injured, while others escaped all harm. One rationale expressed confidence in divine providence, the difficulties of which we have noted. The second approach was to ascribe everything to luck. The third attitude, fatalism, was exemplified by the common affirmation that if a bullet had someone's name on it, then nothing could be done. *The Army and Religion* is full of reports of soldiers' fatalism. As one chaplain put it, 'Theologically most of the men are temporarily fatalists. That seems far enough away from the faith of Christianity.'[31] However, he expressed the hope that such fatalism might lead to a 'renewed interest in the sovereignty of God.' There was a similar ambiguity in a hut worker's comment on such fatalistic attitudes, 'which I should hesitate to call a Christian fatalism, belief in the sovereignty of God.'[32] It should not be assumed that soldiers, officers and chaplains all expressed their belief in terms of just one of the three alternatives of providence, luck and fatalism, for hybrid rationales were common and there was often an ambiguity of language. Thus, in *The Army and Religion,* a private reported: 'Most of the men are fatalists or materialists in so far as they believe that if it is their fate to get shot they will be shot. They do their duty and put their faith in luck.'[33] Even men with a clear religious faith found themselves caught up in the culture of fatalism that was all-pervasive in the theatres of war. Geoffrey Husbands, who had attended a Moravian school and was quite open about his faith to his comrades in the Sherwood Foresters, described an incident in the summer of 1916 near Richebourg-l'Avoué in northern France:

28 Rider, *Reflections on the Battlefield*, pp. 79f.
29 Houseman (ed.) *War Letters of Fallen Englishmen*, p. 116.
30 Barry, 'Faith in the Light of War', p. 43.
31 Cairns (ed.), *The Army and Religion*, p. 160.
32 Ibid., p. 159.
33 Ibid., p. 160.

> an hour or two later [we] entered the dugout … 'Heard the news?' said 'G.R.'. 'No,' said I. 'Corporal Wibberley's killed. Fritz shelled the post and young Wibberley was laid out by a whizzbang. Lucky for you, you'd gone for a bath.' It was a strange coincidence that this should have happened when the original arrangement that I should be there had been cancelled, and it strengthened our fatalistic tendencies for a while.[34]

Chaplains and clergy sometimes saw it as their task to advocate a providential perspective in the face of widespread fatalism or belief in the randomness of death and injury. A fine example of clerical desire to replace notions of luck or fatalism with affirmations of divine providence appeared in this note from the vicar printed in the May 1915 *Monthly Letter* of St. Paul's, Birmingham:

> Brief notes given to me from the mental diary of Sam Skitt, quite lately one of S. Paul's choir boys, now in the Duke of Cornwall's Light Infantry. 'Been through Neuve Chapelle and St. Eloi. … scratched in thigh. … wonderful luck (he meant Divine protection) … we picked off man after man in the trenches.'[35]

Sam Skitt did not, of course, mean 'Divine protection'. Serving at the Front he would probably have been far more conscious of the implications of ascribing his own survival to providence while others died than was his vicar. Tiplady, too, was anxious to re-interpret men's attitudes to match his own belief: 'Men are conscious of a power that is not themselves directing their lives. They feel that in life which the Greek tragedians called Fate. They do not know quite what to call it. Most of them would call it Providence if they spoke frankly and gave it a name at all.'[36]

Just like Sam Skitt's vicar, the Wesleyan chaplain wished to believe that expressions of fatalism or chance were inarticulate ways of affirming divine providence. In contrast, a rather more perceptive chaplain than Tiplady, Geoffrey Gordon, understood that fatalism and faith in God's providence were two quite distinct ways of rationalizing the often apparently random carnage of the conflict. However, he recognized that the effect on the individual might be very similar: '[Fatalism] gives the same calm and courage that comes from a reasoned trust in the Fatherly providence of God, but it does not give a man the recklessness of the Dervish.'[37] Certainly, fatalism – arguably a secularised form of pre-destination – was seen to be preferable to the

34 J.M. Bourne and B. Bushaway (eds.), *Joffrey's War: A Sherwood Forester in the Great War* (Nottingham: Salient Books, 2012), p. 303. The title is derived from Husband's wartime nickname, being a parody of his Christian name.
35 BRO, EP 35/127.
36 Tiplady, *The Soul of The Soldier*, p. 101.
37 G. Gordon, 'The Soldier's Character: II. How are these foundations to be preserved and strengthened?' in T.W. Pym and G. Gordon, *Papers from Picardy by Two Chaplains* (London: Constable, 1917), p. 185.

nihilism inherent in attributing everything to chance. Well before the publication of *The Army and Religion*, its author, David Cairns, had discussed the issue of fatalism in a 1916 article in the *YM* – the magazine of the YMCA. He identified that attitude as 'a just revolt against the notion of a man's life being the sport of chance. It is just like Calvin in the midst of constant and imminent danger laying such emphasis upon God's decrees.'[38] Typical of those whose narratives and hopes were expressed rather ambiguously was the Wesleyan chaplain, C.F. Atherton, formerly a minister in Derby. He wrote to the Mayor telling of the carnage of the 'present campaign'.[39] His account, like many such reports, combined ideas of luck and divine Providence: 'Hope our first dash has succeeded! If not, God help us! We shall have to take pot luck.' After looking forward to a 'ten-fold hell tomorrow', Atherton commented, 'Still a strange providence watches over me; twice I've had wonderful escapes.'[40] Thomas Kettle, who was active in the Irish Literary Revival movement and proud of his Norse ancestry, wrote to his brother on 8 September 1916, 'We are moving up tonight into the battle of the Somme … Somewhere the Choosers of Slain are touching as in our Norse story they used to touch with invisible wands those who are to die. I am calm but desperately anxious to live.'[41] He died on the following day.

During the conflict, stories of providential escapes became a clearly-identifiable and often-repeated narrative form in which the avoidance of death or injury was commonly associated with some meritorious activity on the part of the fortunate person. Chaplain Pat Leonard implicitly acknowledged that in his account of a train crash in which compartments on either side of the one occupied by a group of chaplains were severely damaged. He commented, 'Of course, to complete the story I ought to be able to say that the seven chaplains were all reading their Bibles, but as a matter of fact we were playing card tricks when the crash came!'[42]

While the questions posed to chaplains most often centred on the nature of divine providence, the larger implicit issue was that of divine omnipotence. Lt. Peter Layard of the Suffolk Regiment wrote to his parents in March 1916 with unusual candour:

> I rather hate watching those strafes in a way, because you think of all the poor men being broken and killed – and for what? I don't believe even God knows.

38 *YM*, 22 September 1916, pp. 887-8.
39 As this was published in May 1915, he may well have been referring to his experiences in the second Battle of Ypres.
40 *DDT*, 14 May 1915, p. 2.
41 The Irish Literary Revival was one element of the 'Celtic Revival' or 'Celtic Twilight' movements. It reinvigorated interest in Irish poetry and literature in the late 19th and early 20th century. For Kettle's life, see the memoir written by his wife, in T.M. Kettle and M.S. Kettle, *The Ways of War* (London: Constable, 1917), p. 41. Houseman (ed.) *War Letters of Fallen Englishmen*, p. 168. In old Norse, the 'choosers of the slain' were the Valkyries.
42 Leonard, *The Fighting Padre*, p. 137.

> Any faith in religion I ever had is most frightfully shaken by things I've seen, and it's incredible that if God could make a 17-inch shell not explode – it seems incredible that he lets them explode.[43]

Readers of the *Baptist Times and Freeman* in December 1916 were told of a Brotherhood meeting in France organized by a chaplain to discuss, 'Why doesn't God stop the War?' The assumptions thought to be implicit in the question were analysed: 'First, that this war is evidence that all that is meant by religion is a delusion … The other assumption is that granted God exists and that He is good, then he ought to stop the war.' The chaplain had pointed out that there was another false assumption being made,

> namely that Omnipotence means power to do anything. It does not; rather it is the power to choose between inescapable possibilities. Omnipotence cannot make truth false or make light without darkness. Neither can it make man … without giving him freedom, and with freedom there must be the possibility of abuse. Therefore God cannot stop the war without robbing man of his moral freedom, which would be a worse tragedy than the worst war.[44]

Such reports had more than a narrative purpose; they were also a means of propagating appropriate answers to this inescapable question and this particular one was the dominant response to the problem throughout the First World War. Supporting his argument that divine omnipotence cannot do anything, the chaplain had pointed out that throughout the Old Testament God lamented that he could not get Israel to obey him. An element of humour had been provided by the man who had asserted that God could stop the war if he liked: 'He turned Lot's wife into a pillar of salt. Why doesn't he do the same with the Germans?'

Geoffrey Gordon observed that the question was being asked 'by thousands of people in the ranks, and at home.'[45] His conclusion was that, 'Disquisitions upon free will, and the argument that the failure is not the failure of God or of Christianity, but due to man's misuse of God's gifts, may possibly convince the head, but they do not satisfy.' His answer was similar to that of Studdert Kennedy, albeit expressed less trenchantly: 'The world suffers, but God is no absent spectator above, beyond, serene, but in it, of it, down in the depths of its suffering and its woe. God Himself upon the Cross.' That last phrase is indicative of something less than full-blown patripassianism, but it was not far short of offering that response to the question of divine omnipotence.

43 Houseman (ed.) *War Letters of Fallen Englishmen*, pp. 171f.
44 *BTF*, 29 December 1916, pp. 307f.
45 Gordon, 'The Soldier's Character', pp. 198f.

Omnipotence and Providence on the Home Front

As we have noted, these issues were not sprung *de novo* upon an unsuspecting Church. They had been engaged with for millennia, and the standard answers had become ingrained in the every-day language of church life. For example, the November 1915 issue of the St Giles', Matlock parish magazine included this comment, 'Death continues to take its toll of our young warriors and it seems sometimes as if the best were being picked out and taken.'[46] Similarly, a section of the United Methodist *Long Eaton and Stapleford Circuit Quarterly Journal* in 1916 headed 'The Reaper' referred to the death of a young girl in this way:

> we had prayed that under the devoted care of her loved ones and with the return of the warm weather she would become strong and have a long and happy life. A wise Father has willed it otherwise and she has gone to a fairer clime to be an angel. We assure her parents and grandparents of our tenderest sympathy and remembrance, and pray that they may have grace to bow to God's all-wise and loving will.[47]

So, when a year later, it reported the death of Sgt. John Turner under the same heading, it was with a similar expression of belief that his death, if not actively willed by God, had been permitted by him: 'We had hoped he would be spared, but a higher power has permitted him to fall, reverently we bow to such permission and wait for the "morning". He did his duty and a hero's reward is his.'[48] Such was the common response to death that persists in parts of the British Church to this day. That expression of orthodox faith, founded on a traditional understanding of divine omnipotence, was not as directly and obviously challenged in the East Midlands as it was by the exigencies of the Western Front. No doubt it gave comfort to the faithful and in peacetime had offered an acceptable narrative of the loss of a loved one. 'He only takes the best' remains a commonly-heard affirmation a century later, even in post-modern and post-Christian Britain.

Soon after the outbreak of war, the Bishop of Bristol addressed the 'old problem of Psalmists, of prophets, of the Book of Job, [which] confronts us anew', while admitting that he was unable to give a 'full answer'. He pointed to the 'remarkable conviction that the war is really a contest for the supremacy of spiritual as against material force' and declared that 'The Church must make the most of this turning of men's minds towards a simpler faith.' He then moved on to affirm the breaking-down of

46 DRO, D 6265/1/2.

47 NRO, NC/MR/2/62. *UM Long Eaton and Stapleford Circuit Quarterly Journal,* July-Sept 1916.

48 NRO, NC/MR/2/62. *UM Long Eaton and Stapleford Circuit Quarterly Journal,* Oct-Dec 1917.

class barriers, without – as far as the detailed report suggests – really addressing directly the 'old problem' that 'confronts us anew'.[49] The solution offered by the Vicar of Tamworth to the familiar questions distinguished two methods of divine intervention, 'from without and from within'.[50] God, he wrote, could blot out those who fight, as he had in Sodom and Gomorrah, but this would not satisfy our idea of his love and justice. Christ was sent not to destroy mankind but to save it. 'Then there is only one way of stopping the war, and that is by killing out of man the motives that make him fight.' Along with so many others, the vicar also stressed that divine omnipotence did not constrain human free-will.

For a Baptist pastor in Barnstaple, the Revd. D.J. Llewellyn, his very similar answer to the question, 'can God stop the war? … a question which so many are asking with tears that well from a breaking heart', was illustrated by the example of two men fighting.[51] God could strike them dead, but it would be better for him to make them ashamed of themselves and to settle their quarrel. God was not a despot and his government was paternal and moral. He had always respected human free will and that freedom limited his omnipotence. A speaker at a 'Pleasant Sunday Afternoon' meeting on the Isle of Man was reported as answering the question, 'Is God a failure' by taking as his illustration the sinking of the *Titanic*.[52] Was that God's fault, he asked, or that of those 'who ordered full speed in the presence of ice?' Such responses typified the standard response to the challenge to divine omnipotence that the war was perceived to constitute. However, the reply that God does not constrain human free-will raised a number of problems, such as how God might be able to respond to prayer, and whether divine omnipotence had any meaning at all, given the ability of the human race to re-model the planet and to cause so much destruction. Few preachers appear to have engaged with such issues. Moreover, to say that free-will trumped omnipotence was arguably to say that God could not stop the war.

Some, however, took a different view. As noted in chapter 2, Charles Gore, Bishop of Oxford, believed that the war was a judgment of God, and far from God being unable to prevent the war or reduce its cost, he had at the very least allowed it happen. An editorial piece by the Revd. J. Grange Radford in the *Methodist Recorder* in March 1915 took a similar position.[53] Addressing the familiar question, 'Why doesn't God stop the war?' the writer's response was first to express the traditional understanding of omnipotence that, as with all things, war was always under the complete control of God's will and could not take place 'without the express permission of God.' To argue otherwise was to say that Satan has a 'liberty of access' to this world and thus 'destroy the sovereign providence of the one Lord.' (As noted in chapter 2, the Archbishop

49 Address to Diocesan Conference, reported in *Western Daily Press*, 8 October 1914, p. 6.
50 *Tamworth Herald*, 16 February 1918, p. 3.
51 *North Devon Journal*, 20 April 1916, p. 3.
52 *Isle of Man Examiner*, 23 March 1918, p. 3.
53 *MR*, 14 March 1915, p. 4.

of Canterbury himself had described the war as the 'work of the devil'.) The *Recorder* article stated that God had permitted the war 'to utilise it for the highest good of the race which he has made and redeemed.' Radford then drew parallels with times in Old Testament history when God had worked for good through foreign armies. 'It is equally true that God has hired Prussian militarism and its engines of destruction to use them for the advancement of his Kingdom.' God, he wrote, used war to effect his chastisements and God did not stop the war because those chastisements were not yet finished. Perhaps surprisingly, no letters or other responses to the article were printed in subsequent issues.

The *Christian World Pulpit* published numerous sermons examining omnipotence and providence during the war. That the majority were from Nonconformist ministers may reflect the readership of the weekly newspaper, the traditional importance of the sermon in Nonconformist worship and possibly also the willingness and ability of those outside the established Church to adopt a slightly more detached and critical perspective on the theological questions posed by the war. 'Why does God not intervene?' was the familiar issue considered by the Presbyterian minister James Burns in a sermon published in December 1914, his text being taken from Isaiah ch. 64: 'Oh that Thou would'st rend the heavens, that Thou would'st come down … that the nations may tremble at Thy presence!'[54] People were asking questions, he said:

> Where, in this awful conflict, does God come in? If there is a God, has he hidden himself? Or is he indifferent? Or does He leave the world to take care of itself? Or has He no power to intervene? If he has the power, why does he not exercise it? Why does He not rend the heavens, and come down?

After noting the difficult conditions in which the writers of both Old and New Testaments expressed their unquestioning faith in God, Burns stated, 'No one ever suffered in this world as Christ suffered. … But Christ did not call upon God to intervene.' Burns' first argument was that of free will, stating that for God to intervene would reduce human beings to the state of automata. Moreover, if people asked God to intervene to stop the war, he must intervene in everything. God intervened through his Spirit, through human conscience and through 'the still small voice of love. … It is this intervention which aids, but which does not overrule the human will.' God was intervening, argued Burns, through the hearts of men. Burns ended his sermon with a rhetorical flourish, calling on his listeners and readers to 'cast aside our sloth, our faint-heartedness, our weak and shallow sentiment, and to gird on the armour and fight.' One can but speculate on the most appropriate rousing hymn about spiritual warfare, full of military imagery, which might have followed the sermon. Burns' stress on the suffering of Christ in a sermon preached in 1914 is notable as a corrective to analyses which have suggested that such rhetoric of suffering was the consequence

54 J. Burns, 'Why does God not intervene?' in *CWP*, 2 December 1914, pp. 363-5.

of the mounting losses of the later years of the conflict. Narratives containing all the elements of the Church's response, including its call to arms, its debates over providence and its likening of combatants' sacrificial suffering to that of Christ, can be found from the first year of the war.[55]

The Revd. W.E. Orchard, a pacifist who in 1932 would be received into the Roman Catholic Church, was during the war the minister of the King's Weigh House Church in Mayfair, London, one of Congregationalism's most prominent churches. In a 1914 sermon, he addressed the question of divine omnipotence, his introduction identifying omnipotence as 'the essential attribute of Godhead. If God is not almighty, He is not God.'[56] Yet, Orchard argued, difficulties that form the 'stock theological perplexities of little children' soon emerge – such as whether God could create a stick with only one end. The answer was that God could not do impossible things. Moreover, God cannot do that which is morally wrong. He recognised that in a scientific age, 'one feels how useless it is to pray for … a change in the weather. … And this recognition has wakened the doubt whether we can pray for anything at all.' After an analysis of modern thought, considering ideas of personal freedom, activism, evolution and human progress, Orchard suggested that 'Omnipotence is not irrational. God cannot do anything foolish or evil.' Furthermore, God cannot coerce man in any way. Only in his closing paragraphs did Orchard make any direct reference to the conflict that was clearly the motivation for his sermon. For God to coerce humanity would indicate his impotence to lead mankind in accordance with his own nature, he argued. In Orchard's sermon, clearly, was a much more subtle exposition of the nature of divine omnipotence than that suggested by so many Old Testament narratives. Indeed, the lack of biblical references is notable, the text from Mark 10:27, 'All things are possible with God' being the 'peg' on which he hung his message and the only direct Biblical reference in the whole of the sermon.[57] His argument was fundamentally that God would be acting contrary to his own nature to constrain human freedom. While from the earliest days of the conflict, its outbreak had been seen as a consequence of human free-will being exercised by the aggressors, Orchard's unequivocal assertion that God was unable to coerce human activity so as to bring the war to an end was never more than a minority view among preachers.

At the annual meeting of the Bradford Congregational Council in early 1915, Bertram Smith preached on 'Our doctrine of providence and the war'.[58] His argument had much in common with that of Burns, addressing the 'seemingly unending

55 See also Michael Austin's critique of the suggestion that the Church of England's nationalism and its anxious enquiry about divine providence formed two distinct consecutive phases in M. Austin, *Like a Swift Hurricane* (Chesterfield: Mereton Priory Press, 2014), pp. 11f.

56 W.E. Orchard, 'Omnipotence' in *CWP*, 16 December 1914, pp. 394-7.

57 It would be hard to find a better example of the adage about preaching that 'a text without a context is a pretext' for advancing views not necessarily founded on the text.

58 B. Smith, 'Our doctrine of providence and the war' in *CWP*, 3 March 1915, pp. 137-9.

task of reconciling the presence in the same universe of the Infinite and the Finite, of a God all-powerful and all-good, and man with real powers of self-determination.' Like many others, Smith affirmed that the problem of pain and evil was not limited to the war. For him, the divine purpose in the creation of the world was the evolution of human souls after the pattern of Jesus:

> And men of the Jesus temper can only be evolved as over against an unfinished cosmos, a world of hostile microbes, of earthquakes, lightning and storms, and in a society of fellow-men, inheriting the savage instincts of a prehistoric past. … The glorious outcome of the struggle has been the Jesus spirit.

Then came an assertion of the idea which we shall explore in greater detail in the next chapter; that of the redemptive nature of a soldier's death in the cause of righteousness. If the war stood within the Divine order, 'then every soldier dying on the battlefield is giving his life as a ransom for many … every death is a vicarious sacrifice and once more the blood of the martyrs will be the seed of the Church.' Finally, Smith declared, the doctrine of the Incarnation denies that God is outside of human life. Rather, 'In our afflictions He is afflicted. He indwells humanity as He indwelt Jesus. The sorrows of these painful processes of redemption are God's as well as man's.' This was, for Smith, 'the only doctrine of Providence and the war that is deep enough and broad enough to sustain our courage and comfort our hearts.'

A sermon, 'Does God Care' preached by the Baptist F.C. Spurr in the Regent's Park College chapel on 29 August 1915 was published in the *Baptist Times and Freeman*. He stated,

> It is because we believe Him to be supremely wise, powerful and good, and because we have the record of His mighty works … that a new problem arises at every new crisis when he seems to be inactive, and so even the best of men find themselves saying: 'Could not He who has done all that have caused that this should not be?'[59]

Was it God's love or his power or wisdom that was at fault? He suggested that the war was 'due wholly to the malicious stupidity and sin of men. God has not failed. It is man that has failed, and God, omnipotent, loving, and wise, has allowed man's folly for the moment to have its way.'

In contrast to the standard expositions holding man's abuse of God-given free will responsible for the suffering of the war and asserting that a moral God could not over-rule human autonomy, a sermon by the Wesleyan minister Thomas Westerdale published in the Church's magazine allowed no such delegation of authority and power: 'In both realms – natural and spiritual – we are met everywhere with

59 *BTF*, 3 September 1915, pp. 574f.

overwhelming evidence of a controlling and intelligent activity.'[60] Foundational to his case was his argument from design for the existence of God which differed little from that of Isaac Newton in 1713 or Paley's watchmaker analogy a hundred years later, but which had been increasingly challenged by the scientific developments of the previous century.[61] Westerdale found his evidence in 'the regularity of our food supply, the marvellous forms of beauty that everywhere prevail, the inexhaustible fathomless treasures that are always being discovered.' However, he suggested, 'We get a shock when an earthquake comes, and thirty-three thousand souls are hurried into eternity.'[62] It was, of course, the Lisbon earthquake of 1755 that had famously challenged Voltaire's acceptance of the argument from design. Westerdale then argued that the fact that in such circumstances, 'the human mind remains so sure and steady, the human heart so trustworthy' was a 'witness to the almightiness and glory of God.' Having asserted that, 'The fact that no calamity ... has ever been able to make but a temporary impression either upon the world's sub-total of happiness or ... of progress, is an unfailing assurance of a divine and over-ruling controllership', Westerdale then commented, 'It is not fair to interpret God's great world purpose by localized transactions.' One wonders if, even in June 1915, those involved would have accepted his description and certainly it would become far less palatable later in the war. In keeping with the very traditional tone of his sermon, he concluded with a flourish: 'to say that this terrible war is the obliteration of an over-ruling Providence is only the measure of our incapacity to think the thoughts of God at all.' Furthermore, 'the Original Thinker, Planner, Creator of all things, has not abdicated His throne, but reigns in ever increasing magnificence and power.' In other words, from a divine perspective and time-scale, the war should not be seen as being of a significance that was sufficient to undermine true faith.

In contrast to Westerdale's argument, addressing the 1916 Baptist Spring Assembly, the Revd. W.W.B. Emery declared, 'That the war is a challenge to our faith I take for granted.'[63] However, he recognised that the same challenges come from 'every railway accident, colliery explosion, or shipwreck. It is only the scale of the calamity that is new. ... But the scale makes a real difference.' It had caused many to rethink their belief in an almighty and loving God. Such doubt, he argued, was a serious thing, since

60 T.E. Westderdale, 'Providence and World-Storms' in *Wesleyan Methodist Magazine*, June 1915, pp. 425-29.

61 'This most elegant system of the sun, planets, and comets could not have arisen without the design and dominion of an intelligent and powerful being." Isaac Newton, quoted in J.W.V. Huyssteen (ed.), *Encyclopedia of Science and Religion*, (London, 2003), p. 621; W. Paley, *Natural Theology: or, Evidences of the Existence and Attributes of the Deity (12th ed.)* (London, 1809), p. 1. The French author Bernard Le Bovier de Fontenelle had used a similar analogy in 1686; see W. Durrant and A. Durant, *The Story of Civilization: The Age of Louis XIV, 1648-1715* (New York, 1963), p. 618.

62 This was possibly a reference to the 1908 earthquake in Messina, Italy.

63 W.W.B Emery, 'The Challenge of the War to Belief in Providence' in *Supplement to the BTF*, 5 May 1916, pp. III-V.

belief in providence was essential to 'vital religion'. Emery made explicit what many other preachers may have believed but did not state: 'Belief in Providence is essentially a faith in God, not an induction from observed facts. Cold and dispassionate intelligence can never settle the question whether things are ruled by chance or by God.' Therefore, 'The challenge [of the war] is directed against the form and quality of our belief rather than against the great fact of Providence.' We may contrast Westerdale's 'localised transaction' with Emery's 'catastrophe'. He then offered a succinct exposition of the place of Providence within the totality of the Christian faith:

> There is reason to suspect that much nominal and professed Christianity is little more than theism, tempered by Christian ideas of love and goodness. This is, indeed, challenged by the war, and is impaled, I think, on the old dilemma: 'If God is all-powerful He is not all-good, and if he is all-good he is not all-powerful.' Genuine Christian belief is much more than belief in an omnipotent God, perfect in goodness and universally benevolent. It is belief in the God of the Bible and of the Cross, a God whose Almighty power is matched by an inflexible righteousness and an infinite, self-sacrificing and redeeming love.

Emery argued that suffering was an inevitable consequence of sin that is contrary to God's moral order and so is simply part of the providential order. Therefore, 'God "permits" suffering, simply standing aside and allowing the evil course to work itself out to the bitter end. … Suffering is ordered by the will of God, yet it is not 'the will of God.' In the discussion that followed the address, F.C. Spurr asked rhetorically, 'What is God doing in this war?' and answered, 'God is teaching man in this war by allowing him to be burnt so that he should let the fire alone in the future.'

The Final Years

As the war dragged on, the questions about divine providence and omnipotence continued to be asked, both in the theatres of war and on the home front. As the third anniversary of the start of the conflict was marked, the *Methodist Recorder* carried an advertisement for a booklet that claimed to offer 'A straightforward answer to a perplexing question – "Why God does not stop the war".'[64] Most of the published answers were very similar to those of earlier years and the influence of belief in chance and fatalism was unabated. The 1917 New Year Message from the President of the Baptist Union, the Revd. Thomas Phillips, was – quoting the Prayer Book version of Psalm 129 – 'Good luck in the name of the Lord.'[65] 'All the churches need good luck', he stated. In the review of the state of British religion which followed, there

64 *MR*, 23 August 1917, front page.

65 *BTF*, 5 January 1917, p. 4; Psalm 129:8: 'So that they who go by say not so much as, The Lord prosper you; we wish you good luck in the Name of the Lord.'

was no recognition that the use of the word 'luck' might in any way be seen as undermining belief in divine providence. Most scholars suggest that 'the Blessing of the Lord' reflects the meaning of the Hebrew rather better than did the 1539 'Great Bible', from which the Prayer Book Psalter quoted by Phillips was taken. Perhaps this was an example of a Church leader using ambiguous language in the manner that was commonplace among combatants. Alternatively, he may simply have meant 'good fortune'.

In the same year, the Congregationalist minister Robert Horton considered 'Why does not God stop the war?' suggesting that the question was put scornfully by unbelievers and wistfully by Christians.[66] A list of related questions followed, not dissimilar to those posed by James Burns two years earlier. The failure to find answers to those questions was, suggested Horton, 'The reason why the Churches are practically empty, the reason of the religious indifference which is stealing over the whole world. ... And the longer the war lasts the more rapidly faith declines.' He recognised that modern warfare was far worse than in previous times and argued that God could destroy the Kaiser and his followers who have 'intoxicated and perverted' Germany, just as he destroyed the 100,000 strong army of Sennacherib.[67] However, 'it is not God's way to override our human freedom; it is not God's way to force men into sanity, humility, charity and wisdom.' Horton did not seek to reconcile that analysis with the story of the destruction of Sennacherib to which he had just made reference. Moreover, he argued, if God were to respond to all the human sin that he sees, then all 'scorners of divine power' would be open to divine punishment. 'What nations would evade doom? ... could even our country stand before Him?' To take this argument to its conclusion would practically bring the human race to an end. His somewhat florid conclusion was to affirm that God 'waits and spares and hopes and trusts that out of the unutterable guilt and sin of man may yet come the glory of liberty and of truth and of purity and love.' It is hard not to read in these words the fading but clearly still-glowing embers of Edwardian optimism. As with all such sermons, we cannot tell how they were received, nor the extent to which they provided answers helpful to those for whom problems regarding providence and omnipotence remained a challenge to their faith.

Towards the end of 1917, Wesleyan minister Arthur Hoyle told readers of the *Methodist Recorder* that he had been challenged, 'What about Providence, now?'[68] After over three years of conflict, the 'now' was particularly pertinent. The war, he wrote, was bringing the doctrine of divine providence before the world in a big way. In the past, questions about it had arisen from 'poor inconveniences' like why it had rained on Whit-Sunday and the Sunday School Anniversary. But now, in view of the war, 'we are able to grasp the grandeur of the theme.' His first point was that,

66 R.F. Horton, 'Why does God not stop the war?' in *CWP*, 14 February 1917, pp. 73-75.
67 II Kings chs. 18 and 19.
68 *MR*, 8 November 1917, p. 9.

'It is entirely impossible to understand the Government of the universe, but it is not impossible to make the best of it.' As had Emery, Hoyle argued that making sense of it without faith was impossible. Second, he called for a wider view of divine purpose and progress, noting the development of science, knowledge and civilisation. There was, he claimed, an 'upward sweep'. Patient waiting was required and nothing could serve as well as 'humble waiting'. As the Psalmist wrote, he concluded, 'Wait, I say, upon the Lord.' Again we can detect elements of the pre-war Edwardian optimism in the 'upward sweep' of the human race and the march of progress towards a better tomorrow. Looking at the whole thrust of Hoyle's argument, it can be seen to be a re-presentation of the argument of William Cowper's 18th century hymn *God moves in a mysterious way*, which was very popular in the pre-war period.[69] Pertinent lines include 'Deep in unfathomable mines / Of never failing skill / He treasures up his bright designs / And works his sovereign will'; 'Blind unbelief is sure to err, / And scan his work in vain' and 'His purposes will ripen fast / Unfolding ever hour; / The bud may have a bitter taste, / But sweet will be the flower.' Again, we cannot know how his readers reacted to his call for a 'long view' of God's providential purposes, when the 'bitterness' of the 'bud' had been tasted by so many people by 1917.

Armistice

Still serving with the Sherwood Foresters in the autumn of 1918, but now in a reserve battalion in bomber training near Sunderland, Geoffrey Husbands recalled the events of November 1918:

> All week 'Armistice', that mystic and blessed word, had been in the air with incessant rumours that the war was almost over, and at Bethesda chapel that night the coming of peace seemed very near ... We sang with deeper feeling and more than the usual heartiness that a favourite hymn evokes at any time: 'Now thank we all our God' and as the service ended and we poured out into the darkness of the streets it did indeed seem that we were right at the end of an epoch.[70]

With the signing of the Armistice, the end of the fighting if not the formal peace had come. Westerdale's 'localised transaction' and Emery's 'catastrophe' was over, although the discourses and narratives in the immediate post-war period offered no new insights into the questions of omnipotence and providence. Writing from Christ Church Vicarage, Chesterfield on 25 November 1918, the Revd. James Ducker assured his readers, 'In answer to the prayers of our people, the supreme valour of sailors and soldiers, and the wonderful steadfastness of the nation, with our Allies, God has given to us the victory in this world war. Right has triumphed over might.

69 L. Adey, *Class and Idol in the English Hymn* (Vancouver, 1988), p. 75.
70 Bourne and Bushaway (eds.), *Joffrey's War*, pp. 580-1.

Truly there is a God that judgeth the earth.'[71] For the parishioners of Daybrook in Nottinghamshire, the affirmation was that 'Our hearts are filled with thankfulness to Almighty God because in His mercy, He has seen fit to bring this terrible War to an end and to give us the Victory. … We can see now that God has been working his purpose out.'[72] If there had been doubts about why God had not stopped the war in more than four years, there was no apparent question about who should be thanked for bringing it to an end. All that questioning was in the past as the nation looked to the future. As far as the public face of the Church was concerned – and quite probably as far as many faithful worshippers were concerned – those difficult questions had been resolved by the victorious end of the conflict. A little more reflective was the superintendent minister of the United Methodist Long Eaton and Stapleford Circuit who wrote, 'Faith has been wrestling with problems and doubts and fears. It has been tested severely, and has survived the test. … The war, with all its glorious heroism and all its horrible misery, is but an incident in the eternal conflict between light and darkness, good and evil.'[73]

When the Peace Treaty was signed at Versailles on 28 June 1919, the King issued a 'Proclamation' which opened unambiguously, 'Whereas it has pleased Almighty God to bring to a close the late wide-spread and sanguinary War in which We were engaged against Germany and her Allies; We, therefore … call for public and solemn acknowledgement …'[74] It called for appropriate worship and prayers across the country, instructing the Archbishops and Bishops and 'exhorting the General Assembly of the Church of Scotland and all Spiritual Authorities and ministers of religion' to make suitable arrangements. Consequently, the Archbishops issued a 'Form of Thanksgiving and Prayer' to be used throughout England, Wales and Berwick-upon-Tweed on Sunday 6 July, 'being the Day appointed for Thanksgiving to Almighty God'.[75] The first prayer, a Collect to be used in the order of Holy Communion started, 'O God, who makest wars to cease, and by whose might aid the violence of our enemies hath been restrained.' The second expressed the hope that 'this world may be … peaceably ordered by thy governance' while the third espoused the hope of continuing progress and advancement redolent of the optimism of an earlier age, praying 'that in tranquillity thy Kingdom may go forward, till the earth be filled with the knowledge of thy love.' As the vicar of Daybrook had put it, the pre-war belief that God was 'working

71 DRO, D 2083/12/5

72 *DayBrook Parish Magazine 1916-18*, December 1918, NRO, PR 19,762/4. *God is working his purpose out as year succeeds to year* was a popular hymn first published in 1894, included in the pre-war *English Hymnal* and *Hymns Ancient and Modern* and further popularised in *Songs of Praise* and the *Methodist Hymn Book* afterwards.

73 NRO, NC/MR/2/62, *UM Long Eaton and Stapleford Circuit Quarterly Journal*, Apr-Jun 1915.

74 Proclamation by the King, 1 July 1919, copy at DRO, 2006 A/PI 19/8 (folded in the *Somercotes Parish Magazine*).

75 Copy at DRO, D 1847 A/PI 35.

his purpose out' could now be reasserted with confidence. In many churches, a hymn which had been written by John Oxenham in 1916 in preparation for the peace 'which, please God, cannot now be long delayed' was sung:

> We thank Thee, O our God, for this
> Long fought-for, hoped-for, prayed-for peace;
> Thou dost cast down, and Thou upraise,
> Thy hand doth order all our ways.[76]

Looking Back

In 1930, an article published in *The Expository Times* offered another examination of the doctrine of providence.[77] The author, Norman Hook, first reviewed its history, noting that belief in 'the parochial God of the village' had led to a deterministic view of God's providence so, that for example, when a child was born to a family whose resources were already strained, responsibility was ascribed to providence, and no doubt God would provide for it in his own way: 'A similar notion applied to death. Everyman had his appointed time to die, and if that time had come, nothing could save him. A typical example of such determinism was the average Tommy in the trenches.' In reality, Hook argued, such deaths were the outcome of natural law, rather than the result of divine decision, and he suggested that the catastrophe of the war had almost killed 'this parochial God of the village ... Almost, but not quite.' Consequently, people had lost a grip of the true idea of God's providence. Hook concluded first that in a rational universe, 'God cannot rightly be expected to intervene in the manner of *Deus ex machina*.' (Literally 'God from the machine', the term means an unexpected miraculous intervention.) Second, he argued, we must assume some sort of Divine self-limitation. Third, we are therefore driven to see providence in the spheres of the mental and the spiritual. He concluded: 'It may be that these centres are the only true foci of a rational apprehension of the divine Providence.' Hook's paper expressed in a more structured form many of the tentative answers to the wartime questions of providence and omnipotence. His suggestion that providence operated only 'in the spheres of the mental and the spiritual' was functionally equivalent to the view that, for whatever reason, God did not intervene in any way that would conflict with natural law or with human free will. Such solutions were, of course, vulnerable to Gordon's complaint that while they might possibly 'convince the head', they do not 'satisfy'.

76 J. Oxenham, *The King's Highway* (London: Methuen, 1916), p. 157. Used, for example, at Matlock: DRO, D 4296/21/2 and Chapel-en-le-Frith: DRO, D 6771/9/6/1.

77 N. Hook, 'The Doctrine of Providence' in *The Expository Times*, vol. 41 (1930), pp. 359-62.

Conclusion

Despite all the arguments that the war did not pose any new questions about divine providence but only repeated them on an hitherto unimaginable scale and that a moral God could not use his power to overcome human free will, it is clear that throughout the conflict there was widespread questioning of why God did not intervene. Some clergy pointed to the suffering of Christ and others affirmed the ultimate victory of God's purposes, but indubitably, the advocacy of belief in an omnipotent God who, in Lt. Peter Layard's words, could stop a 17-inch shell but chose not to, was untenable for most preachers. As we have seen, a variety of solutions was offered, effectively redefining the understanding of divine omnipotence. Soldiers' avoidance of injury or death could be attributed to one of three causes; divine providence, fatalism or pure chance. While the first led to the unacceptable conclusion that God was directing shells and bullets, the prospect of life and death being purely a matter of chance was similarly unappealing. Consequently, there was an understandable attraction in the fatalism that characterised the attitudes of millions of soldiers. Both chaplains and clergy on the home front attempted to 'Christianise' such expressions of luck and fatalism, seeking to make more orthodox the responses of 'folk-religion' to the human cost of the conflict.

However, W.W.B. Emery's argument that 'Belief in Providence is essentially a faith in God, not an induction from observed facts' was perhaps the only response that did not inevitably lead to further questions and therefore to further attempts at greater theological precision about the nature of divine omnipotence. He was asserting that cold argument without faith could never resolve such questions. The problem was that they were being asked by many people outside the churches, including those whose religious faith was limited to a basic belief in the existence of God and in life after death. For them, belief in divine providence, however genuinely desired, became less tenable as the war took an increasing toll on the combatant nations. Discussions about the nature of omnipotence and providence hardly helped the bereaved to make theological and moral sense of their losses. Rather, they sought re-assurance that there was a purpose in the deaths of loved ones, especially when it seemed that the war was not being won. From the earliest days of the conflict, meaning and purpose were found in the language of sacrifice and in the way in which the memorialisation of the Great War used that language and preserved it for future generations. In the next chapter, we shall discuss the origins and very varied uses of that language in both the theatres of war and Britain.

5

Sacrifice and Memorialisation

Sacrifice

Sacrifice was arguably the dominant trope of the First World War and when preceded by the word 'supreme' was used on innumerable occasions to refer to the loss of life. Moreover, there developed a language of loss in which making that 'supreme sacrifice' was described not simply as a passive act, but rather as the product of a conscious decision if not to die, then to follow a path – such as enlistment or action in the heat of a battle – which might well lead to death. In his seminal work *The Great War and Modern Memory*, Paul Fussell identified 'sacrifice' as one of the elements of 'high diction' that he believed was one of the 'ultimate casualties' of the war.[1] Subsequently there have been challenges to his thesis, most notably from Martin Stephen in his *The Price of Pity* and then Dan Todman with *The Great War: Myth and Memory*.[2] Stephen argued that the language of sacrifice among ordinary soldiers was founded on neither ignorance about the war nor mindless jingoism, but rather it 'represented the love that men can feel for each other in the midst of appalling hate.'[3] Todman asserted that Fussell himself was 'spectacularly ignorant of the military history of the war.'[4] Moreover, the example that Fussell used of the 'astonishing' staying power of sacrifice does rather support Todman's critique. Fussell quoted a 1918 book, *SOS Stand To!*, which the author Reginald Grant had dedicated 'to the memory of the lads who served with me in the "Sacrifice Battery", and who gave their lives that those behind might live.' Contrary to Fussell's interpretation, this was not an ideological or theological statement and certainly not 'high diction', but rather a factual military description of an artillery battery often deployed forward with the infantry to offer a rearguard action

1 P. Fussell, *The Great War and Modern Memory* (London: OUP, 1975).
2 M. Stephen, *The Price of Pity* (London: Pen and Sword Books, 1996); D. Todman, *The Great War: Myth and Memory* (London: Continuum, 2005), p. 158.
3 Stephen, *The Price of Pity*, pp. 231f.
4 Todman, *The Great War: Myth and Memory*, p. 22.

during a retreat necessitated by an enemy advance. 'Those behind' were literally those soldiers to the rear of the retreating forces and, therefore, those most vulnerable and most likely to be sacrificed. The term was certainly used in the American Civil War and in *SOS Stand To!* it was explained by Reginald Grant thus:

> I was ordered to take my gun to a position known as the sacrifice gun position, three hundred yards back of the front line trench. It derives its name, 'sacrifice gun', from the fact that rarely, if ever, in case of a heavy enemy raid, does the gun or any of its crew escape.[5]

Grant's description exemplified one end of the spectrum of meaning and interpretation of the word 'sacrifice' during the war, describing a military tactic without any ethical or religious significance. More often, 'sacrifice' was used to describe a variety of activities from the material sacrifices by civilians whose lives were affected but not endangered by the conflict to the 'great' or 'supreme' sacrifice of lives laid down in the cause of justice and freedom. Then it formed an element of Fussell's 'high diction', albeit one which, as we shall see, retained its power long after the end of the conflict. Moreover, such use to describe the death of combatants was inextricable from the dominant religious language and belief of the time.

In making their case that, contrary to Fussell's argument, 'sacrificial ideology survived and remained relevant in determining how men interpreted their experiences during wartime', Alexander Watson and Patrick Porter defined the 'ideology of sacrifice' as 'shorthand for a diffuse body of values, concepts and themes extolling the righteousness of laying down one's life for a greater good.' They showed that on both sides of the conflict, while the upper and middle classes employed the 'high diction' of valour, sacrifice and honour, further down the social scale similar ideas were expressed with a 'far less lofty vocabulary'.[6] However, their analysis of the development of the ideology of sacrifice did not do justice to its religious element. So much of the evidence which they cited was religious: Sir Henry Havelock, killed in the Indian Mutiny and depicted as a Christian soldier; Lloyd George's talk of 'the great pinnacle of Sacrifice, pointing like a rugged finger to Heaven' or statements about sacrifice made by the Catholic Second Lieutenant Stephen Hewett or the 'devout Cambridge Anglican', Captain Barclay Buxton, or 'the young, devout high Anglican Grenadier Guards officer, Harold Macmillan'. Watson and Porter rightly drew attention to the way in which Macmillan and countless others could recognise the horror of the battlefield while asserting that 'the act of death in battle is noble and glorious'.[7] However, their conclusions did not reflect the fact that the majority of their anecdotal evidence of

5 R. Grant, *S.O.S. Stand To!* (London: Appleton & Co., 1918), p. v.
6 A. Watson and P. Porter, *Bereaved and aggrieved: combat motivation and the ideology of sacrifice in the First World War*. Historical Research, vol. 83, no. 219 (February 2010), p. 147.
7 Macmillan deposit, Bodleian Library, letter to mother, 2/2/41-3.

the British perspective was either expressed in religious terms or by deeply religious men – or both.

Chaplain Kenneth Best was explicit in founding his call for sacrifice on the example of Christ, writing in his diary on Sunday 5 September 1915,

> Evening service at 4th East Lancs on the cliffs above Gully Beach. … Are we doing God's service in the war, i.e. do we come prepared to make the supreme sacrifice or to get honour and glory and feel we are doing our duty at the least possible expense of ease and peril? '*Take my yoke upon you and learn of me.*' He set his face steadfastly to go to certain death. '*Take my yoke*' involves Christianity and self: the Christian bears the load.[8]

On the other hand, the motivating factors encouraging sacrifice among the lower ranks, who were generally less articulate than their officers and who rarely recorded their thoughts in detail, were often unclear. In the *Army and Religion* report, David Cairns concluded that, 'In the main, there seems to be no clear linking up of the symbol of their own sacrifices with the sacrifice of Christ.'[9] From the vast number of reports from serving officers and chaplains that he presented, two in particular are illuminating. First, the RAMC sergeant who affirmed, 'But the instinct of self-sacrifice is one of the best and one of the commonest instincts in men, and the Church does right to sanctify it', and second the artillery officer who noted, 'one can see day after day countless acts of unselfishness and self-sacrifice which show that the essence of the Christian life is there in practice if not in theory.'[10] Cairns' own conclusion was that many soldiers thought that religion was solely to do 'with the individual and with the other world' and had nothing to do with the virtues which they practise.[11] *The Army and Religion* was typical of innumerable wartime narratives, not least from chaplains, in repeatedly stressing the sacrifices made by millions of men and women. However, it is clear that there was no conscious link in the minds of many between the religion which most of them professed, albeit often nominally, and the sacrificial acts which they performed. It was simply part of the culture of the time; hence the sergeant's support for the Church's 'sanctification' of those acts. Cairns himself addressed the question, 'Why, it is said, should we claim these virtues as due to Christian influence? Why not say that they are simply human?'[12] In terms of military virtues, he concluded that the evidence was 'indecisive', but he saw in the generosity to the vanquished,

8 G. Roynon (ed.), *War Diaries: A Chaplain at Gallipoli: The Great War Diaries of Kenneth Best* (London: Simon & Schuster, 2011), p. 209.
9 Cairns, *Army and Religion*, p. 41.
10 Ibid., pp. 44 and 132.
11 Ibid., p. 411.
12 Ibid., p. 362.

humility and chivalry, the 'influence of the Son of Man'. He continued, 'If these are not Christian virtues, they are astonishingly like them.'[13]

In addressing this question, we are dealing first with the nature of unarticulated 'diffusive Christianity' which was discussed in chapter 1 and second with the broader culture of British society in the first quarter of the 20th century; an indisputably Christian one, irrespective of the church-going practices of the majority of the population. One obvious indicator of this was the manner in which key elements in both the structures of the State, such as the educational, legislative and judicial systems, and a massive network of voluntary organisations, charities and campaigning groups had ecclesiastical origins. Furthermore, to enquire what British society would have been like without those elements, and how the idea of sacrifice (and, indeed, concepts of chivalry, fair play and support for the underdog) would have been understood in a hypothetical non-Christian Britain of the period is meaningless. Clearly, the Church sought to identify in every sacrificial act the teaching and influence of the Christian faith, with the sacrifice of Christ as the exemplar. Certainly, for many people, including the committed Christians whom Watson and Porter identified, that example was a model for their lives. The teaching of the Church had become infused into British culture, even if, as the evidence of the *Army and Religion* report suggested, most of the soldiers were not conscious that the ideals of chivalry and sacrifice to which they aspired had their origins in the Christian culture of their country. The idea of sacrifice in the Great War should be recognized as being understood primarily as a Christian concept, not least because of its widespread dependence on the visual and literary imagery of the sacrifice of Christ on the cross. As Adrian Gregory put it, 'The idea of redemptive sacrifice was second nature to the population, whether they realized it or not.'[14]

Salvation through Sacrifice

A novel development, which became discredited when gratitude for victory was succeeded by the critical retrospection of the late 1920s onwards, was the belief that an act of heroic sacrifice in a good and holy cause was a guarantee of eternal salvation, irrespective of the faith or life-style of the fallen soldier. One of the strongest exponents of this idea was Winnington-Ingram, who was happy to state of every fallen soldier:

> You must not think of your dear one far away; he is close to you in that blessed spiritual communion. ... When that full-bodied, happy-starred spirit shoots into the spirit world, he finds there the Lord who loved him, and understands him,

13 Ibid., p. 364.
14 Gregory, *The Last Great War*, p. 156.

> and Who has a life ready for him which he can enjoy... It is not for ever, the parting. You will see him again with your own eyes.[15]

David Cairns commented, 'The idea of salvation by death in battle for one's country has been widely prevalent, and is one of those points in which the religion of the trenches has rather a Moslem than a Christian colour.'[16] Later, he wrote, 'The cult of sacrifice is near idolatry. I have heard a minister say that each soldier killed ... is as true a sacrifice for his dear ones as Christ's on Calvary. This is simply untrue.'[17] This was a constant theme of the Bishop of London's preaching as he himself affirmed, declaring in a sermon in December 1915, 'As I have said a thousand times, I look upon it as a war for purity. I look upon everyone who dies in it as a martyr.'[18] What has been less clear is how representative such high-profile declarations of salvation through sacrifice were of the views of ordinary clergy, parishioners and combatants. While a quantitative assessment is problematic, it is evident that the rhetoric of martyrdom was commonplace from very early in the conflict. For example, in preparation for the Intercession Services in January 1915, the chairman of the Newcastle Free Church Council told an interviewer, 'in prosecuting this war we were protecting all that was dear in civilisation, and that the soldiers who laid down their lives were as true martyrs for freedom as ever died at the stake.'[19] At a meeting of the Surrey Congregational Union in March 1915, the speaker affirmed, 'It was to the honour of the Allies that they had seen the spiritual nature of this war. It was that which made our soldiers martyrs.'[20] In the same month, John Redmond M.P. declared at the Free Trade Hall in Manchester that, 'Every Irish soldier who gave his life on the battlefield died for Ireland as truly as any of Ireland's martyrs in the past.'[21] A local newspaper report of the 'noble sacrifice' of a soldier of the Black Watch, who threw himself at the muzzle of a machine gun, saving 'hundreds of his comrades' lives' appeared under the heading, 'A hero and a martyr'.[22] A poem published in memory of a Derbyshire soldier, headed 'A railway clerk, a year ago', declared, 'He fell, a martyr for his nation.'[23]

Hymns were frequently chosen to express the confident belief that there could only be one eternal destination for those who had fallen in battle. At a Memorial Service

15 Extract from address at memorial service, London Rifle Brigade, 19 June 1915, quoted in S.C. Carpenter, *Winnington-Ingram: The biography of Arthur Foley Winnington-Ingram, Bishop of London* (London: Hodder & Stoughton, 1949), p. 290.
16 Cairns, *The Army and Religion*, p. 17.
17 Ibid., p. 44.
18 A.F. Winnington-Ingram, 'A Word of Cheer', *CWP*, 8 Dec. 1915, pp. 353–5. For a detailed analysis of the historiography of this much-quoted and much-misquoted sermon, see Bell, 'Malign or Maligned?'
19 *Newcastle Journal*, 1 January 1915, p. 6.
20 *Surrey Mirror*, 5 March 1915, p. 5.
21 *Lichfield Mercury*, 19 March 1915, p. 2.
22 *Newcastle Journal*, 12 October 1915, p. 3.
23 *DDT*, 14 August 1915, p. 3.

in St. Paul's Cathedral in May 1915, every hymn was of that nature.[24] The first was, *Brief life is here our portion*, including '...eternal rest; / For mortals and for sinners / A mansion with the blest.' Later in the service came:

> The saints of God! their conflict past,
> And life's long battle won at last,
> No more they need the shield or sword,
> They cast them down before their Lord:
> O happy saints! forever blest,
> At Jesus' feet how safe your rest!

First published in 1870, that hymn is yet another example of hymns originally written about purely spiritual conflict being applied to the new context of a battle which was seen as both military and spiritual. The last two hymns were identical in tone: 'Let saints on earth in concert sing / With those whose work is done' and 'Now the labourer's task is o'er; / Now the battle day is past'. With such a repeated affirmation, it was hardly necessary for the preacher, the Bishop of London, to proclaim of the fallen, 'They did not want to die; they loved life; they looked forward to a happy life here; ... They asked for life and they will have it. He has given them a long life for ever and ever.'[25] An editorial in the *Exeter and Plymouth Gazette* on the day after Anzac Day in 1916 affirmed that, 'our heroes from the Antipodes ... died the death of martyrs – they had made the supreme sacrifice on the altar of patriotism and love of right, and have won the great reward promised to all who give their lives for their friends.'[26]

It should be recognised that when used colloquially as in the examples above, not every speaker or writer necessarily understood 'martyr' to express the certainty that every soldier who had died in action had obtained eternal salvation though their own sacrificial death, as Winnington-Ingram had stated in the memorial services for Canadian soldiers and for the London Rifle Brigade. Nevertheless, since true martyrs were assured of eternal salvation, many – perhaps most – hearers or readers would have interpreted such affirmations of martyrdom in that way. Other church leaders, however, spoke out against the cult of the martyr. One was the Revd. F.J. Ellis, who at the United Methodist Conference in July 1915 implicitly criticized the Bishop of London, who 'had placed the soldier in the category of the martyr'.[27] However, 'He was not prepared to say that a man killed in the field of battle is outside the power of penitence and conversion.' While traditional Nonconformist teaching would have abhorred prayers for the dead, on the grounds that at the moment of death a person's

24 *Form of Prayer used at The Memorial Service on Monday, May 10th, 1915, at 8 p.m. for the Canadian Soldiers who have fallen in the War.* Copy in SAB.
25 Text of sermon printed with Order of Service and newspaper reports of service in a pamphlet, in SAB.
26 *Exeter and Plymouth Gazette*, 26 April 1916, p. 3.
27 *Exeter and Plymouth Gazette*, 15 July 1915, p. 5.

eternal future is determined by his or her faith, Ellis' somewhat ambiguous comment was clearly intended to offer some consolation to bereaved families desperate to be reassured about the salvation of their loved ones. Such 'theological concessions for pastoral reasons', as Snape put it in *God and the Great War*, became commonplace.[28] Furthermore, preachers were generally and understandably silent about the existence of hell and the possibility that the eternal destination of the 'glorious dead' might be anywhere other than heaven. While it may be correct to distinguish between the Church of England, in which the majority had ceased to be believe in hell, and the more conservative Nonconformist denominations in which the reality of hell continued to be widely accepted, the scale of loss in the First World War served to eradicate hell from most preachers' vocabularies.[29]

In Nottinghamshire and Derbyshire, the rhetoric of both sacrifice and martyrdom was prominent in clerical discourse and public worship. In January 1915 a National Day of Intercession was observed nationwide. A report in the *DDT* drew attention to the 'striking sentence' in the order of service: 'We have made great efforts and sacrifices for what our conscience tells us is the cause of right, and of freedom, and, with the blessing of God, we are ready to make still further more.'[30] Writing in the same month, the Bishop of Southwell asserted, 'Sacrifice is the law of life: through death the buried seed is quickened into life: the blood of the martyrs is the seed of the Church. True also is it that the blood of our sons, mingled with the blood of Him who died for truth and righteousness, will be the seed of a newer and purer England.'[31] Edwyn Hoskyns may not have quite gone so far as advocating the idea of salvation through a soldier's own death, but the close juxtaposition of 'the blood of the martyrs' and 'the blood of our sons' could be read as an attempt to imply such an idea while being able to deny that he had explicitly proclaimed it.

While the decision made in mid-1915 to prohibit the repatriation of the dead (and the previous requirement that all repatriation expenses be borne by the family) meant that there were very few local funerals of combatants who had died abroad, memorial services were on many occasions held for individual soldiers in their home towns or villages. Across the memorial services of the first months of the war, usually commemorating officers and men who were already in the Army when the war had started, a variety of perspectives was offered. Some sermons reflected a retrospective disenchantment with the pre-war years, and a hope that the conflict would be cathartic. For example, a Torquay vicar asserted,

28 Snape in *God and the Great War*, Radio 3, 9 November 2014; comment made at 31:54.

29 See M.F. Snape, 'Civilians, Soldiers and Perceptions of the Afterlife in Britain during the First World War' in P. Clarke and T. Claydon (eds.), *The Church, the Afterlife and the Fate of the Soul* in *Studies in Church History*, 45 (Woodbridge: Ecclesiastical History Society, 2009), pp. 371-403 at pp. 375f.

30 *DDT*, 4 January 1915, p. 2.

31 *SDM*, Feb.1915, NRO, DR 1/1/12/14/28.

> For the first time in their lives the English speaking people were faced with the realities of their existence. Thousands of them had been living for years in a fool's paradise, taking everything for granted … but now they took nothing for granted. … Things had taken on new values, which they never understood before.[32]

A preacher in Newcastle offered a rather less condemnatory view in his statement that the men of the 'Faithful Durhams',

> had laid down their lives in a just and righteous cause … those left behind rejoiced to know that the true manhood of their sons was as great and as true as ever it had been in the past, and that now, in the 20th century, they were no degenerate race, but a race purified and strengthened by the trouble it was passing through.[33]

Some of the memorial services that took place at Ashbourne Parish Church were reported in the parish magazine, complete with a summary of the service and sermon. In June 1915, a service for Lance-Corporal Alick Ford included the hymn written by Reginald Heber in 1812, 'The Son of God goes forth to war / a kingly crown to gain; / his blood red banner streams afar; / who follows in his train?' The vicar, Canon Morris, preached on 1 John 3:10, 'He laid down His life for us, and we ought to lay down our lives for the brethren.' In August of that year, he preached at a Parade Service on Matthew 16:25, 'Whosoever will save his life shall lose it, and whosoever will lose his life for my sake shall find it', telling the congregation that the words of the text were a paradox, yet 'they were true, and taught the great law of sacrifice, of present suffering for future reward, which ran through the very fibres of existence.' The men who had died 'were following the example of the Master and were prepared to lose their souls that they might save them, that by the sacrifice of the lower life they might attain unto the higher.' In November 1915, Canon Morris preached on 1 Timothy 1:18-19: 'War a good warfare, holding faith and a good conscience', in his sermon stating that Jesus 'came to this earth to fight the greatest war the world had ever known, and to sacrifice His life in its accomplishment.' On Good Friday 1916 he referred to the sacrifices of the previous eighteen months and assured his hearers that, 'the supreme sacrifice of Calvary throws a new light on human sufferings and teaches us that all *who suffer with Him* shall be partakers also of His glory.'[34] There is no evidence to

32 *Aberdeen Journal*, 9 November 1914, p. 4. The reporting as far away as Aberdeen of a service in Torquay may be attributable to the funeral being for the son of the MP for Torquay who had been the first Colonel of the Westminster Dragoons and A.D.C. to the King. (Source: N. Huw-Williams. *A Short History of the Westminster Dragoons 1901 to 1987*, retrieved from http://www.westminsterdragoons.co.uk/Westminster_Dragoons/Library.html 19 May 2015.)

33 *Newcastle Journal*, 9 October 1914, p. 4.

34 All quoted in *Ashburne* [sic] *Parish Magazine*, DRO, D768/2.

suggest that Canon Morris was not representative of his fellow clergy, either locally or nationally. The examples above show that while Morris avoided the explicit language of martyrdom, the message of his sermons was clear: Because Britain's involvement in the war was morally justified and because British combatants were engaged in a spiritual and moral battle as much as a military one, they were assured of a heavenly reward for the sacrifice of their lives, irrespective of their life-styles.

In May 1917, the father of Private Thomas Walters of the 6th Battalion of the Sherwood Foresters and a resident of the Derbyshire village of South Darley received a letter from 2nd Lieutenant A.S.F. Elwood:

> Dear Mr. Walters, I deeply regret to have to inform you of the death of your son, who was killed in action 27/28th April. His end was instantaneous. [In reality his body was never found.] I feel that any words of mine can do but little to allay your grief, but you can take it in the knowledge that your son's life was not given in vain, and that by his sacrifice he has earned the rest and immortality of the martyr.[35]

For self-evident pastoral reasons, the bereaved father was assured that purely though his son's own sacrifice, his immortality was certain. That such declarations challenged both the orthodox Christian view that only Christ's death could be a means to salvation and also the Protestant doctrine of *sola fide* – by faith alone – meaning that salvation is only possible though faith and not though human action, did not prevent such assertions being repeated constantly during the war and its aftermath.

Examining reports of memorial services across England reveals both the common use of certain readings, most notably John 15:13, 'Greater love hath no man than this, that a man lay down his life for his friends' and the hymn *For all the saints who from their labours rest*, which will be considered later in this chapter. Throughout such narratives, the language was of heroism, honour, justice and the voluntary nature of the sacrifices offered. For example, in a 1914 memorial service in Braunton, Devon, the preacher stated, 'There was more than a silver lining to the cloud, inasmuch as it was a glorious death. He had laid down his life for us all. He was more than a soldier; he did not go blindly into battle, but took the larger view of things. He knew what he was fighting for.'[36] At Bidborough in Kent, it was asserted, 'They have passed at one bound from the Army of their earthly King to posts of honour in the glorious army of the King of Heaven. I love to think of them taking their places in the magnificent review of Christ's battalions pictured for us in the epistle for All Saints' Day.'[37]

35 K. Taylor and T. Brown, *A Derbyshire Parish at War* (Bakewell: Country Books, 2000), p. 48.

36 *North Devon Journal*, 10 December 1914, p. 2.

37 *Kent and Sussex Courier*, 13 November 1914, p. 3. The epistle for All Saints' Day in *BCP* is St. John's vision of heaven in Revelation 7:2-11.

Of a memorial service at Horsley in Surrey, the report concluded, 'At the close of the service Scout Barnett sounded the Last Post in honour of the departed hero.'[38] Nationally, the equating of the death of soldiers with that of Jesus was typified by the famous – or by now perhaps infamous – painting by James Clark, *The Great Sacrifice*. Circulated with the Christmas 1914 number of the *Graphic*, a widely-read weekly illustrated newspaper, it was displayed in homes, churches and public buildings and was reprinted in February 1915, being described as 'The most inspired picture of the War'. *The Great Sacrifice* depicted a crucified Christ standing above and looking down on a fallen soldier, a hand resting on Jesus' feet, while all around is the detritus and smoke of the battlefield. The message was self-evident; as Christ had sacrificed his life for his friends, so the dead or dying soldier had done just the same. Both had died in the cause of Right and both had triumphed over death. Padre Kenneth Best, serving in Egypt, reported preaching on *The Great Sacrifice*, urging 'self denial, including wine and women'.[39] Private H. Coulson wrote from the Western Front to his vicar in Derby in April 1917:

> I visited a village church this weekend, one of the finest I have ever seen. ... The walls were covered with framed coloured prints. ... What was most interesting to us was a framed picture, hanging on one of the pillars of the 'Great Sacrifice' and round the picture the names and numbers of British soldiers buried in the cemetery near by. A shelf under the picture carried two vases of flowers, which are kept filled with fresh flowers, and over all is a British flag. A fine tribute surely to our fallen heroes.[40]

James Clark's work had become the focal point for a shrine, literally achieving iconic status. However, while *The Great Sacrifice* has been widely reported in the literature, it should be noted that it was simply the most prominent example of the relating closely, to put it no stronger than that, of Christ's sacrifice to that of the fallen combatants. For example, very soon after *The Great Sacrifice* was printed, a poem was published in *The Church Standard* (one of the publications commonly used as inserts in parish magazines) which included the verse, 'And till he with the Lord shall reappear / His soldier sacrifice shall ever be / A silent witnessing memorial here / Of the great sacrifice of Calvary.'[41] The poet was stating that the soldier's sacrifice was a memorial – perhaps even a re-enactment – of Christ's. At a memorial service at St Alkmund's, Derby, in 1917, the preacher declared,

38 *Surrey Mirror*, 4 December 1914, p. 5.
39 Roynon (ed.), *War Diaries: A Chaplain at Gallipoli*, pp. 188f.
40 Austin, *Almost Like a Dream*, p. 68.
41 *The Church Standard*, May 1915, p. 107. Copy within Colwick Parish Magazine, NRO, PR/9147/2.

> It was a common belief that to live a full life one must reach the age of three score years and ten. This was not so, however, for Christ's life was short, only thirty-three years, with three years of ministry, at the end of which he himself said, 'It is finished.' God had called all those gallant lads to a greater ministry.[42]

Without actually equating the service of the soldiers with that of Christ, or their deaths with his death, the parallels which he drew got very close to doing so: in the relative brevity of their lives, in explicitly noting the commonly-agreed three years of Christ's ministry at a memorial service three years after the start of the war, and in the references to Christ's ministry and the soldiers being called 'to a greater ministry'.

A Case Study in Commemoration

Hugh Valentine Gamble was educated at Mill Hill School and commissioned as an officer on 14 September 1915, aged 26.[43] Serving as a lieutenant with the 2nd Seaforth Highlanders, he was killed in the Battle of Arras on 3 May 1917. The tribute paid to him by his commanding officer exemplifies the language of sacrifice and of confidence in immortality that we have previously observed:

> One cannot help wondering what he would have attained in this life, but perhaps the boys he lived for will gain more from the memory that is left them, with the example of his sacrifice before them all their lives. I shall never cease to miss him, but I cannot grudge him his soldier's death. He knew his duty, and was quite fearless because he was sure of the future. I believe he is radiantly happy.[44]

Ten days after his death, a 'Commemoration Service' was held at the Presbyterian Church in Ealing, London. The order for the service, reproduced in the Appendix, is an exemplar of both the heroic status accorded to the fallen and the confident expression of their immortality.[45] Immediately, one notes the descriptor on the front cover, 'Who fell gloriously near Arras, May 3rd 1917' above the quotation from *Pilgrim's Progress*, 'So he passed over, and all the trumpets sounded for him on the other side' – words which in John Bunyan's work are preceded by, 'Death, where is thy sting … Grave, where is thy victory?' Then, below the photograph of Gamble on the first page was printed the third verse of Robert Browning's *Epilogue*, implicitly identifying him as one who 'never turned his back but marched breast forward, never doubted clouds would break.' In the service itself, after the singing of the Sanctus ('Holy, holy, holy, Lord

42 *DDT*, 26 November 1917, p. 2.

43 N.G. Brett-James and J. Gifford, *Book of Remembrance and war record of Mill Hill School 1914–1919* (London: T. Malcolmson, 1922), pp. 61f.

44 Ibid.

45 *Commemoration Service for Lieut. Hugh Valentine Gamble, 13 May 1917*, copy in SAB – see Appendix A.

God of Hosts, heaven and earth are full of Thy glory'), scripture sentences and prayers, the congregation sang, *For all the saints who from their labours rest*. By 1917, this hymn had come to be seen as the definitive expression of the sacred nature of the conflict and of the immortality of the fallen. The psalms that followed (130 and 23) expressed hope and trust in God. After further prayer, the second hymn, *The strife is o'er, the battle done*, a 17th century Easter hymn, was sung, explicitly affirming the victory of Christ over 'the powers of death' and, therefore, the hope of immortality for those who died in the faith of Christ. Although not identified as such, the Anthem used the words of Tennyson's *Crossing the Bar*, a poem expressing his acceptance of death and written three years before he died, with the request that it be the final poem in all anthologies of his work.[46] The third hymn, *The Son of God goes forth to war*, offered another clear expression of that very close association of combatants in the war with the eternal spiritual battle between good and evil, championed by Christ, and the identification of the fallen as martyrs. The act of commemoration began with an affirmation of Gamble's service as a Boys' Brigade captain and a Scoutmaster and then stated that he had 'heard and nobly answered the call of his Divine Lord and Master to take up arms in defence of the cause of God and righteousness in the present war.' Note that the call to enlist was ascribed to neither Kitchener nor the King, but Christ. The act closed with another quotation from the apocalyptic book of Revelation: 'Be thou faithful unto death, and I will give thee a crown of life.' The hymn, *How bright these glorious spirits shine*, by Isaac Watts, then drew on similar themes from Revelation chapters 5 and 7. The ante-penultimate hymn, *Ask and it shall be given*, is notable first for being written by Hugh Gamble himself, and second for its imagery, not only calling on Jesus to be 'our Captain' – a theme of many hymn-writers – but also praying that Christians, 'clean in mind and body, / We may that strength procure, / King Arthur's knight was given / Because his heart was pure.' As the offertory was taken, members of the Boys' Brigade sang their Company hymn, another composition of Hugh Gamble, which in its opening verse contained so much of the language of spiritual battle which had become almost universally understood to be descriptive of the military conflict now raging:

> God bless our Company; under Thy banner,
> Lord, we assemble to fight against wrong.
> Jesus, Commander, be with us for ever;
> Make us Thy soldiers, brave, loyal and strong.

Finally, after the singing of the first and last verses of *All hail the power of Jesus' name*, and the benediction, the *Hallelujah Chorus* was played. Taken as a whole, we can see in this order further evidence of the conflation of spiritual and earthly warfare in the repeated affirmation of the righteousness of the cause. While avoiding any suggestion

46 H. Tennyson, *Alfred Lord Tennyson – A Memoir – By his son*, vol. ii. (London: Macmillan, 1897), pp. 336f.

of salvation though the soldier's sacrifice, it was insistent that it was Christ who had called Gamble to 'take up arms' and certain that he had become one of 'the Saints who from their labours rest.' Here, too, was the 'high diction' of sacrifice. In the use of Bunyan, Tennyson and Browning and in the Arthurian language of chivalry there was a clear attempt to locate Gamble's heroic service and sacrifice within the context of England's glorious heritage.

Elsewhere, writers looked back to Ancient Greece for an appropriate expression of heroic valour, the Roll of Honour printed for the Herbert Strutt school in Belper, Derbyshire being headed, 'so they gave their bodies to the commonwealth and received praise', a quotation from Thucydides' account of Pericles' funeral oration of 431BC.[47] After the conflict, similar implicit associations with classical Greek heroism and the depiction of slain warriors were expressed in the erection of war memorials evocative of Greek temples. The war memorial at Southport, designed by Reginald Blomfield who was also responsible for the Menin Gate at Ypres and the Cross of Sacrifice, is a fine example of this practice. It consists of two colonnades in the style of Greek temples, together with an obelisk. It, too, includes a quotation from Thucydides.[48]

Prayers for the Dead

One of the changes in religious practice indisputably caused by the Great War was the development beyond Catholicism and Anglo-Catholicism of the practice of offering prayers for the dead. Chaplain Eric Milner-White reported from France that he had met only one chaplain who did not 'pray directly for the dead' while James Moffat noted that support for the practice had even come from the evangelical Bishop Moule.[49] In his book, *Christus Consolator*, first published in 1915, Moule transcribed a hymn that he had been given. Its first verse read, 'For the passing souls we pray; / Saviour, meet them on their way. / Let their trust lay hold on Thee / Ere they touch eternity.'[50] The succeeding three verses were in a similar vein, and the hymn by Lady Coote was also published on single-sheet leaflets for widespread distribution.[51] Robert Beaken has recently noted the correspondence between the evangelical Bishop of Chelmsford, John Watts-Ditchfield and the Archbishop of Canterbury, Randall Davidson, over the possibility that such prayers might form part of the liturgies to be authorised for a national day of intercession planned for 21 August 1914.[52] However, before the end

47 *Programme for Speech Day, 1919*, DRO, D5264/14/7.
48 E. Morris and E. Roberts, *Public Sculpture of Cheshire and Merseyside (excluding Liverpool)* (Liverpool: Liverpool University Press, 2012), pp. 201–3.
49 E. Milner-White, 'Worship and Services' in MacNutt (ed.), *The Church in the Furnace*, p. 180; Moffat, 'The Influence of the War upon the Religious Life', p. 485.
50 H.C.G. Moule, *Christus Consolator: Words for hearts in trouble* (London: SPCK, 1915), p. 91.
51 Leaflet published by A.J. Felton. NRO, PR 7762/11.
52 Beaken, *The Church of England*, pp. 149ff.

of that year, praying for the dead had become commonplace. On 5 November 1914, *The Guardian* reported on a sermon preached by Davidson, in which he had said, 'And surely we are right to be on our guard lest ... we discourage the upraising of the devout soul in prayer for the loved one out of sight.' The Church should not hinder

> the reverent ... trustful prayer of a wounded spirit who feels it is natural and helpful to pray for him whom we shall not greet on earth again, but who, in his Father's loving keeping, still lives and ... still grows from strength to strength in truer purity and in deepened reverence and love.[53]

Unsurprisingly, the practice offered yet another focus for public argument between the different wings of the Church, the pages of that high-church newspaper the *Guardian* regularly featuring the arguments of the protagonists throughout 1915. The prayers approved by the Archbishops for use at the various anniversaries and New Year commemorations during the conflict show a belated and very cautious acceptance of this practice. There was nothing of this nature in the material approved for such services in 1914, 1915 and 1916.[54] However, for August 1917, a new prayer was offered for use in the Holy Communion service: 'O merciful God ... we bless thy holy Name for our brothers who have laid down their lives for their country; and we beseech thee to grant that at the last we with them may obtain eternal joy; though Jesus Christ our Lord.' Here was, indeed, a very discreet petition for the dead. However, in the 'Supplementary Material' for Morning and Evening Prayer, under a rubric referring to the discretion of the minister regarding the use of the prayers was a more explicit petition:

> Almighty and Everlasting God, unto whom no prayer is ever made without hope of thy compassion; We remember before thee our brethren who have laid down their lives in the cause wherein their King and country sent them. Grant that they, who have readily obeyed the call of those to whom thou hast given authority on earth, may be accounted worthy of a place among thy faithful servants in the kingdom of heaven'.[55]

This was sufficient to cause the evangelical Bishop of Liverpool, Francis Chavasse, to complain to Randall Davidson about 'a prayer for the dead more definite and precise than any that has yet appeared.' It was, he wrote, causing 'feelings of distress and resentment in the minds of a large number of Church people.' Chavasse requested

53 *The Guardian*, 5 November 1914, p. 1232.

54 e.g. *A form of Intercession with Almighty God on behalf of His Majesty's ... Forces ... on such occasions as each Bishop shall appoint for his own diocese*, 1914. NRO, PR 7762/5; *A Form of Humble Prayer to Almighty God to be used on Sunday, the third of January 1915....* NRO, PR 7762/6.

55 *Forms of Prayer for Public Use on the fourth and fifth of August 1917*. NRO, PR 7762/8.

that an alternative Form be issued with a *Thanksgiving for the Dead*, his primary objections being that the Church of England did not authorize the public use of such prayers and that there was no scriptural authority for them. Davidson replied that he had been at pains to ensure that the order for Holy Communion did not go 'a hair's breadth beyond' what was in the Prayer Book and he stressed that the use of the prayer in question was discretionary. He had hoped that it would meet the needs of the 'hundreds of thousands' who wished to pray for those 'whose life is now going on beyond our sight.' Davidson argued that such prayers were not forbidden by the doctrines of the Church. His biographer commented that Bishop Knox of Manchester was the only other bishop to join Chavasse in his protest.[56] A year later, two amendments were made to that prayer for use in Holy Communion:

> O merciful God … we bless thy holy Name for thy servants, our brothers and sisters, who have laid down their lives for their country; humbly beseeching thee to grant that we with them may be found worthy to enter into thy everlasting joy; through the merits of thy Son Jesus Christ our Lord.[57]

The first alteration was the inclusion of women – a novel feature at the time – while the second made clear that the hope of entry into eternal or everlasting joy was founded on the 'merits of thy Son Jesus Christ our Lord'. This would seem to offer a corrective to the rhetoric of salvation being obtained though the sacrifice of the fallen. Interestingly, the August 1918 booklet, rather smaller than its predecessor, contained no prayers similar to that which had caused the episcopal protests. However, within the forms to be used in Morning and Evening Prayer issued in January 1918 there was introduced a somewhat tortuous prayer, clearly based on one from *The Order for the Burial of the Dead* from the *Book of Common Prayer* (*BCP*), which expressed thanks to God for 'our brethren who have laid down their lives' before asking God

> shortly to accomplish the number of thine elect, and to hasten thy kingdom; that we, with all those that are departed in the true faith of thy holy Name, may have our perfect consummation and bliss, both in body and soul, in thy eternal and everlasting glory[58]

Again, eternal salvation was explicitly associated with 'true faith'. The Archbishops approved 'Forms of Thanksgiving' to be used on 17 November 1918, the Sunday after

56 Bell, *Randall Davidson*, pp. 828-30.

57 *Forms of Prayer and Thanksgiving to Almighty God to be used on Sunday, the fourth of August, 1918 … issued under the authority of the Archbishops of Canterbury and York.* NRO, PR 7762/10. (The leaflet issued for January 1918 included no similar prayer. NRO, PR7762/9.)

58 *Forms of Prayer and Thanksgiving to Almighty God to be used on the Feast of the Epiphany, the sixth of January, 1918 …* NRO, PR 7762/9.

the cessation of hostilities.[59] One of the prayers which could be offered before the Blessing read,

> We give thee thanks, O Lord, Father almighty, eternal God, for all those thy servants who waxed valiant in the fight and wrought righteousness … and we pray thee that … they may rejoice evermore with all them that hath come out of the great tribulation, and … stand before thy throne … for ever.

While there was no suggestion that the fallen might achieve salvation through their own sacrifices, here was indisputably a prayer for the dead similar to the one which Francis Chavasse had criticised. In an approved form of praise and thanksgiving to be used at Morning or Evening Prayer, a prayer was offered that those had fought the good fight and 'finished their course in thy faith' might, with those offering the prayer, 'be partakers of the inheritance of the Saints in light'. To mark the signing of the Peace Treaty in July 1919, the Archiepiscopally-approved Forms of Thanksgiving included that same prayer.[60] The evidence, therefore, is that Davidson and Lang were willing to approve prayers for the dead, albeit using forms which made it quite clear that only the sacrifice of Christ offered salvation.

Diocesan bishops were, of course, free to authorise forms of prayer in their own dioceses, and local clergy, albeit at the risk of complaints being made against them, might choose to deviate from the officially-approved corpus. As early as November 1915, the service at St. Paul's on the occasion of the Lord Mayor's Procession included this petition: 'For all who die in battle, or through sickness, in this war: that Thou wouldst receive their souls into Thy holy keeping and grant unto them a merciful judgment at the last day.'[61] At a memorial service in Peterborough in July 1919, a prayer was offered that God, 'who by the mouth of thy Son has taught that they greatly love who lay down their lives for others' might grant that 'we who serve Thee still on earth may one day with them be partakers of the inheritance of the Saints in light.'[62] Clearly, this was a prayer about the eternal destiny of those who had died. It is impossible to estimate how widespread was the practice of offering prayers for the dead in local churches during the war and in the memorial services that followed. Anglo-Catholic priests, used to offering prayers and saying Masses for the dead, would have no theological objections to intercessions of that nature and neither would their congregations. Such

59 *Forms of Prayer and Thanksgiving to Almighty God to be used on Sunday, The 17th November 1918, Being the Sunday after the cessation of hostilities between the Allied Powers and the German Empire.* BL, UIN BLL01002197200.

60 *A form of Prayer and Thanksgiving to be used … on Sunday, the 6th July, 1919 …* Copy in SAB.

61 *Form of Service to be used on the occasion of the Lord Mayor's Procession, November 9th, 1915.* Copy in SAB.

62 *Memorial Service for those Railwaymen … Peterborough Cathedral, Sunday July 13th, 1919.* Copy in SAB.

practices would, however, be anathema to the staunch Protestants within the Church, and to the vast majority of, if not all, Nonconformists. It was for the 'middle of the road' Anglican priests to seek to balance traditional orthodoxy with the pastoral needs of their congregations.

Within Nottinghamshire and Derbyshire, evidence of the saying of prayers for the dead is sufficient to confirm their use, but insufficient to make any quantitative assessment. Given the moderate evangelicalism of the Bishop and the relative rarity of Anglo-Catholic parishes compared with, for example, the Birmingham or London dioceses, one would expect such a conclusion. With the widespread distribution of the material approved by the Archbishops and the requirement that, apart from the *BCP*, priests use only forms of prayer approved by their bishops, there was little scope for individual originality, certainly in any printed form. At the unveiling ceremonies for both the memorial Cross and the memorial tablet in Calverton, Nottinghamshire, in May 1921, a quite moderate version of the prayer noted above which had been adapted from the *BCP* burial order was used, including the words, 'we humbly leave in Thy fatherly keeping the souls of our brothers who have laid down their lives ... for the Cause of truth and righteousness.'[63] A prayer at a similar service in Eyam in the same year commended to God the souls 'of Thy servants who have given their lives to defend us.' It continued, 'Accept, O Lord, the offering of their self-sacrifice, and grant to them with all Thy faithful servants, a place of refreshment and peace.'[64] The very same prayer was used in 1919 at Netherseal in Derbyshire,[65] and again at the service in Eyam in 1947 at which the cross was unveiled anew after the addition of the names of those who had died in the Second World War.[66] Variations on this prayer are commonplace in the detailed orders that have been examined.[67]

Unsurprisingly, in the Anglo-Catholic parishes of Birmingham there was less reticence. Both before and after the dedication of a memorial Calvary in Moseley, the Vicar in his parish magazine quoted the Bishop of Oxford at a similar ceremony who had expressed the hope that God, 'in His own good time, and in His own way' would bring those who had died along the way of sacrifice to 'full fruition'.[68] A prayer at a similar service in St. Aidan's, Small Heath, pleaded, 'grant unto the souls of Thy servants departed, the remission of all their sins, that they may obtain the pardon which they have always desired.' Then came the responses: '*V.* Rest eternal, grant unto them, O Lord. / *R.* And let light perpetual : shine upon them. / *V.* May they rest in peace. *R.* Amen.'[69] This is the Roman Catholic prayer 'Eternal Rest' or 'Requiem Æternam',

63 NRO, PR 22,917/2 and /3.
64 DRO, D 2602 A/PI 42/1.
65 DRO, D 1813 A/PI 8/1.
66 DRO, D 2602 A/PI 42/3.
67 e.g. *Memorial dedication for Starkholmes and Riber*, 23 November 1919, DRO, D 1847 A/PI 37 and similarly in a handwritten order for Ticknall, DRO, D 1396 A/PI 9/2(i),
68 *Moseley Parish Church Magazine* 1918, BRO, EP 77/7/1/12,
69 *Dedication of Memorial Calvary*, 9 November 1918, BRO, EP 101/7/4/5.

requesting that souls in purgatory may proceed to heaven. The Vicar of St. Albans, Birmingham, stated in April 1915 that,

> ... the clergy are continually being asked to say Mass for the repose of a soldier or sailor who has given his life for his country. Thank God, we who are Catholics, do not sorrow as others who have no hope; we feel the unspeakable comfort of pleading the Holy Sacrifice in sure and certain hope that those who have died so splendidly are now enjoying refreshment, light, and peace in the nearer Presence of their Father and their God.[70]

The contrast between the extant orders for memorial services in the two dioceses in self-evident. It is a reminder both of the theological and liturgical diversity of the Church of England and of the danger of seeking to draw too firm conclusions, especially quantitative ones, from the available primary sources. After the war, *Songs of Praise* included the hymn, *How can I cease to pray for thee?*[71] and with the benefit of a decade's hindsight, Hensley Henson, writing on the Prayer Book debate, recounted:

> The fearful experience of the Great War effected a revolution in public opinion with respect to the Church's duty towards the dead. In approving the introduction of prayers for the departed into public services, the Bishops did but register and endorse the fact. ... Probably none of their proposals is more congruous with the mind of religious people of every description.[72]

Henson was referring to the revision of the *BCP* approved by the courts of the Church in 1928, but rejected by the House of Commons, in which the burial order included this prayer: 'O Father of all, we pray to thee for those whom we love, but see no longer. Grant them thy peace; let light perpetual shine upon them.'[73] The so-called 'Prayer Book controversy' centred on issues such as reservation and other Anglo-Catholic practices, and the issue of prayers for the dead was a peripheral matter.[74]

Notwithstanding the very public arguments about prayers for the dead at the time, built on the ancient foundations of the controversies of the 16th century, it is clear that

70 *St Alban's Parish Magazine, 1911-1915*. BRO, EP 93 additional material. Acc 2005/018 Box 2, No. 16.

71 Percy Dearmer et. al. (eds.), *Songs of Praise* (London: OUP, 1925) No. 160 and No. 290 in the 1932 *Enlarged* edition.

72 H. Hensley Henson, *The Book and the Vote* (London: Hodder & Stoughton, 1928), pp. 71-73.

73 *The Book of Common Prayer with the additions and deviations proposed in 1928* (London, 1928). Page numbers vary across the many different editions.

74 Davidson referred to the issue in his address to the Lords on 12 December 1927, repeating the argument that he had expressed to Francis Chavasse. In the debate, the Bishop of Durham critically quoted opposition from the 'Protestant underworld'. In the Commons debate, prayers for the dead were not mentioned.

the widespread acceptance of such prayers in the Church of England was one of the most significant influences of the Great War on religious practice and faith in Britain. However, that approval remained far from universal and prayers for the departed again proved to be a contentious issue in the liturgical reforms of the 1960s. No evidence has been found of Nonconformists praying for the dead during the Great War, although almost a century later, the *Methodist Worship Book (MWB)* offered a prayer 'for those whom we love but see no longer', clearly an adapted version of the 1928 prayer.[75] When the draft of the *MWB* was being discussed at the 1998 Methodist Conference, a speaker from the floor drew attention to the ancient prayer, 'May the souls of the faithful, through the mercy of God, rest in peace and rise in glory', identifying it as a prayer for the dead. Both prayers were accepted as elements of liturgies authorised for use in British Methodist Churches without significant debate.[76] What had been highly problematic for most British Protestants in 1913 had become unexceptional for the majority before the end of the 20th century.

Memorialising the War

In the latter years of the conflict and especially once the fighting had ceased, at innumerable civic occasions and church services, the language of sacrifice and martyrdom became increasingly prominent as the nation sought to affirm meaning and find purpose in the loss of life. As Bob Bushaway has written, 'The origin of the theme of sacrifice can be found in the inability of the bereaved to comprehend a more immediate military or political justification for their loss.'[77] Typically, at the dedication of a memorial in Cheltenham in 1918, the Bishop of Gloucester affirmed that the blood of the martyrs had been the seed of the Church before calling on the congregation to 'keep alive the memory of these sacrifices'.[78] A dominant narrative of the closing months of the war and the immediate post-war period was that the survivors of the conflict must strive to make a better world so that the sacrifice of the fallen would not have been in vain. At a service for the unveiling of a war memorial at Littleover, Derby, in June 1917, the Archdeacon of Derby asked, 'To what purpose was all this shedding of blood if it was not going to lead to something better?' He told the congregation that, 'They must show that they were worthy of the sacrifices, and he appealed to all to do their part and make their contribution to the bettering of the world.'[79]

Belief in sacrifice gave the only possible reason for hope on the part of the bereaved. Either they did believe that their loved ones' sacrificial deaths would be divinely

75 *Methodist Worship Book* (Peterborough: Methodist Publishing House, 1999), pp. 458, 469 and 498.

76 Personal recollection as a member of the *Conference Revision Committee* for the *MWB*.

77 Bob Bushaway, 'Name upon Name: The Great War and Remembrance', in R. Porter (ed.), *The Myths of the English* (Cambridge: Polity Press, 1992), p. 149.

78 *Cheltenham Looker-On*, 7 September 1918, p. 8.

79 *DDT*, 30 June 1917, p. 3.

An Army Chaplain tending British graves.

Cosmo Lang, wartime Archbishop of York.

Arthur Winnington-Ingram, Bishop of London, addresses troops in France.

British Soldiers receive communion before battle.

A First Aid Post on the Somme.

The Bishop of London preaching in St Paul's Cathedral

Royal Army Medical Corps unit with its ambulances.

Arthur Winnington-Ingram, Bishop of London, in his chaplain's uniform.

Southport War Memorial.

Randall Davidson,
wartime Archbishop
of Canterbury.

A Chaplain Leads a Service in a Field in France.

Crowds, including American sailors, unable to obtain admission to a crowded Intercession Service at St Paul's Cathedral, 6 January 1918.

Nave of Durham Cathedral.

A Siege Battery of the Royal Garrison Artillery.

Interior of the Guards Chapel, Wellington Barracks.

rewarded or else they had to resign themselves to the futility of their loss. That 'brave little Belgium', for the honour of which men had enlisted in 1914, had been restored as a sovereign state offered scant consolation. Thus, for example, at a memorial service in Derby on 16 Apr 1919, the Bishop of Southwell declared, 'They had made the great sacrifice, and he felt that Christ lived with them, and He lived with them still, and was even now perfecting them. … Their sacrifice was redemptive.'[80] At a service in North Wheatley in the following year, the vicar prayed, 'Accept, O heavenly father, we pray thee, the soldier's sacrifice which these thy sons have made, as a tribute to thy glory and an earnest of their own salvation.'[81] Both statements came very close indeed to attributing the men's salvation to their own sacrifices. Later, when the material and social hopes for post-war Britain had not simply ebbed but been washed away, acts of remembrance which preserved and even enhanced the idea of redemptive sacrifice became the only source of hope.

Again, hymns originally written about spiritual warfare were employed to express the conviction of congregations commemorating the military conflict that those who had died had done so in a just cause and would receive their heavenly reward. Without doubt, the exemplar of the commemoration hymn, nationally and locally, sung in the majority of memorial services in Nottinghamshire and Derbyshire of which records exist was *For all the saints who from their labours rest.* Given popular understanding of the moral validity of the cause, of the nature of the conflict as a spiritual one between good and evil – or even between God and the Devil – and of the dead as glorious martyrs, it could well appear to have been written specifically for the purpose of memorialising the First World War, rather than for All Saints Days and funerals since 1864. According to its verses, Jesus had been 'their captain in the well-fought fight.' The 'soldiers, faithful, true and bold' had fought 'as the saints who nobly fought of old'. Now, they have won 'the victor's crown of gold', and while 'we feebly struggle, they in glory shine'. It continued, 'And when the strife is fierce, the warfare long, / Steals on the ear the distant triumph song, / And hearts are brave again, and arms are strong, /Alleluia!' Then, 'The golden evening brightens in the west; / Soon, soon to faithful warriors cometh rest; / Sweet is the calm of paradise the blessed, Alleluia!' It is hard to conceive of a more complete expression of the shared belief in the sacrificial nature of the losses of the conflict, of the spiritual nature of the war and of the certainty that such martyr deaths could do no other than ensure the eternal salvation of those being remembered. In innumerable memorial dedications across the two counties, and, indeed, across the country, the fallen were accorded martyr status with this hymn. *For All the Saints* was written by William Walsham How, later to become bishop of Wakefield, but it was first published anonymously in *Hymns for Saints' Days, and other Hymns* in 1864 before subsequently appearing in many other hymnbooks. Although it was located in the *Processional* section of the *English Hymnal* (1906), elsewhere it

80 *SDM,* May 1919. NRO, DR 1/1/12/14/32.
81 *Order of service for the unveiling of the war memorial,* 28 July 1920. NRO, 25,873.

was identified for use at 'Festivals of Martyrs and other Holy Days', to celebrate 'The Church Militant and Triumphant', or as a hymn addressing 'Heaven and the life hereafter'.[82] After the war, it would be printed under headings such as, 'The Church Triumphant – the Saints' and 'The Church, Militant and Triumphant'.[83] However, the archives of the 'Church Hymn Book committee' of SPCK, which met frequently 1917 and 1918 to revise the *London Mission Hymnal*, show how the growing use of *For All the Saints* as a celebration of the lives of those who had fallen in the war had largely supplanted its original association with Saints' days and the Church triumphant in heaven. The committee minutes record that in October 1917, it was agreed that the hymn would be in the 'Communion of Saints' section. However, at the very last meeting in December 1918, it was transferred to the 'Processional' section.[84] That simple editorial amendment, recorded without comment, reflected the reality that Walsham How's finest hymn was now seen as being much more about the 'soldiers, faithful, true and bold' of the previous four years than the 'saints who nobly fought of old'.

One of the most comprehensively-documented memorial services took place in the churchyard of Chinley Independent Chapel on 14 April 1923, at which the 'highest war memorial in the Peak' was unveiled. The nature of the chapel as a fiercely-independent chapel, quite separate from the established Church, is significant. Although the vast majority of orders of service, church magazines and newspaper reports extant refer to Anglican practice during and after the war, the evidence from other denominations is largely consistent. In his opening remarks, the chairman of the memorial committee asserted that this was the 'greatest day' in the history of the chapel which had been founded in 1662. *For All the Saints* was duly sung. Then, in his address, the Revd. D. J. Price, pastor of the chapel, stated that while to some present, some of these men were unknown, 'yet everyone present recognised the sublime spirit of self-sacrifice in which they offered up their lives, and for that reason the stone cross reflected the light of that greater cross on which our blessed Redeemer offered his life for us all.' Note the stress on the intentional nature of sacrifice; both of the soldiers being commemorated and of Christ, whose death theirs were seen to some extent to emulate.[85]

This constant repetition of the rhetoric of the theology of sacrifice and martyrdom played an important role in validating the immense loss of life, with one intention before November 1918 being the maintenance of popular support for Britain's engagement in the conflict. First, it gave moral authority to that engagement, characterised

82 *Hymns Ancient and Modern – New Edition*, 1904, no. 437; *The (Wesleyan) Methodist Hymnbook,* 1904, no. 807; *The United Methodist Hymnbook*, 1889, no. 791.
83 *Songs of Praise*, 1925, no. 110; *Methodist Hymnbook*, 1933, no. 832.
84 S.P.C.K. Archives, Cambridge University Library, SPCK, MS A21/1. S.P.C.K is the Society for Promoting Christian Knowledge, an Anglican mission organization founded in 1698.
85 *Order of service and newspaper report with photograph*, DRO, D470/39/1/4.

as 'right' challenging military 'might'. Second, it reasserted the Christian hope of life after death, thus giving comfort and hope to the bereaved. Third, in closely associating the death of combatants with the death of Christ, it sought to elevate those deaths above the grim reality of the actual event, 'revolting only and horrid' as Harold Macmillan so memorably phrased it in a letter to his mother.[86] Moreover, as Bushaway observed, despite the slowly-declining place of religion as disillusionment about the War and its aftermath grew in the late 1920s, the Church held on to its key role as the provider of remembrance ceremonies. It was the explicit expressions of patriotism which fell out of favour.

Within a few years, the emphasis of the approved forms of prayer for the anniversaries of the Armistice changed significantly.[87] No longer was the focus on the sacrifice of the fallen, but rather on dedication to the cause of peace. On the absence of any sense of triumphalism in the recommended liturgy for Armistice Day in 1928, Bushaway quoted a comment made by Thomas Harris in that year: 'This omission is made partly because it is becoming increasingly evident that whatever victory there was in the war was a Pyrrhic victory, but more because paeans of victory seem to modern ears particularly out of place in worship.'[88] In 1929, SPCK published a form of thanksgiving and prayer, 'For use where permitted by authority'.[89] In it was a prayer declaring that those who had laid down their lives in the Great War had 'offered their sacrifice in very truth to Thee.' God was asked to grant those praying 'the strength and solace of unbroken fellowship with them [the fallen] in this life and in the life to come.' An Easter hymn, 'The strife is o'er, the battle done' / Now is the Victor's triumph won', followed. Presumably the reason that the hymn to be sung in the 'Dedication' section of the service was *While shepherds watched their flocks by night* was its reference to the angels singing of peace on earth and ceaseless goodwill from heaven to earth. A 'Service for Armistice Day' published in 1930 commenced with opening sentences which included Micah's prophecy of swords being turned into ploughshares and Jesus' declaration, 'Blessed are the peacemakers; for they shall be called the children of God.'[90] Towards the conclusion of the liturgy, the minister prayed,

> Let us remember before God those of all the nations who fell in the Great War, in silence calling to mind the love of those we see no more, who yet are one with us in the Communion of Saints. ... Holy is the true Light, and passing

86 Bodleian, Macmillan deposit, letter to mother, 2/2/41-3.

87 Such forms of prayer, published by S.P.C.K, were not generally dated. However, it would appear highly probable that the accession stamps on the copies held by the British Library, '8 Nov 29' and '5 Nov 30' respectively, are indicative of the year of publication and first use.

88 Harris, *Christian Public Worship*, p. 194, quoted in Bushaway, 'Name upon Name', p. 152.

89 *A Form of Thanksgiving and Prayer In Remembrance of the Cessation of the Great War ...* (London, 1929). BL, UIN BLL01002197211. Biblical references are to Micah 4:3 and Matthew 5:9.

90 *A Service for Armistice Day* (London: SPCK, 1930). BL, UIN BLL01002197214.

> wonderful, lending radiance to them that endured in the heat of the conflict; from Christ they inherit a home of unfading splendour, wherein they rejoice with gladness evermore.

Note the call to remember those of 'all the nations'. The latter part of this prayer is a translation by G.H. Palmer of a Latin prayer from the Salisbury Diurnal, published in 1926. Clearly, the 'heat of the conflict' was originally a reference to a spiritual battle or to persecution because of faith. As has been repeatedly observed, the conflation of spiritual and military warfare allowed historic texts to be employed to affirm the hope that those who had died 'in the heat of the conflict' would be granted eternal life. A responsive litany followed, including, '*V.* The Lord himself suffered with them and gathered them. / *R.* They live in his sight'. After an opportunity for the congregation to 'give thanks for progress in the cause of peace since the last Armistice Day', the service concluded with the short-lived 'Peace Version' of the National Anthem, which concluded, 'Bid strife and hatred cease, / Bid hope and joy increase, / Spread universal peace, / God save the King!'

Long after the fevered patriotism of 1914-1918 was over, the memorials to the fallen stood as reminders of the religious hope which had accompanied that patriotism. The Cenotaph in London was unusual in containing no religious symbolism – other than that implicit in the meaning of 'cenotaph' – that is 'empty tomb'. However, its designer, Edwin Lutyens stated that, including the flags which formed an integral part of the memorial, the Cenotaph contained at least 22 crosses.[91] Elsewhere, the majority of memorials, plaques and sculptures across Britain re-expressed without any sense of triumphalism the association of national and divine purposes which had validated Britain's role in the war. The text, 'Greater love hath no man than this that he lay down his life for his friends' (John 15:13) appeared on almost 2000 British war memorials, reaffirming the likening of the deaths of the fallen to that of Christ.[92] From a contemporary perspective it is easy to be cynical about the idea that any of those almost a million men consciously laid down their lives. However, in addition to the recorded acts of such self-sacrifice in the heat of the battle, many personal diaries reflect a decision by men to enlist, fully aware of what the consequences might be.[93]

One further element of this 'sanctified nationalism', particularly common in acts of remembrance arranged by the British Legion, must be noted: On 6 July 1947, the people of Eyam in Derbyshire assembled for the unveiling and dedication of a

91 S. Foreman, *From Palace to Power: an illustrated history of Whitehall* (Brighton: The Alpha Press, 1995), p. 130.

92 According to the UK National Inventory of War Memorials at the Imperial War Museum, of all 34,688 WW1 memorials, many of which were in secular locations, 5.5 per cent carried this text.

93 e.g. E. N. Goodridge and J. A. Goodridge (eds.) *The Same Stars Shine: The Great War Diaries of Corporal Ernest Goodridge* (Loughborough: Teamprint, 2000), considered in chapter 8.

memorial to those who had died in the Second World War. As they had done at the previous commemoration on 2 April 1921, they`sang *For all the Saints*.[94] This time, however, before the sounding of Reveille, the order of service included the hymn, *Valiant Hearts:*

> O valiant hearts who to your glory came
> Through dust of conflict and through battle flame;
> Tranquil you lie, your knightly virtue proved,
> Your memory hallowed in the land you loved.
>
> Proudly you gathered, rank on rank, to war
> As who had heard God's message from afar;
> All you had hoped for, all you had, you gave,
> To save mankind—yourselves you scorned to save.

It continued in a similar vein for five more verses. Written by Sir John Stanhope Arkwright in 1919, this hymn became a standard element in annual acts of remembrance. With this couplet in verse five, 'Still, through the veil, the Victor's pitying eyes / Look down to bless our lesser Calvaries', it perpetuated the close association of the deaths of those remembered with that of Christ. Published in the highly popular hymn book *Songs of Praise* in 1925, it embodied the religious nationalism of the conflict for future generations, surviving even through the changed attitudes to the war of the 1960s and 70s. It remains in use to this day, bring sung at the 2015 ANZAC Day commemorations at the Australian War Memorial in Canberra, albeit with the omission of some of the most problematic verses, but ending with the couplet, 'Deep your commitment in that blest abode / Who wait the last clear trumpet call of God'.[95] Still used in some local British remembrance ceremonies, *Valiant Hearts* remains the most obvious and public challenge to Paul Fussell's assertion that one of the 'ultimate casualties' of the First World War was 'high diction'.

Conclusion

The Great War had a lasting impact on the corporate religious life of Britain. First, while prayers for the dead had featured in some orders published by the Church of England prior to the conflict and had been proposed in the Prayer Book revision processes in 1911, their pre-war use had been very limited.[96] However, once war had

94 *Unveiling and dedication of the Memorial … April 3rd 1921*, DRO, D2602 A/PI 42/1; *Unveiling and dedication … 6th July 1947*, DRO, D2603 A/PI 42/3.

95 *Anzac Day 2015: 100th Anniversary of the Gallipoli Landings*, Australian Government publication, copy in SAB.

96 Beaken, *The Church of England and the Home Front 1914-1918*, p. 148.

broken out, they became widely used, officially and unofficially, in the Church of England. While a handful of evangelical bishops objected, their use was defended by Randall Davidson, and they were subsequently included in the 'Deposited' Prayer Book of 1928. Second, just as the presence of refugees had throughout the conflict provided a visible and daily reminder in the villages, towns and cities of Britain of the consequences of the conflict for the people of Belgium, so from 1917 onwards the erection of those 34,688 crosses, plaques, tablets and memorials served to remind the country of the human cost of the conflict. While the development of the annual commemoration at the Cenotaph in London has been well documented, that was simply one event among countless others each November.[97] Increasingly organized by the British Legion, such acts of remembrance expressed the determination of the nation not to forget. In the memorials which were the focus of such acts of remembrance we see set in stone and brass the language of sacrifice which was so prevalent during the years of the war. The most extreme expositions of sacrifice, which viewed the soldiers' own deaths as being redemptive in their own right – thus ensuring the eternal destiny of the fallen – were soon quietly forgotten. However, the simple association of those deaths with the sacrifice of Christ, most obviously expressed in the Johanine quotation, 'Greater love hath no man than this, that he lay down his life for his friends', gave comfort to the bereaved, implicitly assuring them that the sacrifices had not been made in vain.

While support for commemoration flagged in the face of the changing attitudes of the 1970s and 80s, Britain's subsequent engagement in new conflicts and the centenary of the Great War have re-established such events in the life of the nation. Very recently the explicit and significant religious content has been challenged yet most acts of remembrance retain the familiar elements of prayers and hymn-singing.[98] However, although confident assertions about the nature of the 'supreme sacrifice' made by millions of soldiers undoubtedly comforted and gave hope to their families, for a small number of chaplains the idea of a God who was content to accept such sacrifices while remaining removed from and unaffected by them became untenable. By far the most prominent of those men was Geoffrey Studdert Kennedy, to whose advocacy of a God who shares in the suffering of humanity we now turn.

97 A. Gregory, *The Silence of Memory: Armistice Day 1919-1946* (London: Berg, 1994).

98 e.g. D. Snow, 'Remembrance Sunday should not be dominated by religion' in *The Guardian* (on-line edition), 6 November 2014, retrieved from http://www.theguardian.com/commentisfree/2014/nov/06/remembrance-sunday-lack-of-secular-presence on 24 March 2015.

6

Beyond Sacrifice to a Suffering God

Geoffrey Studdert Kennedy

For most clergy and church-goers during the Great War, the conventional answers to the inevitable questions about divine omnipotence and theodicy – the reconciliation of the presence of evil with the existence of a loving God – seem to have provided an adequate response. As we have seen, when coupled with repeated declarations about the importance of sacrifice in the Christian life – and hence in that of a Christian nation – and the likening of the soldiers' 'great sacrifice' to that of Christ, then those explanations formed the standard theological commentary on the conflict. Such explanations were, however, seen as inadequate by a minority, especially by some chaplains and certainly by Geoffrey Studdert Kennedy who served as a chaplain on the Western Front. In one of the anthologies for which he became famous was the poem 'A Sermon'.[1] Astonishingly vitriolic in tone, even for someone as outspoken as Studdert Kennedy, it challenged head-on the assertion that God is in control of everything and that it was his will that the war was happening. Therefore, it was argued, God's purposes and actions must never be challenged. As the title suggested, the poem started with a sermon to the soldiers:

My brethren, the ways of God
No man can understand,
We can but wait in awe and watch
The wonders of His hand.
He dwells in Majesty sublime
Beyond the starry height,
His Wisdom is ineffable,
His Love is infinite.

1 G.A. Studdert Kennedy, *More Rough Rhymes of a Padre* (London: Hodder & Stoughton, 1920), pp. 32–37.

He continued in this vein for stanza after stanza, developing the apparent consequences of belief in divine omnipotence and highlighting the paradox of a loving God who not only allows, but even wills, the suffering of millions:

So bow you down and worship Him,
Kneel humbly and adore
This Infinitely Loving God
Who is the Lord of War.

As the main body of the poem came to its climax, Studdert Kennedy parodied the argument that, however much people pray, ultimately the acts of God are beyond human comprehension:

Remember, rather, all your sins,
And bow to God's decrees.
Seek not to know the plans of God,
But pray upon your knees
That you may love with all your heart,
With all your soul and mind,
This perfect God you cannot know,
Whose face you cannot find.

After 124 lines, the 'sermon' came to an end. Then there was a space, a change of typeface and this damning response:

O, by Thy Cross and Passion, Lord,
By broken hearts that pant
For comfort and for love of Thee,
Deliver us from cant.

From a contemporary perspective, the 'sermon' is clearly recognisable as expounding some of the traditional interpretations of the relationship of God to the Great War, but it does appear to be a grotesque parody of the standard theological responses of chaplains to the standard questions that soldiers posed. However, in a short biographical piece published in 1919, Primitive Methodist minister Arthur Hird stated that Studdert Kennedy 'reproduces one of those gramophone homilies with scrupulous fairness.'[2] It was, apparently, much less of a parody that we might assume. For Studdert Kennedy, it was critically important to reject all understandings of divine power which might suggest that God willed the war or that he could have stopped it but had decided not to act. Furthermore, he could not accept that God was left unmoved

2 A. Hird, 'Woodbine Willie', *Aldersgate Magazine*, April 1919, p. 260.

by human suffering on such a scale and so, for him, the inescapable conclusion was that the God revealed in the suffering Christ was the God who actually shared in the world's suffering. As we shall see, Studdert Kennedy was not the only wartime writer to advocate divine passibility, but he was the only such writer whose work was widely published and read. In itself that raises the question of the influence of his advocacy, an issue to which we shall turn in examining the long-term impact of his work.

Geoffrey Anketell Studdert Kennedy (1883–1929) is commemorated in the Calendar of *Common Worship*, the current liturgical book of the Church of England, on the date of his death, 8 March, with the descriptors 'priest' and 'poet'. For William Temple, he was a 'prophet of social righteousness in the true succession of Henry Scott Holland', while friend and biographer J.K. Mozley wrote that, 'The true prophet is a student of life who penetrates to its meaning in the light of the knowledge of God. Such was Geoffrey Studdert Kennedy.'[3] Certainly he was one of the most famous of the forces chaplains of the First World War and the author of more than 20 popular books of prose and poetry that sold in large numbers in the 1920s. Though Studdert Kennedy's preaching was heavily influenced by his wartime experiences, it also reflected some significant events that had taken place earlier in his life. He was born in St Mary's Vicarage, Quarry Hill, Leeds, on 27 June 1883, the seventh son of the Revd. W.S. Studdert Kennedy.[4] That the vicarage was surrounded by the workhouse, the board school, the brick quarry and a public house is indicative of the nature of the parish in which Studdert Kennedy would later assist his father as a curate.[5] Education at Leeds Grammar School and Trinity College Dublin culminated in his taking first class honours in both classics and divinity in 1902. Two years' teaching at West Kirby on the Wirral were followed, in October 1907, by a year at Ripon Clergy College.[6] On leaving Ripon, his first curacy was in Rugby, where,

> His sermons, from the first, displayed that oratorical quality for which he was to become famous … As to the subject matter of his sermons, he preached with fervour the truth of the Fatherhood of God, and possessed a special power of enabling his hearers to realise the truth of divine personality. If he was inclined to lapse into too journalistic a vein, he had the Rector at hand as a friendly and candid critic.[7]

3 W. Temple, 'G.A. Studdert Kennedy: The Man and His Message' in Mozley, (ed.), *G.A. Studdert Kennedy by his Friends* (London, 1929), p. 209; J.K. Mozley, 'Epilogue' in Mozley, (ed.), *G.A. Studdert Kennedy by his Friends*, p. 246.

4 J.K. Mozley, 'Home Life and Early Years of His Ministry' in Mozley, (ed.), *G.A. Studdert Kennedy by his Friends*, p. 13.

5 Ibid., p. 40.

6 See M.W. Brierley, 'Ripon Hall, Henry Major and the Shaping of English Liberal Theology' in Chapman (ed.), *Ambassadors of Christ*, pp. 89-155.

7 Mozley, 'Home Life and Early Years', p. 56.

If Studdert Kennedy's oratorical style was shaped at Rugby, then it was in his first incumbency in Worcester where the scale of the poverty in his parish motivated a zeal for social justice that would be the primary focus of his post-war work for the Industrial Christian Fellowship. Yet, it is a startling paradox that while Geoffrey Studdert Kennedy was almost certainly the most widely-known British army chaplain of the First World War, the aspect of his work which, almost a century later, is arguably of greatest contemporary significance is the one that remains unrecognized by most accounts of his life and ministry. That aspect is his advocacy of belief in a God who suffers. In his first work, published in 1917, he wrote, 'God suffers now, and is crucified afresh every day. God suffers in every man that suffers. God, the God we love and worship, is no far off God of Power but the comrade God of love.'[8]

This was Studdert Kennedy's response to the question, 'Where is God in all this?' – a question posed by believers in innumerable situations of suffering and distress and one which would be asked on a far greater scale in the face of the Holocaust and the dropping of two atomic bombs a generation later. It is a response which would be developed both in his 1918 book of theological reflection on his experiences of war, *The Hardest Part*, and also in collections of his poems published in 1918, 1920 and 1921.[9] Yet, while he has been described as the most well-known of all the early British passibilists – those who advocate belief in a passible God – his theological contribution has been understated or even ignored.[10] In Studdert Kennedy's own time, much of the marginalization of his theology can be attributed to the contemporary understanding of how and by whom theology was 'done'. Essentially, theological insight and development of thought were seen as the exclusive province of a small and elite group of theologians. Such people, almost invariably men, were typically professors or dons at Oxford, Cambridge or, just occasionally, London or one of the Scottish universities.[11] To that group were added the so-called 'best brains' of the bishops' bench, and the occasional dean or canon.[12] They were *the* theologians. Thus, the biographer of Randall Davidson, Archbishop of Canterbury, could offer without any sense of criticism the comment that his subject was 'not himself a theologian'.[13] Similarly, writing shortly after Studdert Kennedy's death in 1929, former army chaplain D.F. Carey insisted, 'Studdert was the last to make any claim to be a theologian in the exact

8 Studdert Kennedy, 'The Religious Difficulties of the Private Soldier', p. 391.

9 G.A. Studdert Kennedy, *Rough Rhymes of a Padre* (London: Hodder & Stoughton, 1918); *More Rough Rhymes of a Padre*; *Peace Rhymes of a Padre* (London: Hodder & Stoughton, 1920); *The Sorrows of God and Other Poems* (London: Hodder & Stoughton, 1921).

10 M. Brierley, 'Introducing the Early British Passibilists', *Journal for the History of Modern Theology*, 8 (2001), pp. 218–33.

11 Examples of such prominent Oxbridge theologians include S.R. Driver, Charles Gore, Arthur Headlam, Henry Scott Holland, William Sanday and B.H. Streeter.

12 Obvious examples are Hastings Rashdall, Dean of Carlisle, and J. K. Mozley, Canon of St Paul's.

13 Bell, *Randall Davidson*, p. 1135.

sense of the word.'[14] In an environment in which discourse on theology was confined to a highly-educated elite, no ordinary parish priest, let alone an army chaplain with a colourful reputation, was expected to publish original theological ideas or to offer a distinctive answer to the question 'Where is God in all this?' from the Western Front.

There were two consequences of this. First, Studdert Kennedy's work was largely ignored in contemporary academic literature. One searches in vain for any serious engagement with the theological issues raised by *The Hardest Part* or some of his poems. In a public lecture in 1997, Kenneth Woollcombe stated, 'I have studied the books about theology in the 1920s and found one reference to Studdert Kennedy.'[15] Second, when his theology was commented upon it was often treated in a somewhat dismissive and patronising manner. J.K. Mozley wrote the classic historical survey of changing attitudes to divine impassibility, publishing his Cambridge D.D. thesis on this subject in 1926. He also edited what soon became the standard biography of Studdert Kennedy, *G.A. Studdert Kennedy – By His Friends*. In the former work, he wrote:

> The thoughts of *The Hardest Part* came to its author on the battlefield of the West, and their intensity, both in idea and in expression, reveals clearly enough the pressure and tension of such tremendous experiences. But the same theology reappears, and as something which belongs to the heart of religious truth, in later works ...[16]

In Mozley's survey of British theology from 1889 to 1946, he described *The Hardest Part* thus:

> The title was meant to express in an arresting manner the belief that in the experience of suffering it is God, not man, who had most to endure. The book was written under the stress of personal immersion in the war, and its emotional aspect is largely due to that fact.[17]

In stressing the effect of the conditions under which he worked and in apparently feeling the need to excuse the 'emotional aspect' of *The Hardest Part*, Mozley seemed to be implying that something more 'balanced' might have come from the usual sources of theological insight like the senior common rooms of Oxford or Cambridge. Soon after his death, *The Times* carried an obituary for Studdert Kennedy. Although it ran

14 Carey, 'Studdert Kennedy – War Padre', p. 149.

15 R. Holman, *Woodbine Willie: An Unsung Hero of World War One* (Oxford: Lion Books, 2013), p. 178.

16 J.K. Mozley, *The Impassibility of God – A Survey of Christian Thought* (Cambridge: CUP, 1926), p. 160.

17 J.K. Mozley, *Some Tendencies in British Theology from the Publication of Lux Mundi to the Present Day* (London: SPCK, 1952), p. 52.

to around 1,000 words, his advocacy of a suffering God claimed just three lines.[18] A few days later 'an appreciation' by H.R.L. ('Dick') Sheppard was published, also in *The Times*.[19] It paid fulsome tribute to his oratory, his eloquence, his advocacy of Christianity, his lovable nature, his wisdom and his efforts to address the problems of British society in the 1920s. Of his theology there was nothing. This treatment of Studdert Kennedy's theology did not end in the year of his death, however. In 1947 'a friend' edited *The Best of Studdert Kennedy*, bringing together extracts from his poems and prose.[20] Significantly, the vast majority of the poems on God's passibility, most notably 'The Suffering God' and 'The Sorrow of God', were omitted from the anthology.

The Suffering God

From a passibilist perspective, God may be believed to be subject to or able to change in numerous ways, including his will, knowledge, love, joy, anger, sorrow and suffering.[21] In Studdert Kennedy's work and in a range of earlier texts, the consideration of divine passibility focused on the last two of those attributes of God – his sorrow and, especially, his suffering.[22] Although he was not widely recognized as a theologian until after the Second World War, Studdert Kennedy's advocacy of his faith in a God who shares in the world's suffering can be seen to be a key theme in all his wartime writing. In a lengthy introduction to his very first book, *The Hardest Part*, published in 1918, he explained the rationale behind it:

> When a chaplain joins a battalion no one says a word to him about God, but everyone asks him, in a thousand different ways, 'What is God like?' His success or failure as a chaplain really depends upon the answer he gives by word and deed ... This is what I have tried to do in this book.[23]

Throughout, the author wove together a narrative of experiences at the front with reaction to it and reflections on the nature of God. Typical was this episode:

> It's about time to strike up off to the left – on my own. There's the wood in which I've got to find a place for an Aid Post. It's being shelled pretty heavily, I believe

18 *The Times*, 9 March 1929, p. 14.
19 *The Times*, 15 March 1929, p. 23.
20 G.A. Studdert Kennedy, *The Best of Studdert Kennedy* 'edited by a friend', (London: Hodder & Stoughton, 1947).
21 T. Weinandy, *Does God Suffer?* (Notre Dame IN: University of Notre Dame Press, 2000), p. 2.
22 For example, A.M. Fairbairn, *The Place of Christ in Modern Theology* (London: Hodder & Stoughton, 1893) and C.E. Rolt, *The World's Redemption* (London: Longmans, Green & Co., 1913).
23 Studdert Kennedy, *The Hardest Part*, pp. xiii–xiv.

> I'm getting windy again. Damn all nerves! Dear Christ, Who suffered on the Cross and wouldn't take that sleeping stuff, give me strength to be a decent chap. Come on. How I hate being alone. It's rotten. One pal makes all the difference. But He was alone. It's funny how it is always Christ upon the Cross that comforts; never God upon a throne. One needs a Father, and a Father must suffer in His children's sufferings. I could not worship a passionless potentate … I don't know or love the Almighty potentate – my only real God is the suffering Father revealed in the sorrow of Christ.[24]

Studdert Kennedy rejected the traditional understanding of an omnipotent God, an understanding that could lead to the conclusion that God actively willed the war to take place. As was shown in chapter 4, he was not alone in this. However, in his advocacy of a God who not only does not exhibit conventional indicators of omnipotence, but is also a Father who 'must suffer in His children's sufferings', Studdert Kennedy was in a small minority. As we shall see, fellow chaplains F.R. Barry and F.W. Worsley expressed similar ideas. Studdert Kennedy's argument was that only the suffering Christ who reveals a suffering God has meaning and significance for those engaged in the conflict. How could a God who could stop the conflict, but chose not to, be worthy of worship? For those who held the conventional view of God's omnipotence and were content not to challenge the argument that humans must not question the divine will, Studdert Kennedy's use of phrases like 'a passionless potentate' must have stood in stark contrast to the moderated tones of standard theological debate. Recognizing the radical and potentially disturbing thrust of his case, at the end of *The Hardest Part* he responded to the 'hurt' felt by some who had read the proofs of the book:

> We must make clear to ourselves and to the world what we mean when we say 'I believe in God the Father Almighty.' The conditions under which these meditations were made account for the repeated and constant denial of the popular conception. I may have railed at that conception very fiercely, but my raillery is mild and good-natured compared with the outspoken comments of the guns.[25]

Although some of his poems had been circulated since 1916, it was not until 1918 that Studdert Kennedy's first anthology, *Rough Rhymes of a Padre*, was published. The second poem in that volume, 'The Sorrow of God', gave its title to a later collection published in 1921. One of his dialect poems, it addressed the question of theodicy for the soldier in the trenches:

> And I'm damned if I really sees
> 'Ow the God, who 'as made such a cruel world,

24 Ibid., pp. 9f.
25 Ibid., p. 192.

Can 'ave Love in 'Is 'eart for men,
And be deaf to the cries of the men as dies
And never comes 'ome again.[26]

As he would throughout his work, Studdert Kennedy held fast to his belief in a loving God and came to the conclusion that God *must* be sorrowing and suffering as he witnessed the sorrow and suffering of the combatants and their loved ones at home:

And the lovin' God 'E looks down on it all,
On the blood and the mud and the smell.
O God, if it's true, 'ow I pities you,
For ye must be livin' i' 'ell.
...
The sorrows o' God must be 'ard to bear
If 'E really 'as Love in 'Is 'eart,
And the 'ardest part i' the world to play
Must surely be God's part.[27]

In 'Thy Will Be Done', Studdert Kennedy told the story of two soldiers caught up in a gas attack. One of them prayed for God to change the direction of the wind and the other died. This posed an obvious question:

Now, 'ow was it 'E didn't shift that wind,
When I axed in the name o' the Lord?
With the 'orror of death in every breath,
Still I prayed every breath I drawed.[28]

Studdert Kennedy's solution was not, in this poem, to question ideas of divine omnipotence or challenge the widely promoted response that the mysterious ways of God must not be questioned, but rather to see in Christ's Gethsemane–Calvary experience a revelation of a God who suffers:

And why ever the Lord didn't shift that wind
I just couldn't see for my life.
But I've just bin readin' a story 'ere,
Of the night afore Jesus died,
And of 'ow 'E prayed in Gethsemane,
'Ow 'E fell on 'Is face and cried.

26 Studdert Kennedy, *Rough Rhymes*, p. 18.
27 Ibid., p. 19.
28 Ibid., p. 33.

Cried to the Lord Orlmighty above
Till 'E broke in a bloody sweat,
And 'E were the Son of the Lord, 'E were,
And 'E prayed to 'Im 'ard; and yet,
And yet 'E 'ad to go through wiv it, boys,
Just same as pore Bill what died.[29]

As he did in *The Hardest Part*, Studdert Kennedy asserted that the Cross was the true revelation of the divine and a far better disclosure of the nature of God than the picture of a God sitting impassive and unmoved above the scenes of carnage below:

And the Christ who was 'ung on the Cross is Gawd,
True Gawd for me and you,
For the only Gawd that a true man trusts
Is the Gawd what sees it through.[30]

The same theme is found in 'The Suffering God'.[31] Perhaps the importance of this poem to its author is shown by the fact that, apart from the short, witty and self-critical 'Woodbine Willie', it was the very first poem in his 1927 anthology *The Unutterable Beauty*. Written in conventional English, this poem started from the Cross before addressing the relationship of God to a suffering world:

How can it be that God can reign in glory,
Calmly content with what His Love has done,
Reading unmoved the piteous shameful story,
All the vile deeds men do beneath the sun?
...
Father, if He, the Christ, were Thy Revealer,
Truly the First Begotten of the Lord,
Then must Thou be a Suff'rer and a Healer,
Pierced to the heart by the sorrow of the sword.[32]

Other Advocates of Divine Passibility

Orthodox Christian belief in the impassibility of God has its origins in Greek philosophy, but it has long been recognized that there is a tension between the Greek idea of the Absolute Being and the Hebrew conception of a loving Father.

29 Ibid., pp. 33f.
30 Ibid., p. 35.
31 Ibid., p. 58.
32 Ibid., pp. 59f.

Belief in divine impassibility in the face of the suffering of Christ has often been preserved by distinguishing between his passible human nature and his impassible divine nature. Geoffrey Studdert Kennedy was far from being the first person in the history of Christendom to suggest that the suffering of God is not confined to the suffering of Jesus Christ, God incarnate in human form. However, the evidence is that advocacy of a passible God before the First World War was very limited. As noted above, in 1926, J.K. Mozley, a member of the Archbishops' Doctrinal Commission, set up primarily to examine and report on the limits to orthodox belief in the Church of England, published *The Impassibility of God – A Survey of Christian Thought.* This work was produced in response to a request by the Commission that he examine the issue of divine impassibility, but it went far beyond the initial brief in its scope. As Michael Brierley has remarked, the very fact of Mozley's production of such a survey is of significance, showing that within a few years of the end of the Great War there were enough advocates of passibilism to warrant such an enterprise.[33] As he put it, 'Enough passibilism had passed down the theological river by 1926 for it to be recognised as a tributary stream.'[34] Brierley identified numerous omissions in Mozley's survey and offered a chronological list of 47 British passibilists, within which Studdert Kennedy is the 36th entry. This might appear to indicate that he was simply a popular and populist spokesman for an established theological development. There are three reasons, however, to challenge such a conclusion.

First, Brierley failed to distinguish those for whom passibilism was a primary emphasis from those within whose corpus he was able to find some evidence of passibilism – evidence which may well have been atypical of most of that writer's work. For example, the philosopher and theologian Hastings Rashdall wrote and preached extensively on the theme of the Atonement, his *magnum opus* on that subject being published in 1920.[35] While Brierley was right that in one place in that 496-page work he came to a cautiously passibilist conclusion,[36] Rashdall's staunch advocacy of the so-called Abelardian, or 'moral influence', theory of the Atonement was so dominant that to call him a passibilist would be quite misleading, for that theory of the Atonement makes no assertion that the Father shared in the suffering of the Son.

Second, Brierley overlooked contradictory evidence within a writer's work. One obvious example is Timothy Rees, a First World War chaplain and later Bishop of Llandaff. The following lines from his hymn *God is Love, Let Heaven Adore Him* have become perhaps the most widely-used expression of divine passibility in British churches since World War Two:

33 Brierley, 'Introducing the Early British Passibilists', pp. 218-33.
34 Ibid., p. 219.
35 H. Rashdall, *The Idea of Atonement in Christian Theology* (London: Macmillan, 1920).
36 Ibid., pp. 450–52.

And when human hearts are breaking
Under sorrow's iron rod,
That same sorrow, that same aching,
Wrings with pain the heart of God.[37]

However, this must be set against Rees' sermon on the Victorious Christ in which he stated, 'Nothing can disturb the bliss of the Eternal God.'[38] Furthermore, the earliest reference in the literature to that hymn dates from 1939, when it was discovered in the author's personal papers after his death – two decades after the date that Brierley claimed for Rees's passibilism.

Third, in providing a more comprehensive survey of early British passibilism, it was not Brierley's aim to identify the influences of early writers on later ones. For some, it is explicit, most obviously in the case of the respected biblical scholar B.H. Streeter whose article on the subject, published in 1914, commenced with a detailed analysis of historic views of passibility, then stopped almost mid-paragraph to become a glowing tribute to Clarence Rolt's *The World's Redemption*, which Streeter had just discovered. The rest of the article is largely a summary of Rolt's work, which Streeter described as showing 'brilliant style and profound thought.'[39]

Influences on Studdert Kennedy

What, then, were the influences on Studdert Kennedy which led to his advocacy of a suffering God? In one of the most significant post-war books on divine passibility, *The Creative Suffering of God*, Paul Fiddes identified four motives for attributing sorrow and suffering to God.[40] The first is the outcome of a reflection on the nature of love, which concludes that love for one who suffers *must* involve the sharing of feelings and sympathy and that therefore a God of love cannot be unchanged by human suffering. A second motive is Christological and turns on the view that, if Christ's suffering affected the whole person of Christ and not simply his human nature, then 'the event of the cross reveals that weakness and humility are characteristic of God's triune nature.'[41] Furthermore, if Jesus reveals what God is like, then a suffering Jesus reveals a suffering God. Third, the belief that God suffers has been argued on moral grounds, claiming that it would be unjust and immoral for God not to suffer. As Brian Hebblethwaite put it in a much-quoted phrase, 'only a suffering God is morally

37 J.L. Rees (ed.), *Sermons and Hymns by Timothy Rees* (London: Mowbray, 1946), p. 110.
38 Ibid., p. 19. The contrast between the hymn and the sermon was identified by Edward Houghton in his article 'Faith and Doubt in the Modern Hymn', *Expository Times*, 111 (1999), pp. 9–13.
39 B.H. Streeter, 'The Suffering of God', *The Hibbert Journal* (April 1914), pp. 603–11.
40 P. Fiddes, *The Creative Suffering of God* (Oxford, 1988).
41 P. Fiddes, 'Suffering, Divine', in A.E. McGrath (ed.), *The Blackwell Encyclopaedia of Modern Christian Thought* (Oxford: Clarendon, 1994), p. 634.

credible.'[42] Finally, it can be argued that if God is immanent in the world, that he is 'in all', then he must share in the suffering of his creation.

Clearly, the first two arguments were more evident than the latter two in Studdert Kennedy's prose and poetry. However, we should exercise caution before concluding that Studdert Kennedy's impassioned advocacy was simply a development of the arguments of earlier writers who had championed the same reasons for advocating divine passibility. More helpful than a comparative analysis of the arguments employed by the early British passibilists in offering an answer to the origins of his theology and the placing of Studdert Kennedy somewhere in that theological map of tributaries and streams is the approach of Thomas Weinandy, a leading advocate of divine *im*passibility among contemporary theologians. In *Does God Suffer?*, Weinandy identified three reasons for the revolt against belief in an impassible God which started at the end of the nineteenth century and, he suggested, had convinced the majority of theologians before the end of the twentieth.[43] Subsequently, Carolyn Winter termed these three 'pathways' by which different thinkers have come to advocate passibility as philosophical, biblical/theological and socio-cultural.[44] Such an approach is far more fruitful in offering an understanding and evaluation of Studdert Kennedy's work than is an attempt to identify purely theological influences. Even a cursory glance at his work shows that the primary impetus to his writing and his primary pathway to his belief in divine passibility was socio-cultural rather than theological. Furthermore, as Carey's account of a wartime encounter with 'an intellectual but rather cold-blooded brother chaplain' shows, he simply was not interested in the philosophical pathway to passibility:

> Studdert was talking on his favourite theme, 'the sorrow and suffering of God.' The other [chaplain] endeavoured to show him that he was dealing with a metaphysical question and, in addition, was merely reviving the heresy of the early days of Christianity. Studdert blazed out: 'To hell with your metaphysics! I have to show God to 'Ole Bill in the trenches in a way which *he* can understand. I have to show him a God who can command his respect and win his love. And why, may I ask, should a doctrine which was considered a heresy in the fourth century necessarily be heresy still in the twentieth?'[45]

42 B. Hebblethwaite, *The Incarnation: Collected Essays in Christology*, (Cambridge: CUP, 1987), p. 36.
43 Weinandy, *Does God Suffer?*, pp. 1–26.
44 In an unpublished 2005 M.C.S. thesis for Regent College Vancouver, 'Pathways to Passibility: The Emergence of the 'Suffering God' in Twentieth Century Theology', Carolyn Winter explored Weinandy's ideas and coined the term 'pathway', identifying historic examples in each case.
45 Carey, 'Studdert Kennedy – War Padre', pp. 152f.

Studdert Kennedy was not alone in coming to passibilist convictions along the socio-cultural pathway as a consequence of what Weinandy terms 'the contemporary milieu'. Even within the pages of *The Church in the Furnace* in which his advocacy of a suffering God was first published, two other padres promoted belief in divine suffering. The task of F.R. Barry, who would later serve as Bishop of Southwell for 21 years, was to write on 'Faith in the Light of War'. For him, the statement of the Johanine Christ that 'He that hath seen Me hath seen the Father' led directly to this conclusion: 'It … cannot at this time be too much emphasised that we must finally give up the pre-Christian theory that God is incapable of suffering.'[46] Barry's argument was Christological, but the whole thrust of the piece was that his experience of war – and he made particular reference to being with his brigade on the Somme – was the catalyst for the re-examination of his faith. He quoted an officer: 'If God ever governed Europe He certainly does not any longer now.'[47] He stated, 'Certainly a God whose providence 'ordained' the present situation would not be one whom we honestly could worship.'[48] Writing over 50 years later, Barry recalled that the task he and his fellow chaplains had set themselves had been 'to hammer out a working theology which could stand the test of battle-conditions and give men a faith that could overcome the world.'[49] It is difficult to conceive of a better example of Weinandy's 'socio-cultural' pathway to divine passibility. Frederick Worsley considered divine passibility in his analysis of 'Beliefs Emphasised by the War' in the same volume.[50] In his autobiography, Worsley's son commented that his father was influenced by Studdert Kennedy, but it is not clear if that influence pre-dated Worsley's argument which is, in fact, strikingly similar to that of Barry:

> Is He a God of pain, Himself wounded and dolorous, to the sufferer? Is he a God of sorrow, grieved and heart-wrung by human sin? I know only of God as he is revealed to me in Jesus, who pointed to the Father, 'He that hath seen Me hath seen the Father.' … In Jesus I see such overmastering love and gentleness and pity, such complete sympathy and identification with human life, all bound up with manifested intention to empower and heal, that I say, 'Yes; somehow – though I dare not, cannot say how – He suffers in and with the sufferer.'[51]

46 Barry, 'Faith in the Light of War', p. 48.
47 Ibid., p. 42.
48 Ibid., p. 43.
49 F.R. Barry, *Period of My Life* (London: Hodder & Stoughton, 1970), p. 57.
50 Worsley, 'Beliefs Emphasised by the War'.
51 T.C. Worsley, *Flannelled Fool* (London: Hogarth Press, 1985), p. 14. The author paints a sad picture of his father, characterizing him as repeatedly prone to infidelity and to the dereliction of his duties first as Warden of Llandaff Theological College and then as Dean of Llandaff, from which post he hurriedly resigned when an extramarital affair came to the attention of colleagues; Worsley, 'Beliefs Emphasised by the War', p. 81.

While less explicitly connected to his experiences as a chaplain than Barry's article, Worsley's more general references to the war – 'We must not hope to hear Him in the thunder of the heavies nor in the rattle of machine-guns' – identifies him as another advocate of the Christological argument that follows the socio-cultural pathway.[52]

The Pastoral Theologian

Studdert Kennedy arrived at the Western Front at Christmas 1915. It must be recognized that his time at the front itself was limited. The first four months of his chaplaincy were spent at Rouen; he spent time at three infantry training schools and was stationed in the base at Boulogne to play his part in the National Mission of Repentance and Hope, on the orders of Bishop Gwynne, the deputy Chaplain-General, and contrary to his personal preferences.[53] In his account, Carey detailed three 'comparatively short periods in the front line', in June 1916, in 1917 when Studdert Kennedy was attached to a brigade involved in the attack on Messines Ridge, and in 1918 as part of the Allies' final advance.[54] His experience was, of course, far from unique and, over the course of the war, a significant proportion of British military personnel worked well behind the trenches.[55] In 1917 Studdert Kennedy was awarded the Military Cross for 'conspicuous gallantry and devotion to duty' during the attack on Messines Ridge, searching out the wounded while under heavy fire and helping them to the dressing station.[56] Work by Michael Snape and Edward Madigan has shown that much of the immediate post-war rhetoric about the cowardice and ineffectiveness of Anglican chaplains, especially when compared with their Roman Catholic counterparts, was unfair and prejudiced, and Studdert Kennedy was one of over 200 Anglican chaplains awarded the Military Cross.[57] Madigan also noted Studdert Kennedy's remembrance: 'I said the more padres died in battle doing Christian deeds the better.'[58] Such deaths would demonstrate the bravery of the chaplains and their willingness to risk their lives in performing their duties.

We have already seen, first, that Studdert Kennedy was an unexpected source of original theological insight for his contemporaries and, second, that his theology is arguably best understood not as a development of earlier theological endeavour, but rather by seeing his advocacy as a clear example of the socio-cultural pathway to

52 Ibid.
53 Carey, 'Studdert Kennedy – War Padre', p. 130.
54 Ibid., p. 125.
55 Snape, *The Back Parts of War*, p. 158.
56 Carey, 'Studdert Kennedy - War Padre', p. 143.
57 Madigan, *Faith Under Fire*, p. 148
58 E. Madigan, 'Hidden Courage: Post-War Literature and Anglican Army Chaplains on the Western Front', in H. Jones, J. O'Brien and C. Schmidt-Supprian (eds), *Untold War- New Perspectives in First World War Studies*, (Leiden: Brill, 2008), p. 76 and Madigan, *Faith Under Fire*, p. 80.

passibility. How, then, do we relate his work as a padre to his theology? Writing in 2005, Robert Ellis argued convincingly that Studdert Kennedy's war poetry revealed him to be 'what we now think of as a "pastoral theologian".'[59] This is key to understanding his theology. In coming to this conclusion, Ellis saw Studdert Kennedy first as 'someone whose poetic voice has a decidedly personal perspective' but also as one who has a wider perspective than the purely pastoral: 'I mean to speak of the way in which pastoral experience and theologising about it – rather than being the application of theology acquired elsewhere – actually becomes the raw material of that theology.'[60] That Studdert Kennedy's theology was grounded in his experience of war is self-evident. What the contemporary reader can too easily overlook is the novel nature of such an approach at that time, however commonplace it may seem today. Like the belief in a suffering God, the idea of theological developments emerging from new pastoral contexts also gathered pace after the Second World War. As Jürgen Moltmann put it, 'There can be no theology "after Auschwitz" which does not take up the theology *in Auschwitz*.'[61] Twenty years earlier, while many of his contemporaries looked at the war and tried, with little success, to apply 'theology acquired elsewhere' – or else did not try at all – Studdert Kennedy, together with Barry, Worsley and no doubt others, theologized about their pastoral experiences and made them into the raw material for their developing theology of a suffering God. This is fundamental to understanding Studdert Kennedy's theological method. Though probably unaware of it, he was one of the first pastoral theologians. In his discussion of 'The Religious Difficulties of the Private Soldier', Studdert Kennedy began by relating a conversation with another chaplain:

> 'He has not got any,' said my friend the Anglo-Catholic, 'you are doing what everyone else is doing now, reading into the soldier what you find in yourself. ... You think he wants thought because you are a thinker. In reality the private soldier does not think.'[62]

While his friend may well have been right about the typical private soldier, in his engagement with the theological issues that, for him, were raised by the conflict, Studdert Kennedy was arguably the most original British theological thinker and writer to emerge during the Great War and its immediate aftermath. Looking at his work from a post-Holocaust perspective, it is very easy to conclude that he was the most influential advocate of divine passibility prior to 1939. Richard Baukham, one of the most prolific writers in what might be termed the school of Jürgen Moltmann,

59 R. Ellis, 'Geoffrey Studdert Kennedy: The Pastor and the Suffering God', *Transformation*, 22/3, (2005), p. 168.
60 Ibid., p. 170.
61 J. Moltmann, *The Trinity and the Kingdom of God* (London: SCM, 1981), p. 47.
62 Studdert Kennedy, 'The Religious Difficulties', p. 375.

saw Studdert Kennedy as the forerunner of an ever-rising tide of passibilist writing.[63] Conversely, Francis House, writing in 1980, took the view that, once the war was over, that tide had ebbed away.[64] By the time of Studdert Kennedy's death in 1929, it may well have seemed his advocacy of a suffering God had had its day. As the people of Britain wished to commemorate but then put behind them the horrors of the war, so the question, 'where is God in all this?' to which Studdert Kennedy's proclamation of a passible God was an answer, was being asked with much less urgency. Moreover, Studdert Kennedy worked indefatigably for the Industrial Christian Fellowship, touring the country as its missioner and campaigning for social justice. All his post-war writings addressed such issues and, except for his denunciation of war, he appears to have forsaken theological discourse entirely.[65] However, as such questions of social justice became focussed in the political arena of 1920s Britain, the determinedly a-political approach of Studdert Kennedy, who rejected proposals for a Labour-Church alliance from Ernest Bevin but was refused a burial in Westminster Abbey on the grounds that he was a socialist, became marginalised and he became far less influential.[66]

Given the quantities in which his books – and especially his poetic anthologies – were sold, we are left to ponder the influence of his advocacy of a suffering God. We have already noted the absence of any indication that such poems prompted a theological debate. While, as was shown in chapter 4, many preachers engaged with the issues of omnipotence and providence, few addressed divine passibility. Arthur Hird did, in that biographical piece in *Aldersgate Magazine*, but only to the extent of summarising Studdert Kennedy's argument, rather than engaging with it. No press reviews of his poetry seem to have addressed the theology that is at the heart of so much of his work. Typically, the short notice announcing in the *Expository Times* the publication of *Rough Rhymes* simply commented, 'The theme which has taken possession of him is the sorrow and suffering of God' while that for *The Sorrows of God* mentioned only two poems with a specific post-war relevance, 'If ye Forget' and 'Waste', the latter being a condemnation of war.[67] Searching a hundred years' issues of the *Expository Times* reveals a far greater *theological* interest in Studdert Kennedy in the 1980s and 1990s than at any time during his life or immediately after his death.

63 R. Baukham, '"Only the Suffering God can Help": Divine Passibility in Modern Theology', *Themelios*, 9/3 (1984), pp. 6-12, note 31.
64 F. House, 'The Barrier of Impassibility', *Theology*, 83 (1980), pp. 409–15.
65 On Studdert Kennedy's renunciation of war, see S. Bell, 'From Collusion to Condemnation – the evolving voice of "Woodbine Willie"' in A.K. Smith and K. Cowman (eds), *Landscapes and Voices of the Great War* (London: Routledge, 2017).
66 W. Purcell, *Woodbine Willie: a study of the life of Geoffrey Studdert Kennedy* (London: Mowbray, 1982), pp. 177f. (First published in 1962.)
67 *Expository Times*, vol. 20, no. 8 (May 1918), p. 384; *Expository Times*, vol. 36, no. 2 (November 1924), p. 96.

Gordon Wakefield observed in 1995 that the '"rough rhymes" express a theological revolution in his attack on the notion of divine impassibility.'[68]

Of the three contributors to *The Church in the Furnace* who had written of a suffering God, Studdert Kennedy, Worsley and Barry, only the last of them continued to write on theological subjects after the war. In 1968, Russell Barry published 'The Atonement', a wide-ranging analysis of different understandings of that doctrine. He wrote, 'the nature and property of God himself is not only to forgive but to "bear our sins" and so to suffer in the estrangement of his children.' In a footnote, he added, 'God is not one who can have things done to him, he cannot be changed or qualified from without. Yet can he love if he does not suffer in the everyday meaning of the world? In that sense we are probably all "patrispassians".'[69] Barry appears to have been suggesting that in the intervening period, belief in a suffering God, perhaps expressed more moderately than during the Great War, had become conventional. However, when he wrote his autobiography two years later, in a moving and poignant postscript to his final book, Barry referred somewhat enigmatically to his family being afflicted by a 'sudden, overwhelming tragedy', apparently the second time that his daughter had been widowed. He wrote of suffering being one element in the mystery surrounding life and death and, while wanting to assert that God is not the cause of suffering, stated that even Jesus himself 'does not seem to have known the answer' to the question 'Why?' which suffering poses. 'I do not think there is any possibility, in this actual tragic world we know, of believing in God who is a God of love, except through Christ crucified and risen.'[70] While in 1917 Barry had written, 'It ... cannot at this time be too much emphasised that we must finally give up the pre-Christian theory that God is incapable of suffering', there is no indication that he found personal comfort in such belief half a century later.

Conclusion

The case that Studdert Kennedy was the most original British theological thinker during and immediately after the Great War appears undeniable. Yet, as we have seen, although his books of prose and poetry sold in huge numbers, there is no evidence that there was any serious engagement with his advocacy of a suffering God. Once the conflict was over, the pastoral needs which his writing had addressed became less urgent and questions about divine omnipotence, providence and, indeed, passibility, were no longer being asked. Studdert Kennedy focused his energies on the work of the ICF, the Archbishops' Doctrinal Commission, set up in response to controversies caused by the Anglican Modernists in 1922 to determine limits to Anglican

68 G.S. Wakefield, 'God and Some English Poets: 9. Twentieth-Century Trends', *Expository Times*, vol. 106, no. 5 (February 1995), p. 138.

69 F.R. Barry, *The Atonement* (London: Hodder & Stoughton, 1968), pp. 213f.

70 Barry, *Period of My Life*, pp. 216f.

orthodoxy and of which J.K. Mozley was a member, did not report until 1938 and the arguments for belief in divine passibility were forgotten. However, 25 years after the end of the Great War, Auschwitz and Hiroshima raised even more starkly the questions which had troubled Studdert Kennedy and for many Christians made belief in a loving God no longer tenable. Studdert Kennedy's assertion that a truly loving God must necessarily be a suffering God was rediscovered and further developed. In 1980, Jürgen Moltmann concluded,

> [Studdert Kennedy's] book *The Hardest Part* has a prophetic and radical force rather like that of Barth's *Epistle to the Romans*, which came out at about the same time. In fact it deserved even greater attention than Barth's book, for the theology of the suffering God is more important than the theology of the God who is 'Wholly Other'. What was able to stand the test of the battlefields of Flanders and created faith even in the hells there was the discovery of the crucified God.[71]

A few years later, divine passibility was described by one of its critics as 'a theological commonplace' and even as 'a new orthodoxy'.[72] Studdert Kennedy's pastoral theology, largely forgotten in the inter-war period, had achieved a remarkable renaissance.

A second prominent characteristic of religious belief and practice in wartime Britain also appears to have had relatively little long-term impact. Ecumenical co-operation in the theatres of war and ecumenical worship and commemoration in Britain during the conflict were seen as heralding a new era of more cordial inter-Church relationships and also as being indicative that re-union between some denominations might be possible. As we shall see in the next chapter, the optimism of the wartime years was not fulfilled once peace had come.

71 J. Moltmann, *The Trinity and the Kingdom of God*, p. 35. It appears that Moltmann's discovery of Studdert Kennedy post-dated his seminal *The Crucified God*, (London: SCM, 1974).

72 R. Goetz, 'The Suffering God: The Rise of a New Orthodoxy', *The Christian Century*, 103/13 (1986), p. 385.

7

Ecumenism

In addressing the history of ecumenism during the conflict and the immediate post-war period, it is important to look beyond the well-worked narratives of interdenominational and intra-denomination discussions and negotiations to determine what, both in the theatres of war and on the home front, had led to those developments. As we shall see, in 1914 relationships between the Churches were often somewhat frosty. Yet, six years later there was widespread talk of the reunion of the denominations. The most famous expression of that optimism was the *Appeal to All Christian People* from the 1920 Lambeth Conference of Anglican bishops. It was, wrote Alan Wilkinson, 'perhaps the most significant result of the ecumenical spirit which had been so strongly quickened by the war.'[1] A similar phrase, 'the ecumenical spirit of the trenches' was used by Richard Schweitzer in his paper on soldiers' faith and doubt on the Western Front, while Adrian Hastings described the Lambeth *Appeal* as, 'one of the rare ecclesiastical documents which does not get forgotten with the years.'[2] This chapter will discuss the nature of ecumenical activity during the conflict and in the immediate post-war period, setting the evidence from Nottinghamshire, Derbyshire and Birmingham alongside that from the theatres of war within an overview of the national experience. After examining different perspectives of the Lambeth Conference, it will conclude with an assessment of the long-term influence of that wartime 'ecumenical spirit'.

Conflicting Tensions

For all the English Protestant churches, their pre-war internal and external relationships are best characterised as being dominated by a range of competing tensions. The promotion of what became the 1902 Education Act, with its abolition of school

1 Wilkinson, *The Church of England*, p. 207.
2 Schweitzer, 'The Cross and the Trenches' in *War & Society*, pp. 33-57, p. 47; A. Hastings, *A History of English Christianity, 1920-1985* (London: Fount, 1986), p. 97.

boards, the creation of local education authorities and the making of provision for the funding through local taxation of Anglican and Catholic schools, had led to strong opposition from the Free Churches. Subsequently, the use of the 1911 Parliament Act had stopped the Lords from blocking the Welsh Church Act in 1914, which disestablished the Church of England in Wales, largely in response to Welsh Nonconformist objections to the payment of tithes. While the Act did not take effect until 1920, the horror with which it was viewed by many English Anglican clerics is self-evident from the many complaints in their wartime parish magazines. Anglican–Nonconformist relationships, therefore, were hardly cordial as war was declared.

Whenever they contemplated organic church unity, for the Free Churches there was always the competing attraction of Free Church union as a more attainable goal than that of re-union with the Church of England. In the creation and effective operation of the United Board to oversee the work of chaplains from the Baptist, Congregational and Primitive, United and Welsh Calvinistic Methodist Churches, the Board's secretary, Baptist J.H. Shakespeare saw a model for future ecumenism: 'We have seen the working in miniature and for a specific purpose of a partially "United Free Church of England".'[3] Shakespeare used his presidential address at the 1916 Free Church conference entitled, 'The Free Churches at the Crossroads' to propose that a committee be set up to work towards the goal of a federation of Churches on the model of the United States of America.[4] However, as Stuart Mews noted, the creation of a united Free Church would highlight another tension for Nonconformists who both sought greater prominence for their denominations in national life, but also cherished the independence of Nonconformity: 'If a united Free Church was successful in its application to join the establishment, would it still be a defender of the rights of those who challenged the establishment?'[5] That would remain a pertinent question throughout the twentieth century, its significance being lessened only in more recent times by the increasing marginalisation of the established Church of England from the social and political centres of influence.

For some Wesleyan Methodists, with their relatively high view of ordination and over which the 'Legal Hundred' ministers wielded authority as the corporate successors to John Wesley, reunion with the Church of England was a far more attractive prospect. Consequently, the response of the Revd. J.E. Rattenbury, superintendent minister of the West London Mission, to Shakespeare's initiative was to propose to the Bishop of London that unofficial talks between their Churches should take place.[6] There had been some ecumenical successes. The United Methodist Church [UMC] had been formed in 1907, bringing together the Methodist New Connexion, the

3 J.H. Shakespeare, Foreword of F.C. Spurr, *Some Chaplains in Khaki* (London: Allenson, 1916), p. 8.
4 *MR*, 13 April 1916, pp. 4 and 11.
5 Mews, *Religion and English Society in WW1*, pp. 304f.
6 A. Turberfield, *John Scott Lidgett – Archbishop of British Methodism* (Peterborough: Epworth, 2003), pp. 216-20.

United Methodist Free Churches and the Bible Christians, albeit only after several abortive attempts at union with the Primitive Methodists.[7] Within 25 years, the UMC, Primitives and Wesleyans would have united to form the Methodist Church of Great Britain, despite strong opposition from a small group of Wesleyan ministers, led by Rattenbury, who feared that it would be prejudicial to re-union with the Church of England.

For the Church of England, there was a not dissimilar tension between a desire for closer relationships and ultimately re-union with English Nonconformity and the wider issue of the relationship of the Anglican communion as a whole to the churches of the European reformation and of the Catholic and Orthodox traditions. However, the tensions which had the greatest impact on English ecumenical developments in the first quarter of the 20th century were those within the Church of England itself. At the turn of the century there were three broad groupings in the Church of England, generally described as 'Evangelical', 'High Church' and 'Broad Church'. 'The Evangelicals were exhibiting all the marks of a moribund party. … Not the choice of Governments, but their own inferiority in personal quality, was the key to their weakness in the hierarchy.'[8] Thus wrote Herbert Hensley Henson, then Dean of Durham, of the situation in 1913.[9] While his own theological position was well towards the liberal-Catholic end of the spectrum, it was probably not an unfair assessment. Far more influential were the 'High Church' Anglicans. James Munson distinguished between the 'High Church' clergy, whom he saw as the second generation of the Oxford Movement and those who were part of a new generation in the last quarter of the nineteenth century who labelled themselves as Anglo- or English Catholics and were variously called by their opponents Ritualists, Sacerdotalists, Sacramentalists or Romanists.[10]

Two incidents, one in England and one in East Africa, illustrate the manner in which the pre-war tensions within the Anglican Communion affected relationships with other denominations. In June 1911, the Bishop of Hereford, John Percival, welcomed Nonconformist ministers and lay people to a service of Holy Communion in the cathedral, having given sufficient notice for the matter to be discussed beforehand in both houses of Convocation, in correspondence with the Archbishop of Canterbury and in the secular and religious press.[11] The analysis of the Bishop's biog-

7 J. Munsey Turner, 'Methodism in England 1900-1932' in R. Davies et. al. (eds.), *A History of the Methodist Church in Great Britain, vol. 3* (London: Epworth, 1983), pp. 309–361.

8 H. Hensley Henson, *Retrospect of an Unimportant Life*, vol. 1 (London: OUP, 1943), p. 157.

9 Henson was successively Dean of Durham, Bishop of Hereford and Bishop of Durham. See O. Chadwick, *Hensley Henson: a study in the friction between Church and State* (Norwich: Canterbury Press, 1983).

10 J.E.B. Munson, 'The Oxford Movement by the End of the Nineteenth Century: The Anglo-Catholic Clergy', *Church History,* vol. 44, no. 3 (Sept. 1975), pp. 382-395.

11 See, for example, *The Times*, 2 May 1911, p. 6; *The Times*, 5 May 1911, p. 6; *The Times*, 6 May 1911, p. 6; *The Times*, 12 May 1911, p. 6; *The Times*, 12 May 1911, p.10.

rapher, William Temple, is pertinent first because it illustrates the nature of some of the inter-party conflicts of the period and second because of who wrote it, a future bishop and archbishop:

> The whole episode is very illustrative of the position in which the Church of England then habitually found itself with regard to Reunion [between the Church of England and Non-conformist denominations]. A convinced believer in one method of approach announces his intention of following that method on one occasion. A storm arises. A wise representative of opposed convictions makes a formal speech dissociating himself from the proposed action, but expressing deep sympathy with the aim, and refraining from the proposal of any condemnatory resolution. ... In the result the episode occurred and was soon forgotten. Such unity as there was before in the Church of England continued unimpaired, but also, of course, undeepened. The cause of Reunion with separated bodies also remained exactly where it was.[12]

Another internal dispute within the Anglican communion arose from a missionary conference held in Kikuyu, Kenya in 1913 which had considered proposals that would allow for limited inter-communion and the exchange of pulpits in a scheme for a federation of Protestant Christian Churches in East Africa. At the close of the Conference, the evangelical bishops of Uganda and Mombasa shared in a joint communion service in the Scottish Mission Church in which all representatives participated. In response, the Anglo-Catholic Bishop of Zanzibar, Frank Weston, wrote to the Archbishop of Canterbury accusing his episcopal colleagues of 'propagating heresy and committing schism'.[13] The primary issue was the ecclesiology of the Church of England. For the evangelicals and many liberals, it was a post-Reformation Protestant Church. For Weston, it was a Church catholic and apostolic holding fast to the importance of the Apostolic Succession, episcopal ordination and confirmation, all of which he saw as being challenged by the Kikuyu proposals. Typically, Hensley Henson was the first to share his views with the readers of *The Times* Letters pages, addressing the ecclesiological issues raised by Kikuyu:

> I must needs think that the Church owes a deep debt of gratitude to the Bishops of Uganda and Mombasa for their action; and I hold it to be the clear duty of all who value Christian unity and the character of the Church of England as a Reformed Church to give them a whole-hearted support.[14]

12 Temple, *Life of Bishop Percival*, p. 333.
13 H Maynard Smith, *Frank, Bishop of Zanzibar* (London: SPCK, 1926), p. 149.
14 *The Times*, 17 December 1913, p. 14.

Later, he mused in his autobiography, 'Was the Church of England really so plainly committed to the exclusive episcopalianism which the Tractarians had taught, that religious fellowship with non-episcopalian Churches was inadmissible?'[15] As we shall see, both Henson and Weston played significant roles in the Lambeth Conference of 1920 and it was undoubtedly the immense contrast between their polarised pre-war confrontation and the notionally common mind that they shared six years later which contributed to the optimism with which the *Appeal to all Christian People* was promoted.

Ecumenism in Wartime Chaplaincy

In the various theatres of war, Protestant denominational boundaries were frequently blurred. John Arthur, a Church of Scotland minister and missionary, wrote of shared communion services in East Africa and the influence of war in 'bringing the African communities into the wide movement towards a united Church.'[16] Philip 'Tubby' Clayton, an Anglican WW1 chaplain, allowed men of all denominations to receive Communion in the attic chapel of Talbot House in Poperinge.[17] Wesleyan chaplain Thomas Westerdale wrote of 'low-church' Anglican chaplains: 'Strongly evangelical and simple in their discourse are many of these padres. To go to their Communion table, and often as a Wesleyan Tommy have I been invited to do so – despite Kikuyu – is a delight.'[18]

In his analysis of the membership of a Christian Union group set up by the evangelical Anglican chaplain M.S. Evers, Richard Schweitzer noted the involvement of one Nonconformist soldier, but he was probably over-ambitious in drawing any conclusion from that one item of data about the readiness of Nonconformists to join in such activities. Personal relationships between the chaplain and the men would be far more important, and Nonconformists might well have felt more comfortable in a group which stressed personal commitment to Christ than would have many Anglo-Catholics.[19] In *The Church in the Furnace*, M. Linton Smith offered this description of ecumenical relationships in his essay on 'Fellowship in the Church':

> On the one hand the official recognition of the various nonconformist bodies, and the appointment of an adequate supply of chaplains to minister to their somewhat scanty and scattered congregations, have been wholly for good; a real grievance has been removed, and opportunities have been given for friendly co-operation and mutual support. Where the nonconformist chaplain has been

15 Henson, *Retrospect*, vol. 1, p. 161.
16 A. Willis et. al., *Towards a United Church 1913-1947* (London: Edinburgh House Press, 1947), pp. 53-55.
17 Wilkinson, *The Church of England*, p. 308.
18 T.L.B. Westerdale, *Messages from Mars* (London: C.H. Kelly, 1917), p. 83.
19 Schweitzer, 'The Cross and the Trenches: . . . Western Front', p. 47.

> a true nonconformist and set himself to look after his own flock, and to seek to reclaim the wanderers from any fold, relations have been of the pleasantest possible nature; the only friction has occurred where a man has settled down with some unit, claimed it as his own and attempted to minister to all the men therein irrespective of their real denominational connection. … [M]utual arrangements about funerals, occasional joint services on special occasions … or a memorial service after an action, and a general exchange of good offices have led to a real and friendly understanding, which makes for fellowship, even through and across the dividing lines.[20]

Another Anglican chaplain, Pat Leonard, wrote in his diary of ad-hoc ecumenicity:

> When I got back I had a sort of tea-lunch and then made off for my last service – evening at the field hospital in a big ward. Here, I found a Presbyterian padre [Thomson] had also arranged for a service half an hour after mine was timed to commence, so postponed mine and we had a joint service. I took the prayers and lesson, and he gave an excellent address on the wonder of Christ.[21]

Later, he reflected on another similar experience: 'I'm not sure how far I like or approve of joint combined services but perhaps they help to make us know each other better, and so tighten the bands of unity, though not of uniformity, from which Good Lord deliver us.'[22] In an article on 'War Delusions', a senior chaplain in France told readers of *The Guardian* newspaper in November 1917, 'The Church of England padre is constantly impressed by the deep earnestness of many Dissenters. They form their little prayer-meetings and have their Bible-classes … they are the first to rally round the Church of England padre at the voluntary services.'[23]

William Sellers' *With Our Fighting Men*, published in 1915, was typical of many uncritical narratives of the faithful work of chaplains and of the wholly heroic nature of the British 'Tommy'. Sellers' aims were clear: 'I hope and pray that the story recorded in these pages may quicken interest in Christian work among soldiers and sailors, and so help to extend the kingdom of Christ.' We should, therefore, be cautious about his evaluation and interpretation of the pattern of religious practice that he described:

> May I describe one service in a Y.M.C.A. tent? It is Sunday evening. The various Parade services of the morning have been held, the Church of England in the open air, and the Congregationalists and Wesleyans in the tent. But now a

20 M. Linton Smith, 'Fellowship in the Church' in Macnutt (ed.), *The Church in the Furnace*, pp. 99-121, at p. 117.
21 Leonard et. al., *Fighting Padre*, p. 36.
22 Ibid., p. 68.
23 *The Guardian*, 22 November 1917, p. 802.

> sergeant is in charge, and for half an hour he allows the men to choose what hymns they like, and right heartily do they sing. But now an Anglican archdeacon is on the platform, and with eager words and practical advice is urging the soldiers to live as Christian gentlemen. Then follows a Wesleyan minister with many a story and many an appeal. Then a Congregationalist minister, in quieter vein but with restrained earnestness. There are Christian songs between the addresses and many an audible response from the 'Tommies' to the word of exhortation spoken. It is a re-union of the churches, proving that at heart they are all one in Christ Jesus, and it is made possible by the work of the Y.M.C.A.[24]

It was not, of course, a 're-union of the churches'. Denominational barriers, not least in the well-documented competition between the Churches to have 'their' chaplains appointed, were quite clear and embodied in the structures for the oversight of those chaplains.[25] Some chaplains may have permitted – 'encouraged' would be too strong a word – what is sometimes termed 'eucharistic promiscuity'; they may have cared pastorally for soldiers of other traditions and they may have shared in some church parades and, as Sellers described, events in YMCA huts. However, it was not 're-union'.

Ecumenism on the Home Front

In England, in a nation united by loss, grief and a desire to commemorate the fallen, ecclesiastical barriers fell, if only a little, and clergy and ministers of the various Protestant denominations commonly shared in acts of intercession or commemoration. Ethel Bilbrough described in her diary an open-air service held in Kent to mark the fourth anniversary of the war:

> The service was held by the Rector, the Vicar and the Wesleyan minister! [Note the exclamation mark.] Who wisely forgot their doctrinal differences, and agreed to meet as fellow Christians and brothers, thinking of nothing but the widespread need for prayer just now for everyone, apart from any sect or creed. ... The three clerics were all in plain white surplices ... the rector and vicar had abandoned stoles and cassocks and birettas ... while the Wesleyan minister had consented to put on a white surplice for the very first time in his life![26]

However, such experiments could not be taken too far: Charles Raven, an Anglican cleric who later in the war served as a chaplain, told of a united service in April 1915

24 W. Sellers, *With Our Fighting Men at the Front* (London: The Religious Tract Society, 1915), p. 15.
25 See P. Howson, *Muddling Through – The Organisation of British Army Chaplaincy in World War 1* (Solihull: Helion, 2013).
26 E.M. Bilbrough, *My War Diary* (London: Ebury Press, 2014), pp. 216f.

held in a parish church. The Congregationalist and Wesleyan ministers read lessons and the Baptist minister was invited to preach. A week later, the vicar was told by his bishop, 'Perhaps you were justified in asking him to preach. After all, the times are exceptional. But you had no right to allow him to use the pulpit.'[27] As we shall see, the attitudes of bishops and their clergy to such practices varied greatly.

In the East Midlands, evidence of inter-denominational activity during the war is limited. Newspapers in January 1915 carried reports of the National Day of Intercession, suggested by the King, and supported by many denominations – or 'All Sects United' as the headline in the *Derby Daily Telegraph* read.[28] On the first anniversary of the start of the conflict, an open-air service in Derby brought together Anglicans, Methodists, Baptists and members of the Salvation Army, the band of which accompanied well-known hymns.[29] While the tone of most reports of such services was positive, that of a united service held in St Peter's, Derby, in January 1916 noted, 'The congregation was not large.' In some parishes, the intercessory services promoted by the King were ecumenical. The vicar of Darley Abbey, E. Spencer Noakes, commented enthusiastically on a united service held on 4 August 1916, stating that it 'was thoroughly representative of the religious nature of the parish, and it was a real joy to feel that there are occasions on which Church people and Nonconformists can unite.'[30] In April 1919, he invited 'our Nonconformist friends' to join his congregation for the Three Hours' Service on Good Friday and later made a similar invitation to a memorial service to be held on 11 November.[31] The minute book of the Retford Free Church Ministers' Fraternal from 1913 to 1929 described arrangements for a week of prayer and pulpit exchanges in January 1915. A year later, plans were made for the Baptists, Congregationalists and Primitive, United and Wesleyan Methodists to meet for weekday intercessions after the nationwide day of special intercession on 2 January 1916. Such a pattern of united services for the Free Churches was not uncommon. One of the more notable local ecumenical events took place at Duffield, just north of Derby, where in January 1918 all the Nonconformist churches cancelled their Sunday morning services so that their congregations might be present at a united service in the parish church. The vicar 'had charge of the service' and preached. In the evening, the Church of England service in the schoolroom was given up and many were turned away from the 'commodious' Wesleyan church due to lack of space.[32]

While nationally there is virtually no evidence of dissentient Anglican clerics being opposed to Britain's engagement in the conflict and while all the Free Churches, with the exceptions of the Churches of Christ and the Quakers, endorsed military action,

27 C. Raven, 'The New Catholicism II. Interchange of Pulpits' in A. Harvey (ed.), *The Church and the 20th Century* (London: Macmillan, 1936), p. 199.
28 *DDT*, 4 January 1915, p. 2.
29 *DDT*, 30 August 1915, p. 3.
30 *Darley Abbey Parish Magazine*, September 1916, DRO, D3202.
31 *Darley Abbey Parish Magazine*, April 1919 and November 1916, DRO, D3202.
32 *DDT*, 7 January 1918, p. 2.

within Nonconformity there were many individuals whose religious views led them to be conscientious objectors to conscription when it started in 1916. At military tribunals across the country, appeals against compulsory military service, for reasons of belief, personal circumstances or the importance of civilian occupation, were heard. One local account of a confrontation across denominational boundaries illustrated the difficulties encountered by conscientious objectors.[33] The vicar, the Revd. E.A. Hadfield, was the chair of the South Darley tribunal when in March 1916, a United Methodist local preacher, James Frost, whose father was both a local councillor and Primitive Methodist local preacher, sought exemption from military service on the grounds of conscience. The cross-examination was reported in the local press and started with a demand to know why, if his conviction against taking life was long-held, Frost had not preached on the subject. Then he was challenged on whether his denomination required conscientious objection, given that many dissenting ministers were fighting at the front. The questioning continued with the well-worn argument: 'Supposing the Germans came here and they came into your home and you saw one murdering your mother, and another out-raging your sister, what would you do?' 'I really don't know what I would do.' After a repetition of that question, the chairman then quoted Asquith's assertion that the war was a spiritual war, 'a war against the enemies of God and Christianity.' Frost replied, 'I can only repeat I have a conscientious objection to taking life.' His appeal was dismissed, though for various administrative reasons, he never had to serve in the forces. The way in which the tribunal had been conducted led to the publication of many letters on both sides of the argument in the *High Peak News*, and Frost's minister, though not himself a conscientious objector, verified his evidence and supported his case. The story illustrates the prominent role that some clergy played in civic affairs during the conflict and is suggestive of occasional tensions between the Church of England and the Free Churches whose members were not as uniformly supportive of the war as were their leaders.

As far as Birmingham and the West Midlands are concerned, the evidence is indicative of a lower level of wartime ecumenical activity than in the diocese of Southwell. A pre-war testing of ecumenical boundaries which had occurred in 1909 when Hensley Henson had preached at the anniversary service of the Digbeth Institute was still remembered, but similar activities were rare.[34] The President of the Wesleyan Conference spoke at a special meeting for the National Mission in 1916, though the vicar of St James's, Aston, was undoubtedly rather optimistic in claiming that the speaker's presence, 'was a touching tribute to the earnestness with which the great Methodist Church viewed the importance of the National Mission.'[35] The vicar of Redditch attended a Worcestershire Baptists' meeting, Nonconformist ministers were

33 Taylor and Brown, *A Derbyshire Parish at War*, pp. 54-59.
34 See reference to 1909 incident in a comment on the controversy caused by Henson preaching at the City Temple, *Birmingham Gazette*, 25 January 1917, p. 4.
35 *Birmingham Daily Post*, 7 November 1916, p. 8.

present at the institution of the new vicar of Walsall and the local Baptist minister read the lesson on the first Sunday after the Armistice at Yardley Parish Church.[36] At the service in Walsall, the Bishop of Lichfield, John Kempthorne, 'expressed his gratification that there was a growing spirit of mutual understanding and sympathy between the members of the different religious communions in Walsall.' However, there is a distinction to be drawn between the presence and the participation of Nonconformists in Anglican worship. The Dean and Chapter of Worcester invited Nonconformist ministers to take part in offering prayer in the Lady Chapel at the start of 1918, despite the objections of the Bishop, who wrote, 'It is an ill compliment to a minister who by his very profession disputes the Church's teaching to ask him to take part in a service which involved that teaching.'[37] The Bishop of Birmingham, Henry Wakefield, was present at a united service for prayer and intercession in the (Wesleyan) Birmingham Central Hall at the start of 1915, the report listing all the Anglican clergy and Nonconformist ministers in attendance.[38]

For every such service or meeting of which evidence exists, there were no doubt several more unrecorded ecumenical events. Even so, the vast majority of gatherings for prayer or worship were organised by one church or chapel for their own people. Within Birmingham, a major reason for the almost total lack of evidence of the participation of Nonconformist ministers in Anglican worship would seem to be the ecclesiology of the parish churches. Many of the largest were Anglo-Catholic and, therefore, far less willing than 'broad church' or evangelical Anglicans to accept the Free Churches and their ministers as authentically part of the Christian Church. Typifying that ecclesiology, the vicar of St Alban's in central Birmingham wrote to his parishioners in April 1915 about the loss of life in the conflict:

> Thank God, we, who are Catholics, do not sorrow as others who have no hope; we feel the unspeakable comfort of pleading the Holy Sacrifice in sure and certain hope that those who have died so splendidly are now enjoying refreshment, light, and peace in the nearer Presence of their Father and their God. ... you only have to ask one of your priests to say a Requiem, and we will most willingly do so.[39]

Within the archival material from such churches, the language and imagery of the 'Holy Sacrifice' as an exemplar for the supreme sacrifice being made by combatants recur frequently. As in Southwell, on some occasions just the Free Churches united for worship and one service hosted by the large and influential Carrs Lane Congregational Church in July 1916 included elements that would be familiar across

36 (Birmingham) *Evening Despatch*, 28 May 1915, p. 5; *Birmingham Daily Post*, 28 October 1918, p. 7; (Birmingham) *Evening Despatch*, 18 November 1918, p. 1.
37 *Birmingham Daily Mail*, 2 January 1918, p. 3.
38 *Birmingham Daily Mail*, 4 January 1915. p. 4.
39 BRO, EP 93 additional material: Acc 2005/018 box 2, no. 16.

all denominations; the National Anthem, Kipling's *Recessional* and Elgar's *The Spirit of England*.[40] Most often, it was a shared purpose which brought Anglican and Nonconformist churches together, for example to make provision for Belgian refugees or to oppose the showing of a particular film in the city.[41] As in Southwell, the civic space was often the favoured venue, such as Birmingham's Town Hall.[42]

Rarely were any ecclesiological or theological issues which these ecumenical events and services might be thought to raise discussed. A report of a letter from the vicar of Marthall, Cheshire, to his parishioners, published in the *Birmingham Daily Mail* in 1915 perhaps gives an indication of underlying tensions and disagreements within the Church of England, contrasting strongly with the expressions of ecumenical co-operation and mutual affirmation which featured in bishops' letters and public statements. Printed also in the *Manchester Evening News* and the *Liverpool Daily Post*, it asserted that, 'In its attitude to Nonconformity, the Church of England is more parochial, more vindictive, more narrow that ever she was.' While churchmen prayed with Nonconformists, sang their hymns and were on 'friendly terms', he argued, 'when it comes to translating this into a concrete act of brotherhood, then at once comes a trail of derision and denunciation.'[43] Arguably, there is evidence here of the pre-war tensions between the established Church and Nonconformity bubbling under the surface of public friendliness and co-operation. Only in the Manchester paper was there printed a response; an anonymous letter couched in the more familiar language of friendship, kindness and courtesy.[44]

In 1917 the *Birmingham Daily Mail* carried a letter from a 'gratified Baptist' affirming local ecumenical co-operation (including that with Roman Catholics) to succour Belgian refugees and also visits to Nonconformist gatherings and services by Anglican clergy.[45] In the final year of the conflict, the Bishop of Birmingham expressed the hope that one result of the conflict would be, 'such co-operation between the Churches as shall enable them to speak on moral and social questions with all the force of a united Christendom.'[46] Both the Baptist's letter and the episcopal statement are clearly indicative of a quite limited model of ecumenicity, both during the conflict and afterwards.

40 *Birmingham Gazette*, 1 August 1916, p. 5.
41 For example *Birmingham Daily Post*, 23 October 1914, p. 7; (Birmingham) *Evening Despatch*, 20 September 1915, p. 5.
42 *Birmingham Gazette*, 4 January 1915, p. 5.
43 *Birmingham Daily Mail*, 29 January 1915, p. 6.
44 *Manchester Evening News*, 2 February 1915, p. 7.
45 *Birmingham Daily Mail*, 14 June 1917, p. 5.
46 *Bishop's Letter to the Diocese*, published in the parish magazine of St Agnes, Moseley, January 1918, BRO, EP 89/343.

Ecumenism after the conflict

After the Armistice, joint services were commonly held to celebrate the cessation of hostilities. At St Peter's, Belper, on the afternoon of Sunday 17 November 1918, the vicar preached at a 'United Thanksgiving Service' promoted with large posters by the District Council. A handwritten 'order of procession' indicated that the ministers of religion walked to the service behind the country magistrates and councillors, but ahead of the urban district councillors, the 'general public' taking 19th place in the meticulously-organised arrangements.[47] At the thanksgiving and memorial service in Ashbourne parish church on the same day, the Old Testament reading was, according to a report in the parish magazine, 'most impressively read' by the Congregational minister.[48] Towards the end of 1918, the rector of Aston-on-Trent in south Derbyshire invited the local Wesleyan minister to preach in the parish church on the first Sunday after peace was declared, his congregation also being welcome.[49]

Once peace had been declared, more celebrations followed. The King issued a 'Proclamation' stating that the Archbishops had been instructed to compose a form of prayer suitable for the occasion to be used in all churches and chapels. It exhorted the Church of Scotland and 'all Spiritual Authorities and ministers of religion ... to take part as may properly behove them.' At Chapel-en-le-Frith, a United Thanksgiving service was presided over by the vicar, while the Wesleyan minister preached.[50] A few days later, 'the clergy and ministers of all denominations' led the Peace Day celebrations at Bradwell in Derbyshire.[51] At Matlock, a united choir led the singing at a united thanksgiving service.[52] Subsequently, the dedication and unveiling of memorials to the fallen gave further opportunities for joint activities. The order of service for the unveiling of a memorial Cross in the cemetery at Calverton in 1921 included addresses from no fewer than three ministers, their names listed under the rubric '(5 minutes each)'.[53] However, that the unveiling of a tablet inside the parish church in memory of the same 32 men six weeks later apparently included no similar ecumenical involvement illustrates a common limit to post-war ecumenical participation.[54] Although there were exceptions, the vast majority of the ecumenical activity took place in the civic space of towns and villages; in squares, in public cemeteries and around memorials to the fallen. Invitations to Free Church ministers to share in worship in the parish church were rare.

47 DRO, 3022/08.
48 Ashbourne Parish Magazine, December 1918, DRO, D768/16.
49 *DDT*, 8 January 1919, p.2.
50 Chapel-en-le-Frith War Memorial, 5 July 1919, DRO, D6771/9/6/1.
51 DRO, D3109 A/PZ 2/1.
52 Order of Service, Matlock, 29 Jun 1919, DRO, D4296/21/2.
53 NRO, PR 22,917/2.
54 NRO, PR 22,917/3.

Nationally, three events marking the end of the war illustrate the relationship of the Free Churches to English society. In November 1918, the King and Queen attended a thanksgiving service arranged by the Free Church Council in the Albert Hall – the first time that a reigning monarch had attended such an event, albeit one not held in a Nonconformist church building.[55] It was widely viewed as an endorsement of the place of the Free Churches in the national life, earned by their patriotic support of the previous four years. Yet when the Peace was celebrated across the country in June and July 1919 and Randall Davidson preached at St Paul's before the King and Queen, in what *The Times* described as the 'consummating memorial service for them all', the reports suggest only the presence and not the participation of Nonconformist ministers, Davidson declaring,

> ... today this gathered multitude stands together ... Churchmen and Nonconformists side by side, to give definite thoughtful, loyal recognition to the Lord God Almighty for what He has done for us in the years of war, and their issue in a victorious peace. The Lord God Omnipotent reigneth.[56]

On the same day, the Bishop of London joined prominent Free Church ministers and Salvation Army officers in leading a united service of thanksgiving in Trafalgar Square. In his typically rhetorical style, Winnington-Ingram told the congregation, 'that this was the greatest day in their lives. A united Christendom had come out to thank God for the greatest victory ever won by freedom over tyranny.' Meanwhile, in Westminster Abbey, Bishop Ryle preached at another purely Anglican service, as did Cosmo Lang in York Minster.[57] Again, 'united Christendom' had been confined to the civic space.

Apart from commemorations of the conflict, evidence of post-war ecumenical activity in the East Midlands is limited. Throughout the early 1920s, there was an annual exchange of pulpits in Derby in January, although only the Free Churches were involved.[58] In smaller towns and villages, there were occasional exchanges between Anglicans clergy and Nonconformist ministers.[59] Evidence from other parts of England indicates the infrequent nature of such activities: Services jointly organised and led by ministers and clergy in Burnley in summer 1920 were held in the open-air – that is in the civic space rather than any church.[60] At Peterborough in 1919, the exchange took the form of the Dean 'presiding' at a service at a Congregational

55 Wilkinson, *The Church of England*, p. 263.
56 *The Times*, 7 July 1919, pp. 12, 17 and 18.
57 *The Times*, 7 July 1919, p. 18.
58 Advertisements for services in *DDT*, 10 Jan 1920, p. 1; *DDT*, 29 Jan 1921, p. 1; *DDT*, 28 Jan 1922, p. 1; *DDT*, 17 Jan 1925, p. 2.
59 For example, that at Hathern, Leicestershire., involving the Baptist church, *NEP*, 1 Dec 1924, p. 6.
60 *Burnley News*, 21 August 1920, p. 4.

church, while the Wesleyan minister read a lesson in the Cathedral.[61] In 1923, in what was described as a 'unique event', an ecumenical fraternal of Anglican clergy and Free Church ministers in Bocking, Essex, was welcomed to the presbytery by the Roman Catholic priest, who gave them tea and read a 'religious paper'.[62] Once the war had ended, so too had the justification for disregarding the requirements of church law about such matters. While Talbot House had admitted Nonconformist communicants, no such liberality applied to the post-war London base of the Toc-H organisation which sprang from the Talbot House experience, All Hallows by the Tower. Any such attempt would, of course, have resulted in, at the very least, the type of episode discussed by William Temple a decade earlier. Frederick Iremonger, Temple's biographer, offered an analysis of post-war English Christendom which contrasts strongly with the impression which might be drawn from the many accounts of increasingly harmonious ecumenical relationships: 'Few members of the Established and Free Churches knew anything of one another's faith and worship, and by most of them any aspirations after unity were regarded with an almost cynical indifference.' Adjacent parish churches and chapels would have no fellowship or understanding between them, he wrote. While those at 'S. Gregory Thaumaturgus' would look down on the 'Saints in Lantern Yard', the latter were 'almost ecstatically unanimous ... that the entire congregation of S. Gregory's – with its 'goings on' .... would burn in all eternity in Hell.'[63] Even allowing for his hyperbolic style, this reminder of the 'church–chapel' divide, commonly accompanied by a sense of mutual suspicion, offers a corrective to a somewhat idealised view of post-war local ecumenical relationships.

Moves for Reunion

While pulpit exchanges and the involvement of Free Church ministers in civic worship which had traditionally been the sole responsibility of the established Church were a feature of both wartime and post-war England – albeit one which remained contested and far from uniformly practised – the closer co-operation of the Church of England with Nonconformity raised the possibility of a reunion of the Protestant Churches of England. During the war, the informal conversations between Anglicans and Wesleyans in London championed by Rattenbury and Winnington-Ingram continued, despite the concerns expressed at the 1917 Wesleyan Conference. One diary entry about those discussions summarised in two lines the fundamental obstacles to Anglican-Methodist re-union, not only in the immediate post-war period, but again in the 1960s 'Conversations' and then in subsequent initiatives. Edward Hicks, Bishop of Lincoln, set the context for a later entry with that for 6 July 1917:

61 *DDT*, 4 Jan 1919, p. 3.
62 *Chelmsford Chronicle*, 16 Feb 1923, p. 4.
63 F.A. Iremonger, *William Temple, Archbishop of Canterbury* (London: OUP, 1948), pp. 454f.

> London Wesleyan ministers want the Bp. Of London to talk to them at their Central Hall about possible reunion with the Church. … It may come to nothing & may only be one of the Bp. Of L.'s bubbles; but it may lead to something very momentous. God grant it.[64]

Six months later, in January 1918, Hicks wrote of the Bishop of Oxford's 'idea that if the Church were disest[ablished] and disend[owed] & B[isho]ps humbled themselves, then the Methodists w[oul]d accept reordination!!!'[65] Establishment, Church wealth and episcopal pomp were indeed all problematic for Nonconformity, but Hicks' punctuation (underlining and three exclamation marks) emphasised the primary issue for Nonconformist ministers; the expectation of Anglo-Catholics and many other Anglicans that a re-union would necessitate a re-ordination of ministers not already episcopally-ordained. Hicks' desire for re-union – 'God grant it' – alongside his clear incredulity about Gore's reported 'idea' epitomises the disconnection between optimistic hope and pragmatic reality that characterised the immediate post-war period. From a contemporary perspective, it is unsurprising that issues such as disestablishment, the wealth of the Church, the power and pomp associated with bishops and the issue of re-ordination would dash the naïve aspirations of Hicks and many others.

In the religious journals and newspapers of the closing months of the war, church re-union – understood to mean that of the Church of England and Nonconformity – became an increasingly important topic. In the *Modern Churchman* of October 1918, G.M. Hanks wrote on 'The Possibilities of Reunion': 'The conscience of Christendom is rapidly becoming quickened to realise that the grievous divisions in the visible Church contribute one of the chief barriers to the victorious sovereignty of Christ in the kingdom of the world.'[66]

A month later, an editorial in that journal drew attention to a series of articles in the church newspaper *The Guardian* contributed by 'distinguished representatives of the CofE and other Churches'. The writer of an article, 'Towards Re-union: a Nonconformist View' in the *Church Quarterly Review* of January 1919 asserted that, 'The comradeship of the padres in the trenches cannot fail to react on the churches at home' before arguing that, 'It is ridiculous for a procession of milk carts to be plying their trade up and down the same street.'[67] At the start of 1919, the issue dominated the church press of all the denominations. The President of the Baptist Union stated that 'our aloofness is doing infinite harm; it is delaying the coming of the Kingdom', while

64 G. Neville (ed.), *The Diaries of Edward Lee Hicks, Bishop of Lincoln, 1910–1919* (Woodbridge: Lincoln Record Society, 1991), p. 182.

65 Ibid., p. 200. Stuart Mews transcribed the entry slightly differently and erroneously dated it as 31 October 1918 – Mews, *Religion and English Society*, p. 309.

66 G.M. Hanks, 'The Possibilities of Reunion' in *The Modern Churchman*, October 1918, p. 614.

67 W.F. Adney, 'Towards Re-union: A Nonconformist View' in *Church Quarterly Review*, CLXXIV, January 1919, pp. 189f.

the President of the Wesleyan Conference suggested that the churches must 'distinguish between the realities of religion and its variable conveniences.'[68] In April 1919, *The Guardian* reported the Bishop of London speaking at a Wesleyan Brotherhood meeting about a re-union scheme with optional re-ordination for Wesleyan ministers 'having signed a protestation that their action is not intended to express adverse judgment on their past ministry.'[69] Two months later, yet another article asserted, 'The recent world-war has given an enormous impetus to the movement towards reunion which had, for some years before it broke out, been steadily growing in force among Christian people.'[70]

However, it should be noted that there was significant resistance to re-union within Nonconformity. For example, Benjamin Nightingale, a leading Congregationalist minister protested:

> It may be possible to standardise a great deal in the world, though I am not so sure of even that; but, the one thing that cannot be standardised is religion! I frankly confess that I hate religious uniformity, whether self-imposed or imposed from without, because I believe that nothing will so surely be the death of all that is best in religion, and so of religion itself.[71]

Another Congregationalist, J.D. Jones, re-affirmed his objection to the possibility of the re-ordination of Nonconformist ministers and proposed a federation of the Free Churches.[72]

Regularising the Exchange of Pulpits

In the last months of the war, asked about the exchange of pulpits with Nonconformist ministers, Hensley Henson had written,

> This interchange of pulpits would appear to be the natural consequence of the remarkable demonstrations of fraternity which have been observed in the vast armies of Englishmen overseas. … Old obstinate barriers of sect and prejudice are too weak to resist the pressure of the new emotion born of common experiences in camp, trench, hospital and stricken field.[73]

68 *The Guardian*, 9 January 1919, p. 32.
69 Noted in *The Modern Churchman*, April 1919, p. 179.
70 J.R. Clark Hall, 'The Problem of Union and Freedom in the Church of Christ' in *The Modern Churchman*, June 1919, pp. 314-326.
71 Reported in *The Guardian*, 9 January 1919, p. 32.
72 Ibid.
73 Entry for 3 August 1918 in Henson, *Retrospect*, vol. 1, p. 299.

Notwithstanding his antipathy to the Nonconformity of his own father, Henson had himself in 1917 consented to preach at the City Temple in London, contrary to Winnington-Ingram's pleading.[74] His lengthy reply to the bishop's letter pulled no punches and drew attention to the limitations to ecumenical activity practised by many Anglicans opposed to pulpit exchanges:

> You appear to suppose that co-operation in civic action, and personal courtesy to non-Anglicans, are the true equivalents of Christian fellowship ... Your large-hearted civic action ... has gone ever along with a determined effort to isolate the Church of England from all *religious* association with Evangelical Christians. ... You addressed a Bible Class of City Templars 'in a neutral hall', and devoted an hour to ecclesiastical debate! The very phrase – a neutral hall – does not suggest fraternity. It belongs to the vocabulary of warfare, suggesting armies in conflict consenting to suspend their fighting for a breathing space.[75]

Winnington-Ingram's biographer mentioned neither the City Temple controversy nor the discussions with the Wesleyans. The bishops of the province of Canterbury considered relationships with Nonconformity at the Convocation in February 1919. The debate started by considering resolutions to permit 'ministers and other members of communions separated from the Church of England' to speak or pray in Anglican churches at special services and meetings with episcopal approval, and to permit Anglican clergy to act similarly in Nonconformist settings. The Bishop of Winchester proposed the resolutions. The Bishop of Oxford objected that the resolutions would include Jews and Unitarians and suggested that 'the tendency of the interchange of pulpits was to divert every denomination from any specific doctrines.' The Bishop of Hereford 'asked that [a] spirit of venture should be applied to this question of reunion' but the Bishop of Gloucester believed that the proposals would divide the Anglican church. The outcome of the debate over two days was the setting up of a joint committee to advise the bishops as to how the desires expressed in the original resolutions could be most appropriately met.[76] A week later, *The Guardian* reported on an address by the Bishop of London, *The Church and the Wesleyans – A Practical Scheme*, given at Kingsway Hall at a meeting at which J.E. Rattenbury had presided. Recognising how he would respond to a Roman Catholic telling him that he had to be re-ordained, Winnington-Ingram proposed that from an agreed date all *future* ordinations should be carried out by both Churches so as to satisfy the members of both traditions, thus creating a transitional period, the length of which would depend 'on the longevity of the existing Wesleyan ministers.'[77] Proposals similar to this formed the basis for the

74 Chadwick, *Hensley Henson,* pp. 8 and 127; Henson, *Retrospect*, vol. 1, pp. 193-203.
75 Henson, *Retrospect*, vol.1, pp. 197-199, letter dated 1 February 1917.
76 'Relations with Nonconformists', *The Guardian*, 20 February 1919, pp. 185f.
77 *The Guardian*, 27 February 1919, p. 213.

formation of the Church of South India and would reappear on several occasions in the succeeding ninety years in various attempts at Anglican-Methodist Union.

At the seventh Christian Union conference, held in the Methodist Kingsway Hall and presided over by J.E. Rattenbury in April 1919, Percy Dearmer spoke on 'The War and Christian Union'. Speaking warmly of the Eastern Church, which, 'overwhelmed by the forces of Mohamedanism … had almost disappeared', he asserted that the Vatican was the chief obstacle to the Reunion of Christendom and urged that in the 'cause of ultimate reunion' the Church of England should look to the episcopal as well as the non-episcopal churches.[78] There was a strong feeling that church law must be amended rather than ignored. For example, *The Guardian*, as might be expected from its generally high-church perspective, published with implicit approval the comments of the Bishop of Birmingham on pulpit exchanges in his diocese:

> I am not in favour of sporadic attempts by interchange of pulpits and such-like means to get into closer touch with our brothers … and I have no particular belief in their usefulness, and probably they are the cause of more objection than they are of permanent benefit to the religion of Christ.[79]

Later in 1919, first the Bishop of Norwich, then seven Nonconformist leaders and subsequently ten other bishops publicly advocated the formal approval of the practice. Randall Davidson wished to postpone his Church's consideration of the issue until after the 1920 Lambeth Conference, while some bishops, such as Frank Weston of Zanzibar, protested on ecclesiological and doctrinal grounds. The correspondence pages of *The Times* were in the autumn of 1919 full of argument and counter-argument involving several bishops. The basis of the Bishop of Norwich's proposals, endorsed by the Nonconformist leaders, was to permit non-Anglicans to be invited to preach in an Anglican church at the request of the incumbent and the church wardens or church council, with the sanction of the bishop, provided that they did not speak about church order unless asked to do so. Furthermore, the preacher should signify his assent to the first three parts of the 1888 Lambeth Quadrilateral which had suggested a basis for church union assent to the scriptures as the standard of faith, to the creeds as 'respectively the baptismal symbol and the sufficient statement of the Christian faith' and to the two sacraments ordained by Christ.[80] It was, of course, the omitted fourth element of the quadrilateral which would prove the sticking point for all discussions of reunion, not only in the aftermath of the 1920 Lambeth Conference, but also subsequently. Clause 4 affirmed, 'The Historic Episcopate, locally adapted in the methods of its administration to the varying needs of the nations and people called of God into

78 'The War and Christian Union – Address by Dr. Percy Dearmer' in *The Guardian*, 10 April 1919, pp. 395f.

79 Quoted from the *Birmingham Diocesan Magazine* in *The Guardian*, 15 April 1919, p. 421.

80 *The Times*, 30 June 1919, p. 9; *The Times*, 30 August 1919, p. 6.

the Unity of His Church.' While the acceptance of the historic episcopate might not be a pre-requisite for the interchange of pulpits, for the majority of Anglicans it was fundamental to their understanding of Church.[81]

In September 1919, the editor of *The Modern Churchman* in discussing the programme for the forthcoming Lambeth Conference suggested that, 'The possibility of the Convocations sanctioning the admission of Nonconformists to Church of England pulpits, and giving permission to women to pray and preach in our churches, caused something of a sensation in Anglo-Catholic circles.'[82] It referred to an article in *The Church Times* about a possible secession, while the issue carried further articles on re-union. When in the following month, 2000 members of the Church of England assembled for the Church Congress in Leicester, the secretary of that city's Free Church Council welcomed them on behalf of fifty local churches. He said that, 'the war had taught them what unity could achieve in national affairs, and they were awakening to the vision of what might be achieved by greater unity in the interests of the higher Kingdom.' In his presidential address, the Bishop of Peterborough, having stressed the importance of unity in matters of international and industrial relations, asserted that, 'The unification of the Christian Church would probably do more to convert the world than all their competing missions put together.'[83] In 1920, a congregation of 7,000, 'which was probably one of the largest in the history of the cathedral' heard J.H. Jowett, minister of Westminster Chapel, London and one of the signatories to the 1919 letter to *The Times*, preach at Durham, albeit only after a vociferous objection from a local vicar has been drowned by spontaneous hymn-singing as the protestor was ejected by the Chief Constable of Durham and three or four policemen.[84] The Bishop, Hensley Henson, while sympathetic to the ideals that had prompted the invitation, absented himself since the matter of the interchange of pulpits was to be reviewed by the Lambeth Conference.[85] Later that year, Dr Jowett engaged in an exchange of pulpits with the vicar of St Paul's, Portman Square.[86]

Lambeth

The story of the 1920 Lambeth Conference and in particular the work of the committee which led to the publication of the *Appeal to All Christian People* has been well-documented. For the Church of England, memories of the pre-war confrontation arising from Kikuyu and the wartime controversy over the appointment of Hensley Henson to the see of Hereford loomed large. The Conference would bring together bishops

81 Text at http://www.lambethconference.org/resolutions/1888/1888-11.cfm accessed 24 November 2014.
82 *The Modern Churchman*, September 1919, p. 467.
83 *Manchester Guardian*, 15 October 1919, p. 4.
84 *The Times*, 16 February 1920, p. 14.
85 *The Times*, 6 February 1920, p. 9.
86 *The Times*, 14 June 1920, p. 9.

of every theological and ecclesiastical position and so disunity within the Anglican communion was a clear danger. George Bell, Davidson's biographer, wrote of the participating bishops, 'Most striking of all was Frank Weston … with his extraordinary mixture of generosity and menace.'[87] Davidson wrote in his diary of the work of the Reunion committee:

> The surprise of the Conference was the line taken by the Bishop of Zanzibar (Weston). Had he been an unknown person who made his debut at this Conference, it would have been said what a wonderful thing it is for the present time to have a Bishop of real learning and eloquence, who is a strong High churchman, and yet holds such liberal, tolerant, kindly views and shows such readiness to see and appreciate the views of those who differ from him, He and Henson became personal friends, and Uganda and Mombassa were continually by his side and they desired that I should be photographed with them as a group.

This was the same Frank Weston who in 1913 had accused those bishops from East Africa of 'propagating heresy and committing schism' and who in 1917 had labelled Henson an 'arch-heretic' and written the book, *The Christ and His Critics*, in protest at Henson's appointment as Bishop of Hereford.[88] Weston's generally uncritical biographer, Maynard Smith, wrote of his subject's attitude in 1917: 'If there is such a thing as abstract hate, I think Frank held it for Dr. Henson; but I am glad to think also that the feeling did not survive the meeting of the two men at the Lambeth Conference.'[89]

Henson's own detailed narrative of Lambeth provided a reminder that the issue of reunion was being considered on a global scale, with bishops from across the Anglican Communion taking part and relating their own experiences of ecumenical relationships. His account of one day of the committee's business indicates how discussion of a wider church union was always in danger of threatening Anglican unity:

> *Thursday, July 15th, 1920.* Shakespeare, the Baptist leader, attended … He pleaded earnestly for 'two small steps.' These were, (1) interchange of pulpits on lines such as those indicated by the Bishop of Norwich. (2) admission to communion at Anglican altars of devout nonconformists where their own churches were inaccessible. The Bishops of S. Albans (Furse) and Zanzibar (Weston) disclosed a hard unyielding temper, and seemed to threaten schism if these points were conceded![90]

87 Bell, *Randall Davidson*, p. 1010.
88 F. Weston, *The Christ and His Critics: An Open Letter to The European Missionaries of his Diocese* (London: Mowbray, 1919).
89 Maynard Smith, *Frank*, p. 181.
90 Henson, *Retrospect*, vol. 2, p.10.

Since the Kikuyu controversy had arisen from similar proposals, Weston's objections could hardly have some as a shock. However, Weston's popularity grew during the Conference and two weeks later, Henson commented,

> It is almost amusing to notice the compliments which are pouring out on this odd prelate who only a few months since was hurling anathemas against all the Bishops for their refusal to excommunicate me as a heretic.[91]

He was somewhat sceptical when Davidson professed that he was 'greatly impressed' by Weston's speeches and general behaviour: 'I told him not to be too confident. Zanzibar was capable of any sudden and surprising turn.'[92] Henson opposed a resolution to inform the public of the 'amazing unanimity' of the Conference, as 'I personally could not go an inch beyond the statement of the Report.' He made no mention in his published memoirs of his alleged friendship with Weston, nor of the reputed souvenir photograph. In his unpublished journal, the primary source for *Retrospect*, Henson noted only being photographed as the bishops sat in their places for the Conference sessions.[93] Maynard Smith, after quoting affirmations of Weston's 'conciliatory spirit [and] large-heartedness' and the 'lofty tone and abandonment of "party"' from the Dean of Canterbury and Bishop of Chelmsford respectively then quoted Henson, who had reportedly written of Weston: 'He was in my belief, a very good unselfish Christian. … It was impossible not to feel his charm even when one execrated his bigotry.'[94] Bell's judgment, writing in 1935, was that

> The Appeal and Resolution were almost unbelievable after everything that had been said before the Conference began. Not only were the lions in the path overcome, but something new and creative had been done, and a great blow struck for the Reunion of Christendom.[95]

However, in his closing reflections on the Conference, Henson had offered a far more realistic analysis than did either Davidson or Bell: 'There is a real desire for union with non-episcopalians, but no adequate perception of the difficulty.'[96] Indications of that 'difficulty', primarily centring on the issue of re-ordination, soon followed. In his private journal, a note recorded towards the end of July was consonant with his consistently dismissive attitude towards his evangelical colleagues at the Conference:

91 Ibid., p.16.
92 Ibid.
93 Durham Cathedral Archives, HHH28, p. 39 (10 July 1920).
94 Maynard Smith, *Frank*, pp. 232-3.
95 Bell, *Randall Davidson*, p. 1014.
96 Henson, *Retrospect*, vol. 2, pp. 22f.

> I am impressed more and more by the ineptitude of Evangelical Bishops. They accept with raptures of thankfulness any tiny unimportant concession, and gladly sacrifice their principles in return. Partly it is their habitual immersion in cant which makes them highly susceptible to emotional appeals & partly their low level of knowledge and intelligence which makes them slow to perceive a point, and unable to appreciate its importance.[97]

The *Appeal to all Christian People* acknowledged 'all who believe in our Lord Jesus Christ and have been baptised into the name of the Holy Trinity as sharing with us in the universal Church of Christ which is His Body' and called for a vision of a united church.[98] It reaffirmed as a basis for 'visible unity' the 'wholehearted acceptance' of the Holy Scriptures, the Nicene Creed (with either it or the Apostles' Creed to be used as the baptismal confession of belief) and the two sacraments of baptism and holy communion. It proposed that the church should have 'a ministry acknowledged by every part of the church as possessing not only the inward call of the Spirit, but also the commission of Christ and the authority of the whole body.' However, rather than asserting that episcopacy was an essential characteristic of the Christian Church (the fourth clause of the 1888 Lambeth Quadrilateral), it instead suggested, 'May we not reasonably claim that the Episcopate is one means of providing such a ministry?' adding, 'It is not that we call in question for a moment the spiritual reality of the ministries of those Communions which do not possess the episcopate.' In order to create a future Church from traditions both within and outside the historic episcopate, the *Appeal* proposed that 'bishops and clergy of our Communion would willingly accept from these [future Church] authorities a form of commission or recognition which would commend our ministry to their congregations.' While later writers such as Roger Lloyd have judged this clause to be a concession to Nonconformity, offering a reciprocal arrangement to acknowledge Anglican and Free Church ministries, Sidney Dark concluded that, since Nonconformists did not dispute the validity of Anglican orders, 'it was assumed that this was a direct approach to the Church of Rome' and he interpreted the provision as indicating episcopal willingness to submit to re-ordination to secure the reunion of Anglicanism and Roman Catholicism.[99] Similarly – and here was the matter on which almost all Anglican-Nonconformist discussions had stalled, and would continue to do so – it stated,

97 Durham Cathedral Archives, HHH28, p. 56 (24 July 1920).

98 Text at http://www.lambethconference.org/resolutions/1920/1920-9.cfm, accessed 24 November 2014.

99 R. Lloyd, *The Church of England 1900–1965* (London: SCM, 1966), p. 409; S. Dark, *Archbishop Davidson and the English Church* (London: Phillip Allen, 1929), p. 156.

> It is our hope that the same motive would lead ministers who have not received it to accept a commission through episcopal ordination, as obtaining for them a ministry throughout the whole fellowship.

Accompanying the *Appeal* was a resolution, reportedly significantly influenced by Frank Weston, which, while disapproving of general schemes of intercommunion or the exchange of pulpits, stated that 'in view of prospects and projects of reunion', a bishop could permit the interchange of pulpits in his own diocese and under certain unspecified conditions allow those baptised but not confirmed to receive communion. Writing in the *Church Times* soon afterwards, Weston explained his vision for a reunited Christendom: 'The visibility of one organism would be due to an undivided College of Bishops, Orthodox, Roman, Anglican, with bishops from the Presbyterian and Free Church communions.'[100] Dark's interpretation that Weston and his supporters had wanted the *Appeal* to reach out in both directions from the Anglican *Via Media* was surely correct.

At the conclusion of the Conference, Cosmo Lang returned to York and preached in the Minster on the Conference and reunion: 'The Press had recognized that it marked a new epoch, for it brought a new spirit and a new outlook to members of the Anglican church.' Some who had hoped for immediate steps towards union might, he said, be disappointed, but, 'Let them remember that all alike, both Bishops who would be regarded as catholic and Bishops who would be regarded as evangelical, united in commending this ideal to the church.'[101] It is clear that both Archbishops, Davidson and Lang, left the Conference with an optimism which was primarily based on the quite unexpected near-unanimity of the bishops representing the geographical and ecclesiological breadth of the Anglican communion, rather than on the substance of the proposals, which had made no real concessions to the concerns of Nonconformity. Much discussion followed in the pages of both the secular and religious press, rehearsing the well-worn arguments about episcopacy and re-ordination.

In a discursive analysis of the whole work of the Conference, Arthur Headlam, Regius Professor of Divinity at Oxford and editor of the *Church Quarterly Review*, identified two 'defects' in the Conference's treatment of difficult questions.[102] The first was 'a certain failure of intellectual precision in the treatment of many problems.'[103] Too often, he suggested, two or three different views were presented but not conciliated. Secondly, he asserted that, 'in most directions it will not readily lead to action.'[104] Turning to re-union, he, too, was keen to emphasise 'the remarkable unity exhibited'.[105] Headlam then quoted at length Frank Weston's account in which he had written, 'The

100 *Church Times,* 20 August 1920, quoted in Maynard Smith, *Frank*, p. 236.
101 *The Times*, 16 August 1920, p. 7.
102 A. Headlam, 'The Lambeth Conference' in *Church Quarterly Review*, Vol. XCI (October 1920), pp. 139-56.
103 Ibid., p. 140.
104 Ibid.
105 Ibid., p. 148.

evident duty of the Conference was to seek for a scheme upon which the bishops as a whole could concentrate their prayers and their labours ... The *Appeal* and its resolutions do exactly represent such a scheme.'[106] Headlam commented,

> If anyone reads the Resolutions he will certainly feel that we owe a great deal of gratitude to the Bishop of Zanzibar . . . We have from time to time in these pages had to criticize his writings ... but certainly his utterances are remarkable evidence of the reality of the spirit of Christian fellowship which inspired the Conference.

It should be noted that he was praising Weston not for any change of view, nor for his accommodation of others' views, but for the spirit in which the discussions took place and in which the text of the *Appeal* was agreed. After an analysis of the proposals for a future united Church, Headlam concluded that 'provided there is a real and earnest desire for union we think that they ought to be capable of being carried out.'[107]

In the succeeding months, the Free Churches made their responses. Meeting in Southampton in September, the assembly of the Congregational Union debated the Lambeth *Appeal*. Concern was expressed that in any united Church, Free Church ministers would have to be re-ordained, while Anglican clergy would only have to be 'recognised'.[108] Yet Anglican orders, it was observed, were not universally accepted. The resolution passed by the Assembly appreciated the 'brotherly and eirenical spirit' of the *Appeal* and recognised that difficulties were in the way which 'reached down to fundamental matters of faith.' The proposer identified the main issue as being 'Apostolic ordination'. While the Assembly reserved judgment until after further discussion, within a month of the close of the Lambeth Conference, the pattern had been set for the response of Nonconformity. In the same month, the Federal Council of the Evangelical Free Churches made a similar response, again welcoming the 'brotherly and eirenical' spirit of the *Appeal*, again reserving final judgment and again identifying what it described as 'fundamental provisions in these proposals which do not command its assent.'[109] As for Weston's 'conciliatory spirit' and 'large-heartedness', when a year later he heard that the Bishop of Manchester had invited Nonconformist ministers to preach, he withdrew all connexion with the Lambeth Conference.[110] In 1921, there started a series of Joint Conferences, bringing together Davidson and Lang, nine diocesan bishops and 25 leading Nonconformists. Even George Bell's very positive and enthusiastic narrative could not disguise the significant divisions that the discussions highlighted. On the thorny issue of re-ordination, he noted that

106 Ibid., pp. 148f.
107 Ibid., p. 153.
108 *The Times*, 1 October 1920, p. 10.
109 *The Times*, 29 September 1920, p. 10.
110 Maynard Smith, *Frank*, p. 240. Maynard Smith suggested that Weston had been misinformed about what the Bishop of Manchester had actually done.

the 'old' bishop of Gloucester, Edgar Gibson, 'was emphatic for episcopal ordination for all ministers officiating fully in the united Church', while the 'new' one, Arthur Headlam, 'wished for mutual recognition of ministers and Sacraments but with the proviso that only episcopally-ordained ministers should officiate in churches accustomed to episcopal ministry.'[111] The Conferences were suspended in 1925, by which time the Archbishops and bishops had declared that in Nonconformist ministries 'are real ministries of Christ's Word and Sacraments in the Universal Church.' Yet, however real, those ministries might in varying degrees be irregular or defective and 'the Anglican church must require episcopal ordination for the ministers of its congregations.'

Throughout the early 1920s, some prominent Anglican clergy and Nonconformist ministers continued to invite their counterparts to preach in their pulpits or share in ecumenical events. For example, in 1921, the Moderator of the Church of Scotland preached at Durham Cathedral, as did the Bishop of Chelmsford at Wesley's Chapel, London.[112] Meanwhile, efforts to persuade the Church of England formally to endorse such practices had a measure of success. In the Upper House of the York Convocation in 1922, the Bishop of Manchester proposed that, with episcopal consent, 'members of Christian communities separated from the Church of England' might speak or pray in consecrated buildings 'on special occasions of public importance or in gatherings for common devotion and mutual edification' provided that what is done is outside the regular services of the Church. Opposing the proposal, Hensley Henson

> ... expressed his anxiety about the risk of the status and use of the churches being pulled down from the high level of devotional regard with which they were at present invested to the kind of level which the ordinary Nonconformist place of worship had.[113]

We have previously noted his antipathy towards Nonconformity, expressed again in this critique of its worship. The Bishop of Manchester's proposals were adopted with Henson's being the only contrary voice. The requirement for episcopal consent meant that any dissentient diocesan bishop could prohibit such practices in his own diocese. Randall Davidson himself visited the Wesleyan Conference in 1923, hearing an address by the President and speaking on Christian reunion. He told his audience that they were 'just now standing together at a juncture in human history, so vast in its import, so measureless in its possibilities.'[114] In 1925, the chairman of the Congregational Union preached at a Sunday evening service in Canterbury Cathedral. 'The Dean of Canterbury had extended an invitation ... with the concurrence of the Archbishop ...

111 Bell, *Randall Davidson*, pp. 1116-1122.
112 *The Times*, 5 December 1921, p. 7; *The Times*, 12 September 1921, p. 5.
113 *The Times*, 16 February 1922, p. 7.
114 Bell, *Randall Davidson*, p. 1123.

expressly in connexion with the Lambeth *Appeal*.'[115] In 1927, the ex-President of the Wesleyan Conference preached in Bradford Cathedral, the report noting that,

> He wore his academic robes. The Bishop of Bradford was present. Last week, the Bishop had spoken at Nonconformist meetings, and on Saturday might he was on a chapel platform with Free Church ministers pleading the cause of temperance.[116]

Just as the identification of a common enemy and a common cause had encouraged wartime ecumenical co-operation, so in 1927 a shared concern about the dangers of alcohol had brought Anglicans and Nonconformists to the same platform. In 1934, in the heated debate that arose from the invitation extended by the Dean of Liverpool to Unitarian ministers to preach in the Cathedral – an act that led to a formal complaint to the Archbishop of York – a correspondent to the *Times*, affirmed,

> It is a pleasure to reflect that sermons have been so preached by eminent nonconformist Divines in several cathedrals – and among them, in Canterbury Cathedral, and also in Westminster Abbey. That is a procedure which accords with the spirit of the Lambeth Conference, especially with the 'Appeal to all Christian People' issued by the Lambeth Conference in 1920.[117]

However, in the same year, an invitation to 'scholars from various Christian denominations' to preach in a 1934 Lenten series at Exeter Cathedral brought both criticism and affirmative comment from across the country.[118]

Fading Hopes

It has to be concluded that there is little evidence that either the wartime ecumenical experiences or the overtures which came from the Lambeth *Appeal* had any significant long-term impact. In Headlam's phrase, the *Appeal* had not readily led to action. That 1934 letter to *The Times* does suggest that pulpit exchanges – even high-profile ones – between Trinitarian Protestant churches had ceased to be seen as controversial by many, but certainly not all, Anglicans. Bishops who had previously permitted or engaged in such practices continued to do so, while some of their colleagues continued to forbid them. Other developments may be attributed to that wartime 'ecumenical spirit', such as Oxford University's decision to allow the awarding of higher theological degrees to non-Anglicans in 1920. Increasingly, Nonconformists and Anglicans

115 *The Times*, 19 January 1925, p. 17.
116 *The Times*, 18 July 1927, p. 16.
117 *The Times*, 31 January 1934, p. 8.
118 *Exeter and Plymouth Gazette*, 9 March 1934, p. 13.

conferred on matters of social concern, exemplified by the Conference on Christian Politics, Economics and Citizenship (COPEC) held at Birmingham in 1924, chaired by William Temple. Three years later, the first *World Conference on Faith and Order* met at Lausanne, with Temple the deputy chair of the group considering the nature of the church. The Orthodox churches, the Anglican communion and Nonconformity were represented, but not Roman Catholicism.[119]

However, the primary focus of the 1920 *Appeal* – 're-union'– had, as far as England was concerned, come to nothing. As Hastings put it, 'For the time being, a long time being, very little would be done by church leaders beyond expressions of polite good will.'[120] Indeed, there is little evidence of any further testing of the boundaries of permissible ecumenical activity. For example, the invitation to Nonconformist ministers and members to receive Holy Communion in Hereford Cathedral made a generation earlier was not repeated, nor was there any serious thought that such practices might be permitted except in the most limited of cases, for any such proposal would have threatened the internal Anglican consensus which the *Appeal* purportedly represented. Just occasionally, clergy would ignore such concerns and Linda Parker has recently noted that Guy Rogers welcomed non-Anglicans to Holy Communion, taking advantage of the protection offered by Ernest Barnes, the Bishop of Birmingham.[121] In 1939, George Bell, Bishop of Chichester used the pages of the *Church Times* to defend arrangements for a communion service to be held at a conference of the 'Friends of Reunion', a group formed in the early 1930s, at which, 'by [his own] permission any baptized communicant member of a Christian Church, present at the conference, will be welcome to communicate.' He cited the 1933 Convocation resolution permitting such arrangements for groups meeting to promote unity, but the necessity for him to defend his action is indicative of the continuing controversial nature of such activities.[122]

Writing in 1929, Dark had expressed cautious optimism:

> Another Lambeth Conference is to open in 1930, and various efforts are to be made to modify the episcopal claim as to bring reunion in England and in the mission field into the realm of practical politics. Dr Davidson will no longer be Archbishop of Canterbury … and Frank Weston is dead. And no man can predict what the decision will be.[123]

119 H.N. Bate (ed.), *Faith and Order: Proceedings of the World Conference* (London: SCM, 1927), pp. 459-75.
120 Hastings, *A History*, p. 99.
121 L. Parker, *Shellshocked Prophets: Former Anglican Army Chaplains in Inter-War Britain* (Solihull: Helion, 2015), pp. 160f.
122 *Church Times*, 24 March 1939, p. 304.
123 Dark, *Archbishop Davidson*, p. 158.

All that was true, but not only had the Bishop of Zanzibar, who had always wanted the Anglican communion to prioritise a reunion with Rome over one with Nonconformity, died, but so had that 'ecumenical spirit which had been so strongly quickened by the war'. The Congregationalist scholar Bernard Manning commented in 1939 that the *Appeal*, 'seemed to alter things, but in cold, actual fact it did not. With the magnificent and unconscious sleight of hand that comes from centuries of practice in the *via media* the Anglicans took back what they seemed to give, and, as usual, wanted it both ways.'[124] Writing in 1941, Guy Rogers, Chaplain to the King, concluded, 'The fact is that the high-water mark of our hopes for reunion was reached at the Lambeth Conference, 1920, and that they have been receding ever since. That Conference came when the loosening effect of war, with its characteristic relaxation of ecclesiastical restrictions on intercommunion, was still strongly felt.'[125]

It is hard to argue with those analyses. In 1911, Temple had written of the furore over the bishop of Hereford's invitation to Holy Communion extended to Free Church ministers and lay people, concluding that 'The cause of Reunion with separated bodies . . . remained exactly where it was.'[126] A decade and more later, despite all the Anglican euphoria over the *Appeal to All Christian People*, that 'cause of Reunion' had also 'remained exactly where it was'.

Conclusion

In his analysis of the proposals of the Lambeth Conference, Arthur Headlam had concluded that 'provided there is a real and earnest desire for union we think that they ought to be capable of being carried out.' No doubt there was a desire in the immediate post-war period for Anglican-Nonconformist reunion, founded on the experience of ecumenical co-operation between the chaplains in the theatres of war and between local churches in England, brought together in a battle against a common enemy and by the same experiences of loss. However, that desire was not sufficiently 'real and earnest' for the Church of England to risk its own precarious unity by making concessions to the Free Churches, nor for those bodies to overcome their opposition to both the ecclesiology of the historic episcopate and the culture of class which was seen to surround it, especially when proposals for re-union might be interpreted as calling into question the validity of their own ministers' ordination. Once the 'common enemy' had been defeated and the work of the Churches was again tidily contained within their well-established structures, the old habits of parallel co-existence re-asserted themselves. The animosity caused by the pre-war education reforms had reduced and even the most militant opponents of Welsh disestablishment recognized that nothing

124 B. Manning, *Essays in Orthodox Dissent* (London: Independent Press, 1939), p. 144.

125 G.T. Rogers, 'Reunion: Defeat or a New Offensive' in *The Modern Churchman*, December 1941, pp. 361-368

126 Temple, *Life of Bishop Percival*, p. 333.

further could be done. At a national level, Anglican and Nonconformist leaders generally treated each other with utmost courtesy while locally there was, no doubt, a wide spectrum of ecumenical relationships, from ones of increasingly strong friendship and co-operation on social matters to others still characterized by the 'derision and denunciation' which had been criticized by the vicar of Marthall in 1915. If the Lambeth Conference in 1920 had indeed offered a rare opportunity for substantive ecumenical progress, that moment had come and gone without being grasped.

In this and previous chapters, an attempt has been made to describe and analyse the influence of the Great War on various aspects of Christian faith and practice in the theatres of war, across Britain and more particularly in Nottinghamshire and Derbyshire. With the exception of chapter 6 which focussed on Studdert Kennedy's advocacy of divine passibility, the scope has been broad, drawing on a wide range of sources and personal experiences. The aim has been to offer a narrative of how the war affected people's understanding of and approaches to different aspects of Christian belief and, apart from Studdert Kennedy, no attempt was made to chart the development of individuals' responses to the conflict. To complement the insights offered by that approach, the purpose of the next chapter is to offer an analysis of the influence of the war on the faith of five individual soldiers.

8

Faith at the Front

In contrast to the overviews offered in the previous chapters, in order to examine more closely the impact of the war on combatant faith – and in particular those whose faith might best be described as 'diffusive' – we now turn to consider the faith of five individual soldiers and how each reacted in terms of their religious practice to the experience of the Great War. Each was very different from the others. For two, the evidence about their faith appears unambiguous; for the remaining three we can but piece together a very limited selection of relevant material to offer the most tentative of conclusions. No claim can sensibly be made that any of them was typical of the majority of British combatants. Rather, together they may well be representative of many others who were less able to express how the conflict affected their faith and, indeed, how their faith influenced their attitude to the war.

Jack Titterton

John Beckett Titterton was born in 1886 in Middleton, a hamlet near the village of Youlgreave in the Derbyshire Dales, the second of four children of Thomas and Elizabeth Titterton. He attested for military service on 6 December 1915, aged 29 years, describing himself as a farmer, single, and living at Rock Farm in Middleton. In his memoirs, he wrote that,

> … the Military did not want to take me, as they said I had all the management of the farm in my hands. This was quite correct, but I offered to instruct my younger brother in management. He had never written a letter or made a cheque out, so I showed him how to do both and during my absence he became quite proficient. He died in Nottingham Infirmary last week [4 March 1968] and my heart is broken thinking of it.[1]

1 *Memoirs of Jack Titterton, Book 8, 'Author, Poet, Philosopher'*, DRO, D 4690/1/3, p. 23.

Titterton joined the Royal Garrison Artillery on 5 May 1916, subsequently serving in France with the 200th Siege Battery. He married Elizabeth Robinson in 1922 and died without children on 9 April 1968, aged 81. The Derbyshire County archives contain a significant amount of material from the hand of Jack Titterton. Some, such as the earliest poems and the much later weather diaries, are dated; the former from 1912 and the latter to the late 1950s and early 60s. That reference to the death of his younger brother, Herbert, indicates that Titterton was writing his memoirs in the last month of his life in 1968 and the similar nature of the exercise books used and the handwriting suggest they were all written in that decade.[2] As with all memoirs written so long after the events that they relate, we must be cautious of the effects both of the fallibility of human memory and of influences on the author's perspective in the intervening period. The limited evidence available indicates that Titterton was far better educated than would be expected of the child of a working-class rural family at that time, for both his poems and his memoirs are full of historical references and literary quotations. His father died when he was 7, and he appears to have been working as an apprentice clerk in Scotland at the time of the 1901 census. That would be consistent with a desire on his part or that of his mother to 'better himself' though training and education.

In the first of his poems, written on 15 October 1912, Jack Titterton offered his *Thoughts on the Balkan Crisis*, using Shakespeare's phrase, 'the dogs of war', characterising the Slavs as 'stalwart' and affirming 'the gallant sons of Greece'. October 1912 saw the start of the first Balkan war, in which an alliance of Serbia, Greece, Montenegro and Bulgaria fought successfully against the Ottoman Empire, capturing almost all of the empire's territory in Europe. Titterton was happy to reflect theologically on the crisis and in doing so demonstrate his familiarity with both Shakespeare and the Bible:

Is there no Justice for this hoary world?
No 'God' above to pity those beneath?
Must Freedom's banner yet remain unfurled?
Shall Honour's sword lie tarnished in its sheath?

Is there no Truth within that ancient Word,
Or has its message ever rung in vain
That they who build their empire with the sword
Shall by the sword be overthrown again?[3]

2 Poems at DRO, D 4690/1/5/1-3; Memoirs at DRO, D 4690/1/1/1-4, D 4690/1/2/1-3 and D 4690/1/3. Folios within the folders of poems are un-numbered.

3 Poems on un-numbered pages in DRO, D4690/1/5/1.

The message of the words of Jesus recorded in Matthew's Gospel, 'Put your sword back into its place; for all those who take the sword will perish by the sword' (Matt. 26:52) recurred again in this poem and later in several others. In the concluding verse Titterton saw the defeat of the Ottoman Empire in Europe as fulfilment of that warning:

> They tilled the stubbles with the levelled spear,
> They pruned the orchards with the reeking blade.
> They sowed in wrath the seeds of hate and fear,
> And from the ripening harvests shrink, dismayed.

His poem, *To a Lady, Whose faith is not of the reasoning order*, appears to have been written between August and October 1914. Although Titterton did not elaborate on his title, the poem was almost certainly written for 'Bess', Miss Elizabeth Robinson, to whom he wrote from the Western Front in 1917 and 1918 and whom he later married.[4] The opening verses expressed directly the age-old problem for the Christian faith of reconciling belief in an omnipotent God of love with human suffering:

> O if there be a God of grace
> Above this toiling world,
> By Whose strong Hand through whirling space
> The planets forth were hurled.
> Why stays he then upon His throne,
> Up yonder in the sky,
> Why looks He down unmoved as stone,
> To see His children die?

Here he was engaging with those questions of providence and omnipotence that, as we have seen, were so frequently asked during the conflict. Rather than being a rejection of conventional faith, the poem was more of a lament that he had lost his. Rather than belittling the recipient's 'child-like trust', he contrasted her reaction to suffering with his own:

> You tell me with your simple faith,
> (I know its child-like trust),
> That Love will rise and conquer Death,
> That God is kind and just.
> I cannot share that blissful hope,
> It brings no help to me.
> My soul has fled beyond its scope
> Upon a shoreless sea.

4 *Letters from 'Jack' to 'Bess'*, DRO, D 849/1-4.

In other poems written before he enlisted, Titterton engaged with various ethical and moral issues posed by the conflict. In *The Belgian Lancers* he lamented that the bravest men were too often those who died first. His poem *'Christian' Warfare* protested that while the religions of the Romans, Vikings and indigenous Americans might have authorised warfare, in the 'Christian age' fighting was done in the name of the God of love. In *The Price of Empire*, his complaint was about the human cost of maintaining that Empire, while in *The Wages of War*, Titterton portrayed Britannia calling people from the ends of the earth to 'give your lives to win the day.' In chapter 3, we noted Titterton's poem, *God of Battles*, as an unusually powerful and vehement repudiation of that title. It ended,

> Still the awful stream rolls onward,
> Still the heroes fall.
> Glory to the God of Battles,
> He is Lord of All.

As for indicators of faith in his somewhat rambling wartime reminiscences, Titterton wrote about a 'Salvation Army lass' in charge of the Salvation Army hut who had asked him if he 'knew Jesus'.[5] He had replied, 'No, and I don't expect to where I am going. It says in the book that a man can't serve two masters and I am sworn in to serve the Sergeant-Major. The Church of England hut was close by. It had 'the famous Woodbine Willie for attraction but he did not attract me.'[6] Titterton also visited the Roman Catholic hut for coffee and duty-free tobacco at bargain prices. On the question of faith and political leadership, he wrote, 'Of course I know that a lot of our great leaders have been religious men. I could quote you plenty of names for that and I have met some myself. But theirs was the religion of the Old Testament and that's where most of mine comes from.'[7] Unlike the 'parsons' whose prayers seemed like speeches to the congregation, he felt that in her prayers, the unidentified Salvation Army girl 'was talking to God, and in a quite confident way that God was listening to her. She was in contact with something that I had never experienced and through her as a medium some of it was searching out to me.'[8] Writing more than 50 years after the event, Titterton saw himself torn between his loyalty to his Sergeant-Major and the invitation to faith of the Salvation Army girl. Perhaps here was a joke based upon the traditionally ambiguous relationship between a Sergeant-Major and the men under him; we cannot be sure. Reflecting later on his survival in the conflict, he wondered, 'Perhaps after all the S.A. girl who interceded for me was listened to. The Book tells

5 DRO, D 4690/1/1/1 pp. 29-36 and DRO, D 4690/1/1/2 p. 49.
6 DRO, D 4690/1/1/1 p. 29.
7 Ibid., p. 35.
8 Ibid., p. 39.

us, "The prayer of the righteous availeth much" and she was a good girl'.[9] There is no evidence that he had been a church-goer before the war or had an active interest in religion, although in a conversation with a French priest and members of his congregation, 'when I said I was Anglican they would still ask if there was anything they could do for me.'[10] Later, he accepted a blessing from the priest, whom he respected, 'recognising him as a man after my own heart.'[11] While he frequented the Church of England and Roman Catholic huts in France, 'I never sampled their spiritual wares. The war had rocked men's religious beliefs and most of us were hard pagans and unbelievers.'[12]

The commune of Saulcourt in the northern part of the Somme is today the location of a small First World War cemetery, forming an extension to the much older church graveyard. Its ruined church was the subject of probably the only one of Titterton's poems written in France. In *A ruined church in the firing line (Saulcourt)* he used the destruction of the church as a metaphor for the destruction of faith caused by the war.

Stop brother; this is holy ground,
Tread soft as you go by;
The tumbled ruins all around
Were once uplifted high.
The faith which gave the word of peace,
That stood to banish fear,
The creed that taught us wars should cease;
Its shattered home is here.

As he had done previously, he contrasted the traditional teaching of the Church about peace with the reality of a conflict between Christian nations. In subsequent verses, he wrote of hearing the cannon's dreadful roar where the statue of the Virgin had stood, of gunners feeding the child of war, and of the strength of those who held firm to their faith that love would triumph over death. In the penultimate verse he returned again to the paradox of Churches that had traditionally opposed violence now supporting the conflict:

They preach the Christ whose dying breath
Pleaded for erring man.
They preach the Sword whose rule is death
Since first the world began.
To faith and love they make appeal,
And with the teaching mate

9 DRO, D 4690/1/1/2 p. 49.
10 DRO, D 4690/1/2/1 p. 8.
11 DRO, D 4690/1/2/1 p. 14.
12 DRO, D 4690/1/1/1 p. 30.

The godless creed of blood and steel,
The hard fierce law of hate.

Finally, Titterton offered a damning indictment of this perceived duplicity and, as he imagined himself departing with his comrade from the scene, he completed the metaphor:

And as we sow, so must we reap,
And as we give, so gain,
Though wolves disguise themselves as sheep,
Wolves shall they remain.
Come, brother, let us take our way,
Tread softly, have a care.
A broken church, I hear you say? –
A broken faith lies there.

What do Jack Titterton's poems reveal about the impact of the conflict on the belief of first a farmer in the Derbyshire Dales and then a gunner serving with the Royal Garrison Artillery? The context for that question is the stark reality that, as was noted in the Introduction, very few people in the war years appear to have recorded their reflections on the influence of the war on their faith. Titterton was unusual in his willingness to challenge the support of the Church for the conflict and to engage with issues like omnipotence and providence. The poem apparently written to his future wife in the opening months of the war, *To a Lady, Whose faith is not of the reasoning order*, suggests that Titterton might have been best described as a reluctant agnostic before August 1914. Indeed, his *Thoughts on the Balkan Crisis* would seem to confirm that conclusion with the couplet, 'Is there no Justice for this hoary world?/ No 'God' above to pity those beneath?' His fiercely-expressed writing had three main targets; first the nations engaging in the conflict, second the Church which was supposed to preach peace but rather proclaimed war, and third the God of War of the Christian nations which were engaged in the conflict. Whereas before August 1914, Jack Titterton had expressed his religious doubts as questions: 'Is there no Justice for this hoary world?' or 'O if there be a God of grace …Why stays he then upon His throne?', in his subsequent work there is not the ambiguity of the rhetorical question. In that one poem written in France, it may seem that we may have the autobiographical evidence that for this soldier of the Great War, the last traces of reluctant agnosticism had been replaced by atheism:

Come, brother, let us take our way,
Tread softly, have a care.
A broken church, I hear you say? –
A broken faith lies there.

So it may seem. And yet, in the Derbyshire archives, written in John Titterton's unmistakeable hand with a ball-point pen – thus dating the transcription if not necessarily the composition after World War 2 – is an untitled poem which concludes:

Oh do not from the task resign
Or think it all in vain.
Nor let your soul in grief repine
When life seems full of pain.

So let each help to share the load
And each one do their best
To keep along the narrow road,
And leave God with the rest.

So when we leave this mortal strife
And earthly troubles cease,
That we may share a fuller life
And find a richer peace.

Clearly, this is not a poem of particular literary merit or spiritual depth. Yet the contrast with the way in which, many years earlier, he had concluded his narrative poem about a broken church and a broken faith is self-evident. Together the two poems offer a corrective to any temptation simplistically to describe Jack Titterton as the gunner who forever lost his faith when faced by a ruined church in a village in the Somme.

James Lochhead Jack

James Lochhead Jack was born in 1880 and served in the South African War with the Argyll and Sutherland Highlanders and with the Scottish Horse. In the Great War, he served with the Scottish Rifles (Cameronians), the West Yorkshire Regiment and the 28th Infantry Brigade, gaining the DSO and bar.[13] He was a professional soldier, and very proud of that fact. During the Great War he kept secret notes in a tiny pocket book and when behind the line, on leave or in hospital he would write those notes up into a diary. After the war he produced two copies of four large foolscap volumes of typescript, integrating the original diary and readily-identifiable subsequent observations, comprising around 200,000 words, accompanied by maps, photographs and original documents. Jack retained one copy and gave the second to the regiments

13 J. Terraine (ed.) *General Jack's Diary* (London: Eyre & Spottiswoode, 1964) and (London: Cassell, 2000). Page references are to the 2000 edition; p. 5.

that he had served.[14] In 1964, soon after Jack's death, John Terraine published about a third of that material as 'General Jack's Diary'. In an epilogue to chapter III of the diary, Jack wrote of his feelings in August 1916 with unusual frankness and at considerable length:

> I was in poor spirits most of this time. The War – especially the Somme – the loss of friends and other matters, rudely shook one's Faith, and not enough responsible occupation as second-in command gave too much time to think about it. It did not seem possible that a gentleman could abandon, as fully as Providence appeared to have done, his servants to the cruelties of the world on the specious grounds that human agency must have a free hand.
>
> 'Except ye *believe in* (not *serve*) Me, ye shall in no wise enter My Kingdom' – a harsh threat, I thought, that no gentleman would utter to any servitor who … nevertheless carried out his duties to the best of his ability, maybe giving his life for them.
>
> Well, I laughed, if this is to be the reward of Service, however lacking the Faith, many will have scored over Providence by giving All, free, gratis and for little or nothing, for the honour, perhaps, of a grave on a battlefield.
>
> As is told in Chapter IV of my diaries, I went my way in Pride and Temper until in the course of years mental balance on this subject, temporarily upset by strain, had been restored.
>
> … My military successes have been, I believe, due mainly to 'luck' sent from Above.[15]

Given the nature of that 'epilogue', the surprising and disappointing conclusion after examining every chapter but one of the full diary is that except for that single entry, James Jack might be described as yet another of those 'silent witnesses' who were discussed in the opening chapter. In a brief pen-portrait included in the published diary, Major General R.C. Money, who had served with Jack both before and after the Great War, described him as being

14 Copies of chapters I, II, V, VI and VII were given to the Cameronians and are held in the regimental archives in the South Lanarkshire museum at Hamilton. A copy of chapter IV was given to the West Yorkshire Regiment and is held in its archives at the York Army Museum. Those are the copies consulted for this study. Only one copy of chapter III was produced and efforts to locate that copy have been unsuccessful.

15 Terraine, *General Jack's Diary*, p. 158. The passage which troubled Jack is not a verbatim quotation of any biblical verse. It may be a paraphrase of Mark 10:15, Matt. 18:3 or Luke 18:7, in which the demand of Jesus is that his hearers 'receive the Kingdom of God', a phrase which does not make the distinction between belief and service which Jack found problematic.

> intensely reserved, inhibited perhaps by shyness. Never once did I hear him mention home, father, mother or relatives. His private world he protected by enacting the parts of his two heroes, the Duke of Wellington and Brigadier Gérard …[16]

Sidney Rogerson, who served under Jack in 1916-17 and was a life-long friend, observed that he 'was peculiarly averse from [sic] showing his feelings, or from admitting any but a few well-tried friends behind the veil which reticence hung before him.'[17] Moreover, as Terraine noted in his introduction, the whole language of combat, with its formal reports and regulated procedures, with men 'proceeding' rather than 'going' and 'assisting' rather than 'helping' creates a 'stiff strait-jacket for emotion and passion'.[18] Clearly, it also curtailed reflection, religious or otherwise, on his own experiences. Just occasionally, it would appear, did he allow that veil of reticence to drop.

We are left, therefore, with a series of brief diary entries, sometimes little more than asides, to place alongside that epilogue in an attempt to understand Jack's attitude to faith during the conflict. On 17 October 1914, while billeted in Sailly-sur-Lys in northern France, he wrote, 'Today I attended church parade – as an example to those whose Faith is still intact. Besides, the practice helps to screw up one's sense of duty.'[19] As it was for Jack Titterton, 'duty' was critically important. For Titterton, there had been a tension between the call of two 'masters'; duty to his Sergeant-Major and duty to Jesus mediated through the Salvation Army girl. Similarly, in his epilogue, James Jack had written of God as a 'gentleman' who had apparently 'abandoned … his servants to the cruelties of the world.' Such personification of God helped both men to frame questions of faith in terms of army life or social behaviour.

On Christmas Day 1914, Jack briefly mused on the paradox of a war fought in the name of the Prince of Peace: 'So passes the first Christmas of the War, far away from the original "Peace and Goodwill to all men" – or is the true message "I came not to bring peace, but a sword"?'[20] A year later, he again highlighted the issue: 'I could not help smiling at the thought of all the Christian peoples at war beseeching the Almighty at this season of goodwill to see to the triumph of their cause – the cause of Right, of course – and to deliver up to them their bloodguilty enemies.'[21] Jack was generally protective of the duty to attend church parades as part of the discipline of the Army. He offered this comment in January 1917: 'We are lenient in excusing men from it – for a sufficient reason. But field-punishment men, defaulters and marked

16 Ibid., p. 16. Gérard was the brave soldier hero of some short stories by Arthur Conan Doyle first published in the *Strand Magazine* 1894–1903.
17 Ibid., p. 14.
18 Ibid., p. 6.
19 Ibid., p. 116.
20 Matthew 10:34.
21 Diary entry, 2 January 1916, Terraine, *General Jack's Diary*, p. 123.

men must always attend, smart and soldierly, to gain Grace.'[22] On another occasion, he lamented the poor attendance of the West Yorkshires at a voluntary parade conducted by a senior chaplain: 'Fortunately, the Cameronians, whose parade is always compulsory, save the situation.'[23] Moreover, Jack was proud that the Cameronians held their parades

> fully armed, according to the two-and-a-quarter-century tradition of the 1st Cameronians. This practice is based on that of our Covenanting forebears who, prior to forming our regiment in 1689, were forced to hold their services on the moors ready to fight the dragoons of Claverhouse.[24]

The historical reference is to the battles between the Episcopalian John Graham of Claverhouse (1648-89) and the Presbyterian Covenanters when he was appointed by Charles II to suppress the Covenanters' outdoor meetings – hence Jack's reference to them worshipping 'fully armed'.[25] Jack, as well as demonstrating his Biblical knowledge, also showed his familiarity with the language of hymnody in his diary entries. In that for 16 August 1917, he noted the losses of the West Yorkshires in the Battle of Langemarck.[26] Of the ten officers who went 'over the top', not one returned and nine were killed, as were 264 other ranks.[27] He wrote, 'So, to my infinite sorrow nearly all my dear West Yorkshire friends were swept away. "How bright their Glorious Spirits shine."'[28] The reference was to the hymn with that first line, written by Isaac Watts, which affirms the Christian hope of eternal life and is a paraphrase of Revelation 7:13-17. A period of sick leave in Spring 1918 was spent in Scotland and London.

> On Sundays in Renfrewshire I always attended Divine Worship, either in the Coat's Memorial Church, built by the family of my hostess, or in Paisley Abbey with my brother. In London the soldierly service in the Guards' Chapel, Wellington Barracks, attracted me most.[29]

Yet, as we noted, in France at the beginning of the conflict, he had attended a church parade, 'as an example to those whose Faith is still intact.' Whether that should that

22 *Diary*, chapter IV, p 37.
23 Ibid., p. 74.
24 *Diary*, 13 January 1915, chapter II, p. 61.
25 This is a hugely-contested period of Scottish history, with competing perspectives offered by defenders of the Jacobites and Covenanters. An account of one encounter is given in D. Love, *Scottish Covenanter Stories: Tales from the Killing Times* (Glasgow: Neil Wilson, 2013), ch. 13.
26 The Battle of Langemarck was part of the third Ypres offensive, commonly referred to as 'Passchendaele'.
27 Terraine, *General Jack's Diary*, p. 240.
28 *Diary*, chapter IV, p. 89.
29 *Diary*, chapter V, p. 1.

be read as meaning 'to those, like me, whose Faith is still intact', or 'to those, unlike me …' we cannot know. A tentative solution to the question may be indicated by a later comment on the war. Recounting the last battle of Ypres in September 1918, Jack recorded watching the 'wounded trickle back along the Menin Road … It always makes me sick to see so many fine fellows mangled and bloody from this God-forsaken War.'[30] Unlike some other writers, Jack was not in the habit of making colloquial references to God. As Terraine observed, his phraseology was usually precise and at times formulaic. Perhaps, therefore, his 'God-forsaken' epithet should be understood more literally than when used by others? Perhaps for Jack, God was inextricably associated with the Britain for which he was proud to fight and in which he 'always attended Divine Worship'. Yet all those 'fine fellows mangled' and the massive scale of suffering proved to Jack that God had indeed forsaken the fields of battle. Consequently, while regular Sunday worship was right in Renfrewshire or London, it seemed pointless, other than as a matter of discipline or duty, in 'God-forsaken' northern France. Jack's 'default' religious practice was 'soldierly' worship in Britain, where God's existence was a given and both his own long-established habit and the tradition of his regiment affirmed such practices and attitudes. However, those periods at the Western Front – especially in 1916 – and all that they had involved had caused a temporary deviation from that norm. In the brief expressions of belief and emotion in the diary of a very private officer we have a glimpse of one man's struggle to reconcile belief in a loving God with the horrors that surrounded him. The inconclusive nature of those glimpses may well be indicative of the reality of James Jack's struggle with faith.

Thomas Higgins

Thomas Higgins was a Lance Corporal (the lowest rank of NCO) in the 1/5th North Staffordshire Regiment of the Territorial Force, with which he served on the Western Front from March 1916 until 1 July 1917, when he was taken as a prisoner of war.[31] His diary is quite different from those of Jack Titterton and James Jack. There are none of the classical or Biblical references of the former and it is no more than a tenth of the size of the latter. The style is colloquial and the vocabulary limited. However, unlike the majority of diaries written during the conflict, it offers the perspective of an ordinary, uneducated soldier. It appears to have been written in 1926, although it was not published until 2005. The opening sentences declared, 'Taken from a diary I kept from 1914-19. What I have written here is true.'[32]

30 Terraine, *General Jack's Diary*, p. 272.

31 T.J. Higgins, *Tommy at Gommecourt* (Leek: Churnet Valley Books, 2005) He enlisted into the 3/5th N. Staffs, but when at the end of 1915, the 1/5th N. Staffs. had been 'smashed up in an attack at Hulloch' the 3/5th N. Staffs. made their numbers up again (p. 12).

32 Ibid., p. 2.

Higgins' first page sets the scene. He was working at the Etruria Steel works in Stoke-on-Trent – to which he returned after the conflict – when war broke out. Everyone, he said, was mad, and men were enlisting in large numbers. Higgins himself 'caught the fever'.[33] Having been 'brought up in the Church', a phrase on which he did not elaborate, Higgins reported without further comment his regular attendances at church parades while billeted at Long Eaton.[34] One early episode, the account of an assembly of companies ready to march off to Stafford having said goodbye to wives and girlfriends, typified the widespread practice noted in the Introduction, of soldiers singing verses of doggerel to well-known hymn tunes:

> What a splendid day it was. While we were forming up to start from Stoke, the chaps were singing this:
> Only one more kit inspection
> Only one more church parade
> Only one more marching order
> Then we'll all go home again…

This was sung to the tune of *What a friend we have in Jesus*.[35] Thomas Higgins also typified combatants' near-universal fatalism as he remembered the crossing to France on 29 March 1916: 'As I stood on deck, and watched the lights of Southampton fade, I took my last look at Old England … I thought of home, my wife and son, and when, if I ever should, see the loved faces again. We all knew that some of us would never see our homes again. But fate will be.'[36] Later, he noted finding a silver crucifix in a ruined house: 'I carried this with me till I got home again.'[37] In such expressions and practices he was, of course, one among millions. In May 1916, his battalion took over the front line trench and very soon came under heavy fire.

> Then the bombardment stopped as suddenly as it had began. The day was just breaking, everything seem so still after the fierce tumult. Then the birds began to sing as they greeted the new day, and it made me think of that ages old saying 'Peace on Earth and Goodwill towards Men.' There were many men killed that night.[38]

It is not evident whether Higgins knew the source of that 'saying.' Quite possibly it was one of many such mottoes and proverbs inculcated into him in childhood which together had helped to form an ethical structure and set of ideals. One particular

33 Ibid., p. 3.
34 Ibid., pp. 45 and 14.
35 Ibid., p. 7.
36 Ibid., p. 17.
37 Ibid., p. 56.
38 Ibid., p. 27.

event dominated Tommy Higgins' account of his service as a soldier, the first day of the Battle of the Somme.

> On the evening of June 30th we fell in to march up to Foncquevillers.[39] The Colonel, Lieut-Col Burnett, made a short speech before we started. 'Well Boys', he said, 'By sunrise tomorrow I hope to see you on the other side of Gommecourt Wood.' By that time or soon after he was dead. Then the whole Battalion started to sing that well-known hymn, 'God be with you till we meet again'. I have never heard that hymn sung with so much meaning as it was sung that evening, by men who were going to face death in all its most terrible forms. Whenever I hear that song now I think of that scene. The setting sun, the men with heads bowed thinking of those so dear to them. Many who sang that night, in a few short hours their voices were stilled for ever.[40]

Higgins' account of 1 July runs to several pages and the narrative does not spare the reader. Having gone over the top, he was knocked out but not seriously injured by a fragment of a shell, leaving him stranded in No Man's Land. 'The smell of blood and dead bodies was sickening. I mentally said goodbye to those I loved, as I did not seem to have a ghost of a chance of living though that day.'[41] In the event, he records being one of around 150 survivors from his battalion, and one of only two in his platoon who had gone over the top and not been killed.[42] After the account of the eve of the Battle of the Somme, Tommy Higgins made no further references to faith, luck, fatalism or religious practice. However, later that month, he offered an insight into the work of Studdert Kennedy, the chaplain whose appearance in a Church of England hut had failed to attract Jack Titterton. Higgins' comment offers a corrective to some scholars' inferences that Studdert Kennedy was too much of a showman to be an effective chaplain:

> July 1916. While in this sector of the trenches I made the acquaintance of the finest parson I ever knew. It was the Rev. Studdert Kennedy, or Woodbine Willy [sic] as the boys called him. He was Chaplain to our Brigade for about 3 months. He was the only Chaplain I ever saw in the trenches. He was in them at all times

39 His battalion formed part of the 137th (Staffordshire) Brigade in the 46th (North Midland) Division. With the 56th London Division they took part in a diversionary attack at Gommecourt, intended to draw German fire away from the main Somme attack.
40 Higgins, *Tommy*, p. 36.
41 Ibid., p. 39.
42 I am grateful to Rodney Atwood for pointing out that in Middlebrook, *First Day on the Somme*, pp. 330f, the 1/5th North Staffs. are not recorded as a battalion with over 500 casualties on 1 July 1916. However, Middlebrook noted that he had taken the lowest estimates from various sources in compiling his list.

> of day or whether Fritz was shelling or not ... I think Woodbine Willy was one of the best.[43]

Studdert Kennedy invited Higgins to be confirmed and a few weeks later the Bishop of Khartoum, the Deputy Chaplain-General Llewellyn Gwynne, confirmed him 'along with a lot more men'. A couple of months later, Higgins recorded a concert in a schoolroom at which Studdert Kennedy sang 'Mother Machree'.[44] Captured in Lens precisely one year after the first day of the Battle of the Somme, Higgins' war was over as far as active participation was concerned. The remainder of his diary recounts a grim existence as a prisoner of war for 16 months, arriving home on 30th December 1918. After two months' POW leave, and one more night in the barracks at Lichfield, 'So ended my life as a soldier in the British Army in the Great War.'[45]

Then in Higgins' manuscript came a number of appendices that are as telling as the narrative of his service. First a poem: 'God and soldiers men adore / In times of War, but not before / When War is over, and things are righted / God is forgotten and Soldiers are slighted.'[46] This is one of many variants of an epigram attributed to Francis Quarles (1592-1644).[47] Undoubtedly, Higgins' concern was more about the 'slighting' of soldiers than the 'forgetting' of God, for under the poem and a heading, '1914' were printed without attribution the words of a promise from that year, 'Your King and Country need you. Go and fight for your Country. You will be looked after when you come back. We shall never see you want.' Then, under a second heading, '1919 to 1926 – Forgotten', Higgins inveighed against the post-war treatment of ex-soldiers, concluding, 'It makes you wonder who have come off best. Those who pulled through, or those who went west.'[48] A selection of 'Songs of the Trenches' followed, with the comment,

> The gem of the lot was the song we sung on the Somme in 1916, as we marched to that inferno, so many of us never came back:
> The bells of hell go ting-a-ling
> For you, but not for me;
> For me the angels sing-a-ling;
> They've got the goods for me,
> Oh, death! Where is thy sting-a-ling?
> Oh, grave! Thy victory?
> The bells of hell go ting-a-ling
> For you but not for me.

43 Higgins, *Tommy*, p. 45.
44 Ibid., p. 47.
45 Ibid., p. 118.
46 Ibid., p. 119.
47 *Oxford Dictionary of Quotations*, 2nd Edn. (London: OUP, 1953), p. 404.
48 Higgins, *Tommy*, p. 119.

This song, a parody of a popular song of the time and an amalgam of a Biblical quotation (St. Paul on the resurrection from 1 Corinthians) and black fatalistic humour, appears in many diaries and memoirs of the conflict.[49] Then, on 1 July 1926, Higgins had added this to his diary:

> July 1st 1916, ten years ago, or to be exact the evening of the 30th June. The 5th North Staff[ord]s were at a place called Humbercamps, about three miles from the firing line. We were to march to Foncquevillers, where we held the front, to make an attack on the Germans who held the wood and the village of Gommecourt in front. It was a beautiful evening and the Battalion stood on parade on a field, the sun was setting in a sea of red and gold. It was a scene I shall see in my memory if I live to be a very old man; and I've tried to convey it in a few verses how affected me; and affects me still whenever I hear that hymn sung even now. 'God be with you 'til we meet again'. … I regard that as a tribute to my comrades who died that day for old England.
>
> The years roll on, as life passes by,
> But leave memories, that will not die.
> Until I go, as all men must,
> Beyond this vale is dust to dust…
>
> And then there fell a silence
> Upon the evening air.
> It seemed as though, eight hundred men
> Were deep in silent prayer…
>
> Then once again was the silence broke,
> As they sang a sweet refrain,
> The hymn they sang; with heart and voice,
> Was 'Til we meet again…
>
> Many of those who sang that song,
> 'Ere another day was done,
> Had crossed into the 'Great Beyond',
> Their course on earth was run…

The poem ran to a total of 11 verses. Higgins had returned to that event which had been for him the defining day of the Great War – as it had been, indeed, for many thousands of others. And yet, rather than dwelling on the carnage of 1 July, he wished to recall the communal hymn-singing of the evening before the battle. The picture that

49 For example, J.C. Dunn, *The War the Infantry Knew* (London: Jane's, 1987), pp. 426f.

he painted of contemplative preparation was entirely consistent with the account from the *Nottingham Evening Post* of a padre leading prayers for the Sherwood Foresters on that same evening which was quoted in Chapter 3. Clearly, the final version of his narrative of 30 June 1916 was written with the benefit of hindsight of the succeeding four and half months of the battle of the Somme, in which around 300,000 men died and well over twice that number were injured. We cannot know now how many men on 30 June 1916 who were 'going to face death in all its most terrible forms' had a sense of what awaited them and Higgins' recollection of that evening could not but be influenced by subsequent events. However, that extended narrative and its recollection a decade later were surely Higgins' way of expressing his hope in the 'Great Beyond', where those who had fallen would meet again – 'at Jesus' feet' as the chorus of 'God be with you till we meet again' puts it.

Ernest Goodridge

Corporal Ernest Goodridge was born in 1892, the son of a Wesleyan Methodist class leader (responsible for the pastoral and spiritual well-being of his 'class' of church members) and a similarly devout and religiously-committed mother.[50] His brother, John, was a Wesleyan minister and the whole family's life revolved around the worship, meetings and activities of Bentley Wesleyan Church, near Doncaster in what was then the West Riding of Yorkshire.[51] On 5 November 1915 he wrote to a friend that 'the greater call had come [to enlist]', asserting that 'we are men of freedom & liberty for which our fathers have shed their life's blood' and commenting that the effect on his parents 'is only the sacrifice which thousands of homes have made.'[52] He enlisted in the Kings Royal Rifle Corps (KRRC) at Leeds a fortnight later. The next few months were spent in training in England before he arrived with the 18th Battalion KRRC in Le Havre on 3 May 1916.[53] On 4 June, Goodridge wrote a long letter to his parents, painting an almost bucolic picture of life in camp, admittedly well behind the lines. 'The cuckoo sings here as well as in England ... God is indeed very kind to us & makes up much that we miss.' He wrote of the fun and excitement of washing day with 100 men passing through the wash-house every half-hour: 'The whole system of this camp is wonderful & the organisation perfect.'[54] Such a positive narrative may perhaps be attributed to a natural optimism, the extensively-documented practice of combatants seeking to reassure and comfort their families to whom they wrote, and the safe location of the camp near Étaples. While at the camp, Goodridge copied a poem into his diary, the concluding stanza of which read,

50 Ernest Goodridge's war diary and letters were published in E.N. & J.A. Goodridge (eds.), *The Same Stars Shine* (Loughborough: Teamprint, 2000).
51 Goodridge (ed.), *Why am I in Paradise: the 'Great War' Diaries of J.B. Goodridge*.
52 E.N. & J.A. Goodridge (eds.) *The Same Stars Shine*, p. 55.
53 Ibid., p. 66,
54 Ibid., pp. 91-3.

On guard or march, O Prince of Peace
My martial steps keep time;
And grant that I may answer, 'Here'
At roll-call & review.
Be thou my Captain and my Guide
And in the conflict shield
Dismiss me to the Warrior rest
On heaven's white tented field.[55]

On 11 June, Ernest wrote a sealed letter, accompanied by another in which he explained his intention

> to make some expression of my wishes as to some of my personal belongings should it be my Master's will to call me to the Higher Service. In doing this I am sure you will not construe it as a lack of faith on my part as to God's Kindness and power to bring me back again safely if it is His Will because I believe with all my heart that He is too wise to err & too good to be unkind.[56]

The long letter continued in a similar vein, wondering if God would spare him 'for further service in His vineyard', reporting on a memorial service for Kitchener and of singing the final hymn 'with such a mixture of glorious manhood drawn from every corner of the globe.' Goodridge attributed the occasional tear when singing familiar hymns to a recognition of God's presence and when he resumed writing on the following day, reported the number of Christian meetings offered, 'with after-Meetings for decision every night', assuring his family that 'God is doing a great work here.' In the sealed letter, being written because he had volunteered to join up immediately with his original battalion, the 18th, he urged his parents to, 'Say "Thy will be done" and mean it.' Only the sacrifice which thousands of others have made would further Christ's kingdom upon Earth. After further personal greetings, he quoted again the first verse of the poem that he had copied into his diary:

Beyond this mortal strife I view
Those white tents stretched away;
No bugler-calls, or war's alarms,
Or muster for the fray;
The wearied soldier dreams again

55 Ibid., p. 88. The poem had been printed in the *Brooklyn Daily Eagle* (New York) on 9 April 1905 (p. 34) above the name of John B. Ketchum. A man of that name fought in the American Civil War and the poem could well date from that conflict, but it has not been possible to confirm its provenance.
56 Ibid., pp. 93-6.

The night's dark work is done,
Guard-mount, relief & sentry gone
Life's battles fought and won.

The letter closed with the instructions for the distribution of his possessions. However, on the following day, Goodridge appended a further note, expanding on his thought and faith. Human love, he wrote, was deep and strong, but could not be compared to God's love, for He alone had placed that love in human hearts. 'He alone is the giver of every good & perfect gift '& if our fellowship below in Jesus be so sweet what heights of rapture shall we know when round his throne we meet.'[57] Any separation caused by his death would only be for a short time. 'Don't waste time with useless mourning but commemorate my translation by renewed consecration. Every virtue I possess & every victory won & every thought of holiness are His alone. Yours lovingly, Ernest.'[58] Whereas his letters were long and discursive, Goodridge's diary entries were usually brief and to the point. For example, 'Mon 12 June. Stiff day on Bull Ring. At Soldiers Christian Association finishing Will & letter home & posted same.'[59]

On 14 June, he was part of a group that was sent to reinforce the battalion on the Ploegsteert front. From 18 to 20 June he wrote another long letter to his family 'from a delightful wood just behind the firing line'. 'Nature is praising God here just the same', he assured his family. A less encouraging note was struck with an account of the Church bell ringing on the previous Sunday evening to warn of a gas attack. He had survived his first 'baptism of fire' – a bombardment from the Germans. 'Naturally I felt a bit windy at first but one gets over this in the company of comrades.' In his diary he reported a visit to a service at the Catholic church in the village; 'very weird but a very reverent business – it did me good though I could not understand it.'[60] Later that month, in a letter to his parents he expressed his joy that he had found himself 'kipping' in the same dugout with two good friends: 'isn't it fine? It is nothing short of Providence the way we have been brought together again.'[61] He reported that when strengthening the trenches at night, 'like Nehemiah we have to carry our Rifle in one

57 He was quoting a line from the hymn, 'All praise to our redeeming Lord' written by Charles Wesley. His letters were full of lines from hymns, some explicitly identified but others forming part of his narrative and comments. The editors listed 33 different hymns and 29 scripture passages referenced by Goodridge.

58 Ibid., pp. 96-8.

59 Ibid., p. 99. The 'Bull Ring' was the parade ground at the Étaples camp. The Soldiers' Christian Association was an auxiliary of the YMCA, formed in 1886. Members were required to accept a comprehensive basis of faith and to have confessed Christ to their comrades for a minimum of three months. See G.J. Byrnell, 'The Soldiers' Christian Association' in *R.A.Ch.D. Quarterly Journal*, Vol. 2, No. 15, (July 1925), pp. 99-102.

60 Ibid., pp. 101-3.

61 Ibid., p. 104. The editors drew attention to the widespread 'imaginative significance' attached to threesomes and the number 3 by soldiers. However, it is arguable whether Goodridge was doing so in this letter.

hand and our spade or pick in the other.' No doubt his parents were familiar with Nehemiah 4:18, 'For the builders, every one had his sword girded by his side, and so builded.' (AV)[62] He continued, 'it is exciting at first to have the bullets whistling over one' and he again thanked 'God's good providence' that he was with his friends. 'God is very good to us and makes our hearts glad many a time by his near presence.'[63] Reflecting in early July on a rough time in the trenches, he assured his family that nothing could harm him 'unless it be our Heavenly Father's Will and such experiences are after all mere tests of faith and character.'[64] Two weeks later, he reported on machine gun bullets cutting the grass above his head and reassured his family 'that having found the secret of life, no harm can befall me except sin … 'The joy of the Lord is with them that fear Him.' Love – Ernest.'[65] A short letter to his parents at the end of July lamented the problem of mosquitoes while another to his brother John reported the sound of 'that true soldier's hymn "onward Christian soldiers" coming from a Church of England parade service in a nearby hut' and assured him that 'I go forward strong in the assurance that "Jesus shall reign where're the Sun doth His successive journeys run."'[66] A letter to a family friend expressed the same assurance, while a diary entry affirmed a new chaplain who had given them each soap and Woodbines.[67] Although the letters written to Goodridge have not survived, in a letter to his parents of 2 August, affirmations of the faith of both his mother and father indicate that his confident expressions of providence and hope were shared by them.[68] Throughout the summer, he wrote at length whenever he was behind the lines. Meanwhile, the Diary entries became a little more detailed. On Sunday 27 August he recorded, 'My consecration this morning is if God in his mercy spares me I will go softly all my days 'One thing have I desired of the Lord that I will seek after &c.' Nevertheless thy will not mine.'[69]

A few days later, the 18th KRRC was involved in the Battle of Flers, involving the first full-scale use of tanks. The Battalion lost 309 men – almost a third of its strength – by 16 September. On that day, Goodridge's diary simply noted, 'Stragglers came in all day.' On 18 September, the battalion was relieved by one from the West Yorks, Goodridge commenting, 'Battalion joined up jiggered.'[70] Two days later he wrote to his family after the severest test that that Battalion had yet faced, expressing

62 Authorised Version
63 Ibid., p. 106.
64 Ibid., p. 108.
65 Ibid., p. 113. The quotation is a translation of Psalm 147:11.
66 Ibid., p. 116. The quotation is the first two lines of a hymn by Isaac Watts, the rest of the verse reading, 'His kingdom stretch from shore to shore, / till moons shall wax and wane no more.'
67 Ibid., p. 117.
68 Ibid., p. 118.
69 The quotation is of Psalm 27:4. Ibid., p. 131.
70 Ibid., pp. 140f.

his disappointment that having trained, slept, eaten and drunk with comrades, he had not been 'with them in the hour of their fiercest trial and would never see them again 'this side [of the] Jordan'.' A letter to John reaffirmed Ernest's faith in 'God's direct guidance in it all, but it is awfully hard to miss the cheery faces of comrades who we had learned to love.'[71] On 24 September, he wrote again, telling of a memorial service for those who had fallen on the 15th and 16th. 'never', he wrote, 'have the fine & wonderful words of the burial service had deeper meaning for me.' At both services, *For all the Saints* had been sung. 'The experiences of the past week have taught us to sing that Hymn in a way to make every line live in our memory.'[72] It is notable, although perhaps not surprising, that notwithstanding his explicitly evangelical faith, he was willing to affirm as 'saints' all those who had died, and declare that for each of them had broken a 'yet more glorious day'. On 3 October 1916, Goodridge wrote to his family as he prepared to go up to the front line again.

> If the business is as we anticipate there are sure to be some of us go west & not being as sure as dear Pa as to what may be God's Will concerning me, I thought I would take this opportunity to open up my heart … I shall always thank God both in time and in eternity for the dear friends who I have met during training particularly …

There followed a list of people, complete with their postal addresses so that they could be contacted, the request being unequivocal: 'Please let them know that I have been called to Higher Service.' After further affirmations of his faith and an expression of concern about how his father might react to Ernest's death, he closed,

> If it be possible think of me as a Guardian spirit watching over you all & beckoning to Higher Heights of Christian experience until that happy day when we shall all be able to sing 'Safe Home Safe Home in Port'.[73] Yours until the dawn shall break & the shadows flee away. With Eternal Love Ernest.[74]

On the following day, the 18th Battalion diary reported the repelling of an early morning bombing raid, in which the enemy was 'easily driven back.' It was probably in that relatively small skirmish that Ernest Goodridge died. It was nine days before his body could be retrieved from the battlefield and buried, although his grave, like so many, was subsequently lost.[75]

71 Ibid., pp. 142f.
72 Ibid., p. 144.
73 A hymn written by John Mason Neale, first published in 1862 and included in the 1904 *(Wesleyan) Methodist Hymnbook* (at 835, not 805 as given by Goodridge's editors).
74 Ibid., pp. 147-9.
75 Ibid., p. 151.

Arthur Graeme West

It could be argued that in a chapter on individual combatants' 'faith at the front' it is illogical to include Arthur Graeme West. Born the son of a retired missionary (described by West's modern editor as being 'of typical narrow and unbending religiosity'), West appears to have lost his faith before August 1914.[76] However, in this discussion of five representative if not necessarily typical soldiers, the writing of West offers the perspective of one who rather than possessing faith saw in his experiences so much to confirm his atheism. If Ernest Goodridge represented one end of a spectrum of faith at the front, then West represented the other. Neither would have convinced the other, but both voices need to be heard and considered if this small sample is to be at all representative.

Arthur Graeme West was born in 1891 and went up to Oxford to read Classics in 1910. Having been a member of the Oxford Officers' Training Corps, he made repeated efforts to enlist, despite his poor eyesight. West succeeded in February 1915, enlisting with the rank of Lance Corporal, and he arrived in France in 1916. In March, West returned to Scotland to train to be an officer and on 20 May wrote in his diary of the men on his course: 'They go to church, a lot of them, on Sundays, partly, I think, because they like the service out of religious sentimentality, partly out of custom, partly to feel themselves a part of normal civilisation again, partly to get off with a choir-girl.'[77]

Clearly, in his account there were resonances with the James Jack's different practices in Britain and France. Towards the end of that month, West described himself as getting 'more perfectly to the state of Stoicism to which I aspire.' However, a few lines later, he wondered if he were approaching a state of Nihilism rather than of Stoicism, 'I sometimes think that nothing is good or has any permanent value whatsoever.'[78] In the same note under the heading 'Ethical Creed', West wrote,

> … and most of all, now, I reject the presumption that I worship a God by Whose never-wronging hand I conceive all the present woe to have been brought upon the now-living generation of mankind. If there is a God at all responsible for governing the earth, I hate and abominate Him – I rather despise Him. But I do not think there is one. We only fall into the habit of calling down curses on a god whom we believe not to exist, because the constant references to his beneficence are so maddening that anger stings us to a retort that is really illogical.

76 A.G. West, with introduction by N. Jones, *Diary of a Dead Officer, Being the Posthumous Papers of Arthur Graeme West* (London: Greenhill Books, 2007). (First published in 1919 with an introduction by C.E.M. Joad.), pp. 10f.

77 Ibid., p. 51. (All page references are to the 2007 publication.)

78 Ibid., p. 71.

In August came a period of leave prior to taking up his commission. In the 1917 edition, the editor C.E.M. Joad described that as a time in which West's 'beliefs in general and his attitude to the war in particular underwent a profound change.' However, as far as his religious belief was concerned, it appears to have been a time of what might better be termed a consolidation of his previous thoughts. He described himself as 'disbelieving utterly' in both Christianity and Christ as an actual figure. So violent was his reaction to the conventional religion that once bound him '– or if it did not bind me, at any rate loomed behind me –' that he 'loathed and scorned' all emotionalism and religious feeling.[79] The reference to religion looming behind him would seem to confirm Jones' assessment that West had lost his faith before the start of the war if, indeed, he ever had a conventional faith. The equating of emotionalism and religious feeling was to some extent explained a little later when he referred to an argument with two friends in which he had favoured science and abstract truth while they had been 'in favour of emotion, denying advance of knowledge and running down science itself as a work of the devil.'[80] It was a time of liberation for him, but also a time of crisis as he wrote a letter intended for his commanding officer, renouncing the war and his own involvement in it. Under circumstances that are not entirely clear, the letter was not sent.

Consequently, September 1916 saw West return to France as an officer. In a period typical of the standard pattern of fighting units rotating between front line duties and periods of recuperation behind the line, there was little opportunity for him to record his thoughts at any length. One diary entry reported him discussing 'ever so slightly' the problems of atheism.[81] A few days earlier he had declared his atheism; now he said that he was a 'respectable atheist.' In the face of objections that there could be no such thing, West wrote,

> Thus we see how men cannot get out of their minds 'the horrid atheist' idea – the idea that intellectual convictions of this sort must of necessity imply some fearful moral laxity. The most religious men are really the extreme Christians or mystics, and the atheists ~ nobody can understand this. These two classes have really occupied their minds with religion.

His last dated diary entry was made on 3 November 1916. West was killed by a sniper early in the morning of 3 April 1917 and was buried near where he fell.[82] Published with his diary in 1917 were ten poems. His original editor, C.E.M Joad, drew attention in his introduction to West's love of literature and poetry, and there is clearly a literary quality to West's own poems which places them above the often somewhat

79 Ibid., p. 93.
80 Ibid., p. 14.
81 Ibid., p. 134.
82 Ibid., pp. 14f.

formulaic and routine 'trench poetry' which abounded during the conflict. Several of the poems addressed the issues of belief and the nature of God to which he had made passing reference in his diary entries. In his poem 'God! How I hate you, you young cheerful men', West offered a blistering attack on the work of the soldier-poet H. Rex Freston, quoting the whole of his poem 'To the Atheists' before offering his response. Freston, who was killed in action in France in January 1916, had written:

> I KNOW that God will never let me die.
> He is too passionate and intense for that.
> See how He swings His great suns through the sky,
> See how He hammers the proud-faced mountains flat.
> He takes a handful of a million years
> And hurls them at the planets ; or he throws
> His red stars at the moon : then with hot tears
> He stoops to kiss one little earthborn rose.
>
> Don't nail God down to rules, and think you know!
> Or God, Who sorrows all a summer's day
> Because a blade of grass has died, will come
> And suck this world up in His lips, and lo!
> Will spit it out a pebble, powdered grey,
> Into the whirl of Infinity's nothingless foam.[83]

While Joad described West as harshly criticising Freston's 'patriotic' poems, 'To the Atheists' might better be described as 'pious.' Some of Freston's work, such as 'Lines written upon a statue of Nelson which stands on the high hills overlooking Portsmouth Harbour' certainly was typical of the strident patriotism that West hated, but in poems like 'To the Atheists', the patriotism is, at most, implicit.[84] It was, rather, Freston's expression of faith that elicited this response from West:

> God! How I hate you, you young cheerful men,
> Whose pious poetry blossoms on your graves
> As soon as you are in them, nurtured up
> By the salt of your corruption and the tears
> Of mothers, local vicars, college deans,
> And flanked by prefaces and photographs
> From all your minor poet friends – the fools –
> Who paint their sentimental elegies

83 H.R. Freston, 'To the Atheists' in *The Quest of Truth and Other Poems* (Oxford: Blackwell, 1916), p. 60.
84 Ibid., pp. 27f.

Where sure, no angel treads; and, living, share
The dead's brief immortality.[85]

After his critique of the genre of posthumous poetry anthologies of which Freston's was a classic example, West turned his attention to the contradiction which he saw between the brutal reality of war and the affirmations of divine love which he read and heard:

... his head
Smashed like an egg-shell, and the warm grey brain
Spattered all bloody on the parados:
Had flashed a torch on his face, and known his friend,
Shot, breathing hardly, in ten minutes—gone!
Yet till God's in His heaven, all is right
In the best possible of worlds. The woe,
Even His scaled eyes must see, is partial, only
A seeming woe, we cannot understand.
God loves us, God looks down on this our strife
And smiles in pity, blows a pipe at times
And calls some warriors home.
We do not die, God would not let us, He is too 'intense',
Too 'passionate', a whole day sorrows He
Because a grass-blade dies ...[86]

The poem ended with this critique of the idea, widely promoted, that the excitement and challenge of the war made it a good time to be alive, and that 'God Himself does seem to walk / The bloody fields of Flanders he so loves!' While West's lack of faith and his rejection of the false comfort which he believed it to offer was just one of several themes in the ten poems in his papers, it was a recurring theme. In 'The End of the Second Year' West wrote in response to a letter affirming that events like the Battle of Jutland were 'history in the making' and therefore worthwhile. He rejected the idea that somehow the battles of the war were part of God's plan and a movement 'toward some supreme perfection', writing autobiographically, 'He lifts his startled face, and finds the Throne / Empty, and turns away, too drunk with Truth / To mind the shame, or feel the loss of God.'[87] In 'The Last God', West declared, 'All Gods are dead, even the great God Pan / is dead at length; the lone inhabitant / of my ever dwindling Pantheon.'[88] The poem 'Spurned by the Gods' portrayed someone climbing with

85 West, *Diary of a Dead Officer*, p. 148.
86 Ibid., p. 149.
87 Ibid., p. 150.
88 Ibid., p. 160.

great difficulty a mountain, seeking to find an un-identified God and then encountering 'The mighty shouts of Gods at festival.'[89] The narrator knelt, offering his life to the God, 'o'er powered by the trembling ecstasy / Of deity's completest immanence.'

> I offered thee myself, my loveliness,
> I kept it all for thee, I was not timid,
> Not coy before the King of Gods — and thou,
> Thou drab uxorious tyrant, sate at feast,
> Champing the meat, and craned thy neck, and leered
> Upon me, naked on the ground …
>
> … 'Loud laughter shook the sides
> Of all the blessed gods'— The blessed gods! And I
> Grew cold and fearful, my disheveled hair
> Was damp with dew, the fires of adoration
> Flickered, burnt blue, and died in smoky doubt.[90]

Conclusion

The five soldiers considered in this chapter were selected to reflect the 'spectrum' of combatant faith identified by Schweitzer.[91] Additionally, the diary, memoirs or letters of each man exhibited a significant characteristic: Titterton's unpublished memoirs and poems unusually and unexpectedly engaged with issues of providence and omnipotence; Jack had written a rare extended self-reflection in the epilogue to chapter 3; Higgins was one of the relatively few soldier (rather than officer) diarists who wrote of his faith response to his experiences; Goodridge was distinctive because of the strength and consistency with which he expressed his faith and West was an exemplar of those who reacted fiercely against the patriotic piety of some soldier poets. While each was no doubt representative of many thousands of combatants, it is impossible to draw any conclusions from the nature of those primary sources about the relative numbers that each might represent. For all the reasons considered in the Introduction, a recognition that Sassoon, Brooke or Gurney were not necessarily typical of most Great War combatants must lead to similar conclusions about Titterton, Jack or Higgins.

However, between Goodridge's confident and unwavering faith – expressed, it should be noted, in fervently pietistic rather than patriotic terms – and West's atheism, the other three men's expressions of faith offer helpful insights into the reality of religious faith in the face of conflict. Titterton responded vehemently against the

89 Ibid., pp. 161-4.
90 Despite the punctuation indicating that West is quoting an earlier source, attempts to identify that source have not been successful.
91 Schweitzer, 'The Cross and the Trenches' in *War and Society*, pp. 36f.

inconsistencies inherent in a faith that spoke of the 'Prince of Peace' supporting the conflict. He apparently sought faith, envied those such as 'Bess' and the Salvation Army girl who had it, and clung on to a belief in a 'fuller life' and a 'richer peace' after death despite his wartime experiences. For Jack, religious practice was inextricably linked to tradition, duty and discipline. The 'norm' was belief in God and associated practices, and the experience of war caused but a temporary perturbation from that default position. For Higgins, the simply articulated faith that he would 'meet again' those many comrades who had fallen on the Somme comforted him through the personal disillusionment of the post-war decade. Together, the narratives of the three men, indicative of neither conventional Christian faith nor an absolute rejection of that faith, exemplify the theism and diffusive Christianity which has been so widely identified as being typical of combatant faith in the First World War. Their witness, placed alongside that of the 'silent witnesses' considered in the Introduction, is undoubtedly more representative of individuals' religious responses to the conflict than those of Ernest Goodridge or Arthur Graeme West.

Conclusion

In the Introduction, we noted the apparently common popular assumption that the Great War caused a 'widespread' loss of faith. While recognizing that measures of personal faith should not be equated with those of religious practice, the research of Clive Field and others had shown that most counts of church membership did not show a significant decline during the conflict, although church attendance did continue to fall gently. In subsequent chapters, a narrative was offered of the responses of combatants, lay civilians and clergy to the questions of faith that the War might have been thought to pose. It was shown that from the outbreak of the conflict, the vast majority was absolutely convinced of the moral justification for Britain's declaration of war, a conviction founded primarily on the need to respond to Germany's invasion of 'brave little Belgium.' Indubitably, the God who had given Britain and her Empire 'divinely-favoured nation' status was on her side in a battle of right against might. It was, argued many, a Holy War, and such a conflation of a military conflict and a spiritual battle validated the use of numerous hymns full of militaristic imagery. The language of the God of Battles and the Lord of Hosts was employed to stress the parallels with the history of the people of Israel. There was a widespread agreement that traditional and simplistic understandings of the nature of divine omnipotence could not be sustained in the face of the immense human cost of the conflict and most theologians and preachers argued that the evil of the war should be attributed to humanity's abuse of its God-given free will. Many combatants clung on to a somewhat confused amalgam of fatalism and belief in Providence, both being preferable to the alternative view that experiences of life or death, injury or a 'near-miss' were entirely random. However, others struggled to maintain any faith in God's providence. Sacrifice became a dominant trope very early in the war. Through image and word, the fallen were likened to the chivalric knights of Arthurian legend and 'dead' was repeatedly prefixed by the adjective 'glorious'. Many affirmed that the salvation of those 'glorious dead' was assured, irrespective of their faith or lifestyles, though some clerics resisted such assertions. Praying for the dead became widely but not universally accepted in the Church of England from the first months of the conflict and this was the most significant change in religious practice caused by the war.

Geoffrey Studdert Kennedy derided the standard response to many theological questions – that the ways of God are beyond human understanding – and was the first popular proponent of divine passibility, the belief that God shares in human suffering. However, despite the popularity of many volumes of his prose and poetry, there is little evidence that his theology was taken seriously and once the conflict was over it was largely forgotten. Similarly, wartime ecumenical co-operation, limited as it was, gave hope to many that some form of organic Christian unity might be possible. However, once hostilities had ceased, the impetus was lost and old divisions within the Church of England and between denominations, especially concerning the importance of episcopal ordination, together constrained any significant ecumenical progress.

Continuing his statistical research into the interwar years, Clive Field plotted the figures for church-going and other religious activity, a task made difficult by the absence of any national religious censuses in that period.[1] He concluded that pre-war trends continued and that much of the fall in attendance figures was attributable to people worshipping less frequently, with fewer church-goers attending every Sunday and many former 'twicers' becoming 'oncers', sometimes as a consequence of the enforced move of Evensong and other services from Sunday evenings to afternoons during the war. His view was that social changes do much to explain the phenomenon of declining attendances.[2] Field's conclusions about the relative stability of the levels of post-war church membership were entirely consistent with the earlier exhaustive analyses of Currie, Gilbert and Horsley.[3] Key figures for the period 1920-30 show a rise in Church of England Easter Day communicants of 4.16 per cent, a membership increase in Wesleyan Methodism of 7.4 per cent and a decline in Baptist membership in England of 0.51 per cent.[4] The numbers of Sunday school scholars fell by 10.35 per cent in the Church of England and by 9.3 per cent across the largest Methodist denominations.[5] However, such statistics take no account of population changes in that period. Neither do they show the figures for gains and losses that together gave effect to the overall changes in membership. Close examination of a wide range of measures of involvement in the Wesleyan Methodist Church from 1913 onwards illustrate trends that were broadly reflected in other denominations.[6] While membership figures rose over the period, despite the entirely to be expected fall during the war, the post-war peak membership as a percentage of the population aged 15+ was reached in 1925–27, before subsequently falling. Similarly, the numbers of new members fell significantly after 1927. While wartime deaths peaked in 1917, that loss was less than that in 1919, presumably as a consequence of the influenza pandemic. During and

1 C. Field, 'Gradualist or Revolutionary Secularization? A Case Study of Religious Belonging in Inter-War Britain, 1918-1939', *Church History and Religious Culture 93* (2013), pp. 57-93.
2 Ibid., p. 90.
3 Currie, Gilbert and Horsley, *Churches and Church-goers.*
4 Ibid., pp. 128f, 143 and 150 respectively.
5 Ibid., p. 167 and derived from pp. 183, 185f and 190.
6 Ibid., pp. 66, 145 and 185f.

after the conflict, there was a marked reduction in the numbers of people ceasing to be members, post-war levels being around two thirds of the 1913 figure. There is no obvious explanation for this, the 'ceased to meet' process usually being instigated by a local church when a member no longer attended regularly.[7] The figures for both membership as a percentage of population and new members indicate that the period of ambivalence towards the war of the late 1920s saw a more significant decline in commitment to the Church than had the immediate post-war years. As far as church attendance was concerned, Field recounted the contemporary accounts of decline.[8] While there were many local attendance surveys during the period, their methodologies often differed and rarely were they repeated in the same area. Figures for Ipswich indicate a drop in church-going of almost a half between 1923 and 1938, and a similar fall in York from 1901 to 1935.[9] However, the fundamental problem with crude measures of church attendance is that, for example, such a decline of 50 per cent could mean either that only half of the earlier congregation worshipped subsequently and they did so just as regularly, or that there were the same number of regular worshippers, but they all went to church half as often. In practice, of course, the reality invariably falls somewhere between those two extremes.

Of the many sources which Field cited, one of particular interest is the visitation returns for the Diocese of Oxford in 1922, in which the report on the parish of Cropredy drew attention to the demoralising influence of returning ex-servicemen who seldom or never worshipped and whose 'example seems to have worked like leaven of evil amongst the elder boys and younger men.'[10] Field quoted numerous comments made by clergy from the Diocese complaining about shrinking congregations and less-frequent church-going. Such anecdotal evidence abounds, but should be set alongside the numerical analyses. Writing in 1975, Stephen Koss quoted Charles Royle, briefly M.P. for Stockport, who had stated that more than 600 local members of the Brotherhood movement had served in the forces, and 'although the big majority came back to the town, only a small number resumed their membership of the Brotherhood.'[11] However, the national statistics for the Movement paint a rather less negative picture. While membership had peaked in 1913 at over 300,000 and fallen to 100,000 by 1919, five years later it had recovered somewhat to 125,000, before declining to 115,000 in 1934.[12] Certainly, the disruption to the men's organisation

7 Until very recent times, there was always a financial pressure on Methodist churches to 'prune' membership lists, since they determined the assessment levied by the circuit, the group of churches that pays ministers' stipends and other related costs.

8 Field, 'Gradualist or Revolutionary Secularization?, pp. 62-8.

9 Ibid, pp. 64f.

10 Ibid., p. 67. Cropredy is a small village 4 miles north of Banbury, Oxfordshire.

11 C. Royle, *Opened Doors* (London: Meat Trades' Journal Co., 1949), p. 37, cited in S. Koss, *Nonconformity in Modern British Politics* (London: Batsford, 1975), p. 1.

12 T. Sykes, 'The Brotherhood Movement' in D.P. Thompson and H.L. Simpson, *Modern Evangelistic Movements* (Glasgow: Thomson & Cowan, 1924), p. 72 and J.W. Tuffley,

caused by the war had been massive, but not as disastrous as might be inferred from the anecdote about Stockport.

Robert Beaken's recently-published study of the influence of the Great War on the Church of England in Colchester clearly differed in its focus from the work discussed in this book.[13] He had confined his research to one denomination and one geographical area, although setting his narrative in a wider context. A particular emphasis was on the role played by the laity, in contrast to many previous studies. Rejecting the earlier analyses of the impact of the conflict of the war on the Churches, he commented that if it were possible to return to 11 November 1918 and tell the clergy, civilian laity and the thousands of troops who had passed through Colchester that the Church of England had had a bad war, 'they would have had great difficulty reconciling that claim with their own experience and would simply not have believed it.'[14] He concluded that the evidence from Colchester does not support the 'myth ... that things were never the same' for the Church of England after the conflict.[15] 'The role played by the First World War in secularisation was not so much the impact of the war upon the Church as its impact upon the wider society in which that Church was located.'[16] Certainly the evidence from Nottinghamshire and Derbyshire is consonant with Beaken's conclusions about Colchester's experience.

As was noted in chapter 4, this was how Geoffrey Husbands had recalled the events of November 1918:

> We sang with deeper feeling and more than the usual heartiness that a favourite hymn evokes at any time: 'Now thank we all our God' and as the service ended and we poured out into the darkness of the streets it did indeed seem that we were right at the end of an epoch.[17]

Undoubtedly, the cessation of hostilities at the 11th hour of the 11th day of that month brought a welcome transformation of the daily lives of tens of millions of people across Europe. While the demobilisation of the men who had enlisted or been conscripted 'for the duration or three years' would take many months, and while the Influenza pandemic in 1918–1920 would have a higher global death-toll than the war itself, Husbands' sense of the end of an epoch was surely justified. The combatant countries had experienced four years that had been quite unlike any others in their history. Well over ten million people had died, large areas of northern France and Belgium had been

Grain from Galilee (London: Headley, 1935), p. 115. I am grateful to Andy Vail for pointing me towards these somewhat elusive membership figures for the Brotherhood movement.

13 Beaken, *The Church of England and the Home Front.*

14 Ibid., p. 234.

15 Ibid., p. 245.

16 Ibid., p. 246.

17 Bourne and Bushaway (eds.), *Joffrey's War*, pp. 580f.

destroyed and the conflict had affected countries across the globe. While the losses did not justify the rhetoric of a 'lost generation', they dwarfed the cost of all previous wars.[18] Nevertheless, the evidence of the primary sources examined in this study, set alongside the statistical work done by Currie, Gilbert, Horsley and Field, indicate that the impact of the Great War on both the faith and the religious practices of the people of Britain was very limited. That membership figures held up until the late 1920s, while church attendances declined, does suggest a change in the frequency of religious observance of many regular worshippers, as a consequence of the social changes and technological developments of the 1920s. The growing attraction of the cinema, radio and leisure activities such as cycling, following on from the social disruption of the conflict, most probably had a greater impact on religious practice than did the loss of faith caused by the horrors of the war.[19]

How, then, may we explain the very limited influence of the conflict on the faith and religious practices of the people of Britain? A number of factors may be adduced to explain the resilience of their Christian faith. The first derives from the perhaps surprising way in which some men looked back on their wartime experiences. The post-war reflections of two officers and one chaplain, all articulate and intelligent, must suffice as examples: Sidney Rogerson served with the West Yorkshire Regiment and wrote his memoirs in response to the expressions of disillusionment of the late 1920s and early 1930s. The judgments offered in his *Twelve Days on the Somme*, first published in 1933, can be seen to be as influenced by Rogerson's post-war experiences as much as by those of 1916:

> We were privileged, in short, to see a reign of goodwill among men, which the piping times of peace, with all their organized charity, their free meals, free hospitals, and Sunday sermons have never equalled. Despite all the Christian fellowship and international peace, there is more animosity, uncharitableness and lack of fellowship in one business office now than in a Brigade of infantry in France then. Otherwise we could not have stood the strain.[20]

Similarly, writing his memoirs of the Great War during the Second World War, former chaplain Robert Rider suggested that the communal life of army days had introduced men to 'a life of comradeship, sacrifice and service that surpasses the fellowship of the average Christian society.'[21] Guy Chapman, who had served with the Royal Fusiliers,

18 On the 'lost generation' rhetoric, see Corrigan, *Mud, Blood and Poppycock*, pp. 52-76.

19 Perceived threats to traditional Sunday observance pre-dated the war; see the narrative of an ecumenical Conference in 1906 on this issue in Bell, *Randall Davidson*, pp. 506f. On the challenge of leisure activities see Wilkinson, *Dissent or Conform?*, pp. 58f. and pp. 64-66.

20 S. Rogerson, *Twelve Days on the Somme: A memoir of the trenches, November 1916* (London: Greenhill Books, 2006), p. 61.

21 Rider, *Reflections on the Battlefield*, p. 145.

looked back on his war-service with affection, appending this comment to his diary entries:

> Apart from the badly-dressed young woman who came into Chapman & Dodd's office one bitterly cold January day in 1924, the battalion is the only wholly good thing in my life. To the years between 1914 and 1918 I owe everything of lasting value in my make-up. For any cost I paid in physical and mental vigour they gave me back a supreme fulfillment I should never otherwise have had.[22]

While Chapman was hugely critical of the way in which the war had been waged and of amateurish officers and national leaders and had a distinguished post-war career as a historian, he could nevertheless describe his battalion as the second-best thing after his wife in his life.[23] None of the writers minimised the horrors of his experience of the conflict. They were, however, able to be positive about them. Especially from the context of the early 1930s, the war years could seem to have a somewhat romantic attraction – a time when British society was united against a common enemy, when the effects of class divisions were to some extent mitigated by that shared purpose, and men were bound together under the constant threat of injury or death in a genuine spirit of comradeship.[24] While it would be unwise to exaggerate the significance of such recollections, they offer yet another corrective to the 'mud and futility' narratives which, taken alone, could not but be suggestive that a loss of faith was commonplace.

A second factor that served to limit the impact of the conflict on people's faith was the detachment that was noted in chapter 1. Theologians, clerics and lay people alike were all, in general, either unwilling or simply unable to engage with the theological issues which the war might be thought to raise. Few were equipped, for example, to discuss the nature of divine providence in the light of the war. Those that did engage with such questions almost invariably did so sharing the view of George Bell described in chapter 2, that 'on 4 August, 1914, England was morally bound to go to war' and this attitude could not but have blunted the perceived impact of the War on faith.[25] Moreover, the standard response that the ways of God 'pass all understanding', so derided by Studdert Kennedy, appears to have been adequate for many believers.

Third, it seems reasonable to suggest that the deferential culture of Edwardian England served to reduce the deleterious influence of the conflict on faith. In the discussion of Jack Titterton's attitude to religious belief in chapter 8, we noted his dilemma – real or jocular – caused by the perceived rival claims of loyalty to God, mediated through the Salvation Army girl, and that to the Army. 'It says in the Book

22 G. Chapman, *A Kind of Survivor: The Autobiography of Guy Chapman* (London: Gollancz, 1975), p. 280.
23 Ibid., pp. 58-61.
24 See S. Bell, 'Collapsing Class Barriers – another Myth of the Trenches?' in *Crucible: The Christian Journal of Social Ethics* (April-Jun 2014), pp. 35-42.
25 Bell (ed.), *The War and the Kingdom*, p. 4.

that a man can't serve two masters and I am sworn in to serve the Sergeant Major.'[26] Deference was a significant characteristic of both civilian and military cultures, and, while it cannot be proven, in a society in which the challenging or questioning of one's human masters remained generally counter-cultural, it would seem likely that such attitudes militated against the challenging or questioning of God. The contrast with the very different social context of, for example, the 1960s, is self-evident.

Arguably the most significant factor in the long-term resilience of people's faith is exemplified both by Husbands' narrative and by the 'Proclamation' by the King on the signing of the Treaty of Versailles that was noted in chapter 3. Not only had Britain won the war but, as the soldiers' singing of 'Now thank we all our God' indicated and as the King's words made explicit, it was God who should be thanked for the victory. Thus, the confident expressions throughout the conflict of God being 'on our side' had been proved to have been fully justified and all the assertions of the moral authority of Britain's declaration of war on Germany were shown to be totally vindicated. At the beginning of 1918, such an outcome had been far from certain. On New Year's Eve 1917, Randall Davidson confided to Edward Talbot, Bishop of Winchester, 'I own to feeling the general situation as regards the war to be exceedingly anxious.'[27] Writing in his diary on the following day, Frederick Robinson of Cobham, Surrey, wondered when the 'awful nightmare' would end. The country was becoming 'tired out' and he questioned if people would ever live 'normal lives' again.[28] Publicly, of course, no such doubts were expressed; the war must be won. While it would be futile to engage in counter-factual conjecture to wonder what the impact on the faith of the people of Britain might had been if the war had been lost, it is clear that the victory validated all the assertions of the previous four years about the righteousness of the cause. God had, indeed, been 'on our side' and there was, therefore, no reason to question his providential purposes.

Significantly, James Moffat had suggested in the middle of the conflict that its impact on British religion would not be great: 'I shall begin frankly by expressing my opinion that the influence of the war upon the religious situation is not nearly so powerful as an outsider might expect. I would even go farther and predict that it is not likely to leave any far-reaching changes behind it.'[29] In the event, Moffat's prediction appears to have been fulfilled. For a host of reasons, the impact of the First World War on the faith and religious practices of the people of Britain was far less than that of the social changes of the succeeding years.

26 DRO, D4690/1/1/1, p. 34.
27 Bell, *Randall Davidson*, p. 850.
28 Unpublished diary in the Imperial War Museum archives quoted in M. Brown, *The Imperial War Museum Book of 1918: Year of Victory* (London: Pan Books, 1999), p. xxii.
29 Moffat, 'The Influence of the War upon the Religious Life', p. 482.

Appendix

The Commemoration Service for Lieut. Hugh Valentine Gamble, 13 May 1917.

The Presbyterian Church of England.

ST. ANDREW'S CHURCH, EALING, W.

Commemoration Service

SUNDAY, MAY 13TH, 1917,

AT 6.30 P.M.

Lieut. Hugh Valentine Gamble

(2nd Battalion Seaforth Highlanders),

Captain of the 11th Thames Valley (St. Andrew's Church, Ealing) Company of the Boys' Brigade;

Scoutmaster of the 2nd Ealing Troop of Boy Scouts;

Who fell gloriously near Arras,

May 3rd, 1917.

'So he passed over, and all the trumpets sounded for him on the other side.'

'One who never turned his back, but marched breast forward,
Never doubted clouds would break;
Never dreamed, though right were worsted, wrong would
triumph;
Held we fall to rise, are baffled to fight better,
Sleep to wake.'

The above portrait (Arthur Hawes, late Lock and Whitfield, Ealing) is reproduced in response to the request of friends.

Order of Service.

1. The Sanctus.

(*The Congregation are requested to rise with the Choir, to join in the singing of the Sanctus, and to remain standing during the reading of the sentences.*)

Holy, holy, holy, Lord God of Hosts: heaven and earth are full of Thy glory. Glory be to Thee, O Lord most high. Amen.

2. The Sentences.

3. Prayer and The Lord's Prayer.

4. Hymn.

For all the saints who from their labours rest,
Who Thee by faith before the world confessed,
Thy name, O Jesus, be for ever blest.
Alleluia!

Thou wast their Rock, their Fortress, and their Might;
Thou, Lord, their Captain in the well-fought fight;
Thou, in the darkness drear, their one true Light. Alleluia!

O may Thy soldiers, faithful, true, and bold,
Fight as the saints who nobly fought of old,
And win, with them, the victor's crown of gold. Alleluia!

O blest communion! fellowship divine!
We feebly struggle, they in glory shine;
Yet all are one in Thee, for all are Thine.
Alleluia!

And when the strife is fierce, the warfare long,
Steals on the ear the distant triumph song,
And hearts are brave again, and arms are strong.
Alleluia !

The golden evening brightens in the west ;
Soon, soon to faithful warriors cometh rest ;
Sweet is the calm of Paradise the blest.
Alleluia !

But, lo ! there breaks a yet more glorious day :
The saints triumphant rise in bright array ;
The King of Glory passes on His way.
Alleluia !

From earth's wide bounds, from ocean's farthest coast,
Through gates of pearl streams in the countless host,
Singing to Father, Son, and Holy Ghost,
'Alleluia !'
Amen.

5. Reading of Holy Scripture. (Psalms cxxx, xxiii.)

6. Prayer.

7. Hymn.

Alleluia ! Alleluia ! Alleluia !

The strife is o'er, the battle done ;
The victory of life is won ;
The song of triumph has begun,—
'Alleluia !'

The powers of death have done their worst,
But Christ their legions hath dispersed ;
Let shouts of holy joy outburst,—
'Alleluia !'

The three sad days have quickly sped;
He rises glorious from the dead;
All glory to our risen Head! 'Alleluia!'

He brake the fast-bound chains of hell;
The bars from heaven's high portals fell;
Let hymns of praise His triumph tell.
'Alleluia!'

Lord, by the stripes which wounded Thee,
From death's dread sting Thy servants free,
That we may live, and sing to Thee,
'Alleluia!'
AMEN.

8. READING OF HOLY SCRIPTURE. (St. John xiv, 1–3 and 27, 28; Rev. vi, 9–17.)

9. ANTHEM.

SUNSET and evening star,
And one clear call for me!
And may there be no moaning of the bar
When I put out to sea,
But such a tide as moving seems asleep,
Too full for sound and foam,
When that which drew from out the boundless deep
Turns again home.

Twilight and evening bell,
And after that the dark!
And may there be no sadness of farewell
When I embark;
For, though from out our bourne of time and place
The flood may bear me far,
I hope to see my Pilot face to face
When I have crost the bar.
AMEN.

10. THE LITANY OF INTERCESSION.

(*The Congregation are invited to join in the response, "We beseech Thee to hear us, O Lord."*)

11. HYMN.

THE Son of God goes forth to war,
  A kingly crown to gain ;
His blood-red banner streams afar :
  Who follows in His train ?

Who best can drink His cup of woe,
  Triumphant over pain,
Who patient bears His cross below,
  He follows in His train.

The martyr first, whose eagle eye
  Could pierce beyond the grave,
Who saw his Master in the sky,
  And called on Him to save ;

Like Him, with pardon on his tongue
  In midst of mortal pain,
He prayed for them that did the wrong :
  Who follows in his train ?

A glorious band, the chosen few
  On whom the Spirit came,
Twelve valiant saints, their hope they knew
  And mocked the cross and flame ;

They met the tyrant's brandished steel,
  The lion's gory mane ;
They bowed their necks the death to feel :
  Who follows in their train ?

A noble army, men and boys,
  The matron and the maid,
Around the Saviour's throne rejoice,
  In robes of light arrayed ;

They climbed the steep ascent of heaven
  Through peril, toil, and pain :
O God, to us may grace be given
  To follow in their train !

AMEN.

12. THE COMMEMORATION.

WE commemorate in this Service the life and devotion even unto death of Lieutenant Hugh V. Gamble, of the 2nd Batt. Seaforth Highlanders, Captain of the 11th Thames Valley Company of the Boys' Brigade, Scoutmaster of the 2nd Ealing Troop, who heard and nobly answered the call of his Divine Lord and Master to take up arms in defence of the cause of God and righteousness in the present war; who was a good soldier of Jesus Christ and of his country, and who passed home to glory, as he fought gallantly in the Battle of Arras, on 3rd May, 1917. 'Be thou faithful unto death, and I will give thee a crown of life.'

13. PRAYER.

14. HYMN.

How bright these glorious spirits shine!
Whence all their white array?
How came they to the blissful seats
Of everlasting day?

Lo! these are they from sufferings great
Who came to realms of light,
And in the blood of Christ have washed
Those robes which shine so bright.

Now, with triumphal palms, they stand
Before the throne on high,
And serve the God they love, amidst
The glories of the sky.

His presence fills each heart with joy,
Tunes every mouth to sing;
By day, by night, the sacred courts
With glad hosannas ring.

Hunger and thirst are felt no more,
  Nor suns with scorching ray;
God is their Sun, Whose cheering beams
  Diffuse eternal day.

The Lamb Which dwells amidst the throne
  Shall o'er them still preside,
Feed them with nourishment divine,
  And all their footsteps guide.

'Mong pastures green He'll lead His flock,
  Where living streams appear;
And God the Lord from every eye
  Shall wipe off every tear.

To Him Who sits upon the throne,
  The God Whom we adore,
And to the Lamb That once was slain,
  Be glory evermore!

AMEN.

15. THE ADDRESS.

16. HYMN.

Ask and it shall be given;
  Thy promise, Lord, we plead;
For life is spread before us
  And many gifts we need,
If stedfastly and surely
  We seek to win the crown
That comes to those who follow
  The plans by God laid down.

Clean in Thy sight, Redeemer,
  We pray that we may be
From every sinful action
  And foolish word set free;
That, clean in mind and body,
  We may that strength procure.
King Arthur's knight was given
  Because his heart was pure.

We would be brave, our Captain,
For Thee to live and fight ;
Give us that fearless spirit
Which dares to stand for right.
Though comrades jeer or threaten,
Though tempted oft to fall,
Lord, make us brave to serve Thee
In things both great and small.

To live for those around us ;
To think of others first ;
To ease the heavy burden ;
All chains of bondage burst.
Make this, O Lord, our purpose ;
And, as we labour thus,
Accept such gifts for Jesus,
Who gave Himself for us. AMEN.

Written by Hugh V. Gamble.

17. THE OFFERTORY.

(During which the boys of the Brigade will sing the Company Hymn, of which Lieutenant Gamble was the author.)

GOD bless our Company ; under Thy banner,
Lord, we assemble to fight against wrong.
Jesus, Commander, be with us for ever ;
Make us Thy soldiers, brave, loyal, and strong.

God bless our Company ; may deeds of valour
Mark every boy who has carried our name,
True noble actions and thoughts pure and kindly,
That in Thine Army we all may win fame.

God bless our Company ; all who have left us,
Scattered far from us, on life's varied ways.
May they be cheered, Lord, and kept strong and faithful
When they remember their Boys' Brigade days.

God bless our Company ; and when the bugle
Sounds for parade, when our life here is o'er,
May none be missing, O Lord, at that roll-call ;
Friends, reunited, to part never more.
AMEN.

18. Hymn.

All hail, the power of Jesus' name!
  Let angels prostrate fall;
Bring forth the royal diadem
  To crown Him Lord of all.

O that, with yonder sacred throng,
  We at His feet may fall,
Join in the everlasting song,
  And crown Him Lord of all!

Amen.

19. The Benediction.

20. Organ Voluntary.

(The Congregation are requested to stand whilst the 'Hallelujah Chorus' is played.)

'These are they which follow the Lamb whithersoever He goeth' *(Rev. xiv, 4).*

'His servants shall serve Him' *(Rev. xxii, 3).*

A Note on Secondary Sources

The historiography of the British Churches and the First World War is dominated by one as yet unpublished thesis and one very widely-read book. Stuart Mews' 1973 Cambridge Ph.D. thesis, *Religion and English Society in the First World War* had as its primary focus the Church of England and it remains the foundational document for work in this area.[1] Alan Wilkinson's seminal *The Church of England and the First World War*, published in 1978, recounted the Church's work in both the theatres of battle and England.[2] Gathering together an impressive range of printed sources, it remains by far the most-quoted work on the subject. However, it made no use of unpublished primary sources (such as the Davidson papers at Lambeth Palace) and too often took at face value the rhetoric of the writers of the 1930s for whom little positive could be said about the conflict. Since it pre-dated the work both of the revisionist historians of the last thirty years and of more recent scholars who have reassessed the work of the Forces' chaplains, *The Church of England and the First World War* has become somewhat dated.[3] Albert Marrin's *The Last Crusade* had been published four years before Wilkinson's work.[4] As may be seen when examining the contribution of the Bishop of London to the rhetoric of a 'Holy War' (chapter 2), Marrin was more cautious than Wilkinson in offering critical judgments which appear to have been influenced by the era in which they were written. That was the period in which Alan Clark's *The Donkeys* and the musical *Oh! What a Lovely War* had both shaped public

1 S. Mews, *Religion and English Society in the First World War*, unpublished Ph.D. thesis, University of Cambridge, 1973. I understood from a telephone conversation with Dr. Mews in March 2011 that this work, much quoted by later writers, might be published, but it has yet to appear. Quotations from the thesis are by kind permission of the author.

2 A. Wilkinson, *The Church of England and the First World War* (London: SCM, 1978).

3 For analyses of the influence of writers in the immediate post-war period on later perceptions of the role of chaplains in the conflict, see E. Madigan, *Faith Under Fire: Anglican Chaplains and the Great War* (Basingstoke: Palgrave Macmillan, 2011), M. Snape; 'Church of England Army Chaplains in the First World War: Goodbye to "Goodbye to All That"', *Journal of Ecclesiastical History*, Vol. 62, No. 2, (April 2011), pp. 318-45 and various papers in M. Snape and E. Madigan (eds.), *The Clergy in Khaki: New Perspectives on British Army Chaplaincy in the First World War* (Farnham: Ashgate, 2013).

4 A. Marrin, *The Last Crusade: The Church of England in the First World War* (Durham, NC: Duke University Press, 1974).

perceptions of the conflict, the Vietnam War was in progress and the Campaign for Nuclear Disarmament had influenced a generation of Anglican clergy.[5] In his later *Dissent or Conform?* Alan Wilkinson included a chapter on English Nonconformity and the war.[6] Subsequently, I have attempted a single-chapter summary of the Church of England's engagement with the First World War.[7] The primary focus of these volumes was ecclesiastical rather than theological, discussing the Churches' response to the conflict and examining how they were affected organisationally and practically, both nationally and locally.[8] An article by Richard Schweitzer, 'The Cross and the Trenches', considering the faith and doubts of British soldiers in the Great War and then a book with the same title with a scope widened to include American soldiers addressed some of the issues considered in this study.[9] However, the latter's brief analysis of religion on the home front made no attempt to assess the experience of ordinary citizens, focussing rather on prominent people such as Vera Brittain. Between the publication of Schweitzer's article and his book, Snape and Parker's chapter on belief and religiosity during the conflict discussed many of the key characteristics of wartime faith and religious practice which have been developed in subsequent work.[10]

Turning to broadcast media, a Radio 3 programme, *God and the Great* War, first broadcast on 9 November 2014, included interviews with Michael Snape and Martin Purdy in which they sought to address some of the long-standing prejudicial perceptions of the Churches' involvement in the conflict.[11] Adrian Gregory also spoke about the importance of ideas of redemptive sacrifice and belief in the afterlife. Similarly, Michael Snape, Georgina Byrne and I contributed to a Radio 4 programme in the

5 A. Clark, *The Donkeys* (London: Hutchinson, 1961); The 1963 stage musical *Oh, What a Lovely War* was adapted by Joan Littlewood from a radio play by Charles Chilton. In turn, it was developed into a 1969 musical film directed by Richard Attenborough. See M. Grimley, 'The Church and the Bomb: Anglicans and the Campaign for Nuclear Disarmament, c. 1958–1984' in S.G. Parker and T. Lawson (eds.), *God and War* (Farnham: Ashgate, 2012), pp. 147-164.

6 A. Wilkinson, *Dissent or Conform? War, Peace and the English Churches, 1900–1945* (London: SCM, 1986), pp. 21-53.

7 S. Bell, 'The Church of England and the First World War' in Parker and Lawson (eds.), *God and War*, pp. 33-59.

8 In his review of my chapter in *God and War*, Wilkinson again confused the conflict's influence on faith with its influence on the Church, challenging my conclusion that the war 'had little impact on the faith of the Church' by pointing to liturgical change, self-government, new paths towards ordination and new possibilities for women's ministry, among other developments: *Church Times*, 19 April 2013, p. 34.

9 R. Schweitzer, 'The Cross and the Trenches: Religious Faith and Doubt Among Some British Soldiers on the Western Front' in *War and Society*, Vol. 16, No. 2 (October 1998), pp. 33-57; R. Schweitzer, *The Cross and the Trenches: Religious Faith and Doubt Among British and American Great War Soldiers* (Westport, 2003).

10 Snape and Parker, 'Keeping Faith and Coping'.

11 *God and the Great War*, Radio 3, first broadcast 9 November 2014, 18:45. Recording available at http://www.bbc.co.uk/programmes/b04nql0m, retrieved 11 January 2016.

Beyond Belief series broadcast in the week of the centenary of the Battle of the Somme, addressing the primary focus of this book, the impact of the war on popular faith.[12]

Of more general books examining British society during the conflict, Catriona Pennell's *A Kingdom United*, a compendious analysis of responses to the outbreak of war, merits particular note. Using a large range of material from local archives across Britain, she re-examined one of the myths of the First World War, that men enlisted without serious thought: 'For those men who enlisted because of patriotism, it should be noted that "love of country" was not a form of national hysteria or jingoism. It was a considered, reflective sense of obligation.'[13] While it must be recognised that not all men enlisted for entirely altruistic reasons, Pennell's rebuttal of the myth of mass hysteria is significant for this study in setting the broader social context for the Churches' responses to the start of the war. In October 2015, Robert Beaken published an analysis of the influence of the war on the Church of England, focussing on the civilians and soldiers of wartime Colchester.[14] While his secondary sources included most of the narratives commonly used by scholars of conflict and religion in that period, the broad range of primary sources from Colchester and Essex on which Beaken drew formed a large corpus of previously-unexamined material. Clearly, his work focussing on Colchester was contemporaneous with the emphasis of this book's examination of church life and belief on experiences in Nottinghamshire and Derbyshire. While recognising the distinction between evaluating the war's impact on a religious denomination and that on people's faith, his conclusions are consonant with those reached in this volume.

12 *Beyond Belief: Battle of the Somme*, Radio 4, first broadcast 27 June 2016, 16:30. Recording available at http://www.bbc.co.uk/programmes/b07h6n1q, retrieved 27 October 2016.

13 C. Pennell, *A Kingdom United* (London: OUP, 2012), p. 159.

14 R. Beaken, *The Church of England and the Home Front 1914-1918: Civilians, Soldiers and Religion in Wartime Colchester* (Woodbridge: Boydell & Brewer, 2015).

Bibliography

Archives

Birmingham City Archives, Library of Birmingham.
University of Birmingham Special Collections: The YMCA archive.
Bodleian Library, Oxford: The diary of the Revd. Andrew Clark: MSS. Eng. hist. e. 88-177c.
Bodleian Library, Oxford: The personal papers of Maurice Harold Macmillan, 1st Earl of Stockton (1894-1986).
University Library, Cambridge, The Society for Promoting Christian Knowledge collection.
The Cameronians (Scottish Rifles) Archives, Low Marks Museum, Hamilton, Lanarkshire: The Diary of James Lochhead Jack, chapters I, II, V, VI and VII.
Derbyshire Archives, Matlock.
Durham Cathedral Archives: Bishop Henson Papers.
Nottinghamshire Archives, Nottingham.
The West Yorkshire Regiment Archives, the York Army Museum, York: The Diary of James Lochhead Jack, chapter IV.

Hymnbooks and Liturgical Books

Book of Common Prayer with the additions and deviations proposed in 1928 (1928).
Fellowship Hymn-Book (1909)
Hymns Ancient and Modern – New Edition (1904)
Methodist Hymn Book (1933)
Methodist Worship Book (1999)
Songs of Praise – Enlarged edition (1932)
Songs of Praise (1925)
United Methodist Hymnbook (1889)
(Wesleyan) Methodist Hymnbook (1904)

Newspapers and Magazines

Aberdeen Journal
Aldersgate Magazine
Baptist Times and Freeman
Bedfordshire Times and Independent
Biggleswade Chronicle
Birmingham Daily Mail
Birmingham Daily Post
Birmingham Gazette
British Weekly
Burnley Express
Burnley News
C.R. The Chronicle of the Community of the Resurrection.
Chelmsford Chronicle
Christian World Pulpit
The Church Standard
The Commonwealth, A Christian Social Magazine
The Cornishman
Coventry Evening Telegraph
Dawn of Day
Derby Daily Telegraph
Dundee Courier
(Birmingham) *Evening Despatch*
(Dundee) *Evening Telegraph*
Exeter and Plymouth Gazette
Guardian
Hull Daily Mail
Isle of Man Examiner
Kent and Sussex Courier
Lichfield Mercury
Luton Times and Advertiser
The Manchester Courier and Lancashire General Advertiser
Manchester Evening News
Methodist Recorder
Newcastle Journal
North Devon Journal
Nottingham Evening Post
Primitive Methodist Leader
Sheffield Evening Telegraph
Southwell Diocesan Messenger
The Spectator
Surrey Mirror

Tamworth Herald
The Times
Wesleyan Methodist Magazine
Western Daily Press
Western Gazette
Western Times
Y.M. – The British Empire YMCA Weekly

Published Primary Sources

W.F. Adney, "Towards Re-union: A Nonconformist View" in *Church Quarterly Review*, CLXXIV (January 1919), pp. 189-190.
F.R. Barry, *The Atonement* (London: Hodder & Stoughton, 1968).
—— *Period of My Life* (London: Hodder & Stoughton, 1970).
H.N. Bate (ed.), F*aith and Order: Proceedings of the World Conference* (London: SCM, 1927).
K. Best and G. Roynon (ed), *A Chaplain at Gallipoli: The Great War Diaries of Kenneth Best* (London: Simon & Schuster, 2011).
E.M. Bilbrough, *My War Diary* (London: Ebury Press, 2014).
A. Bishop and M. Bostridge (eds.), *Letters from a Lost Generation* (London: Virago, 2008).
J.D. Borthwick, *Poems and Songs on the South African War* (Montreal: the Gazette Publishing Co., 1901).
J.M. Bourne and B. Bushaway (eds.), *Joffrey's War: A Sherwood Forester in the Great War* (Nottingham: Salient Books, 2012).
N.G. Brett-James and J. Gifford, *Book of Remembrance and war record of Mill Hill School 1914-1919* (London: T. Malcomson, 1922).
G.J. Byrnell, "The Soldiers' Christian Association" in *R.A.Ch.D. Quarterly Journal*, vol. 2, no. 15, (July 1925), pp. 99-102.
D.S. Cairns (ed.), *The Army and Religion* (London: Macmillan, 1919).
J. Carrol, *The Besiegers' Prayer; or, A Christian Nation's Appeal to the God of Battles for Success in the Righteous War* (Toronto: The Guardian Office, 1855).
G. Chapman, *A Kind of Survivor: The Autobiography of Guy Chapman* (London: Gollancz, 1975).
J.R. Clark Hall, "The Problem of Union and Freedom in the Church of Christ" in *The Modern Churchman* (June 1919), pp. 314-326.
P.D. Clayton, *Tales of Talbot House* (London: Chatto & Windus, 1919).
A. Clutton-Brock, "6. The Cure for War" in *Papers for Wartime* (London: OUP, 1914).
M. Dearmer, *Letters from a Field Hospital* (London: Macmillan, 1915).
P. Dearmer, *Songs of Praise Discussed* (London: OUP, 1933).
J.C. Dunn, *The War the Infantry Knew* (London: Jane's, 1987).
A.M. Fairbairn, *The Place of Christ in Modern Theology* (London: Hodder & Stoughton, 1893).

R. Fielding and J. Waller (ed.), *War Letters to a Wife* (Staplehurst: Spellmount, 2001).
H.R. Freston, *The Quest of Truth and Other Poems* (Oxford: Blackwell, 1916).
F.J. Gillman, *The Story of our Hymns* (London: Swarthmore, 1921).
E. N. Goodridge and J. A. Goodridge (eds) *The Same Stars Shine: The Great War Diaries of Corporal Ernest Goodridge* (Loughborough: Teamprint, 2000).
H.L. Goudge (and others), G.K.A. Bell, (ed) *The War and the Kingdom of God*, (London: Longmans, Green & Co., 1915).
R. Grant, *S.O.S. Stand To!* (London: Appleton & Co., 1918).
D. Hankey, *A Student in Arms* (London: Melrose,1916).
——*A Student in Arms Second Series* (London: Melrose, 1917);
G.M. Hanks, "The Possibilities of Reunion" in *The Modern Churchman* (October 1918), p. 614.
T.L. Harris, *Christian Public Worship* (New York: Doubleday, 1928).
A. Harvey (ed.), The *Church and the 20th Century* (London: Macmillan, 1936).
A. Headlam, 'The Lambeth Conference' in *Church Quarterly Review*, vol. XCI (October 1920), pp. 139-56.
H.H. Henson, *Westminster Sermons* (London: James Clark, 1910).
—— *The Book and the Vote* (London: Hodder & Stoughton, 1928).
——*Retrospect of an Unimportant Life, vol. 1* (London: OUP, 1943).
T.J. Higgins, *Tommy at Gommecourt* (Leek: Churnet Valley Books, 2005).
N. Hook, "The Doctrine of Providence" in *The Expository Times*, 1930, vol. 41, pp. 359-62.
L. Houseman (ed.) *War Letters of Fallen Englishmen* (London: Gollancz, 1930) reprinted with Foreword by J. Winter (Philadelphia: Pine Street Books, 2002).
F.A. Iremonger, *William Temple, Archbishop of Canterbury* (London: OUP, 1948).
The Editor (L.P. Jacks), "A Theological Holiday – and After", *The Hibbert Journal*, vol. XIV, no. 1 (October 1915), pp. 1-14.
T.M. Kettle and M.S. Kettle, *The Ways of War* (London: Constable, 1917).
P. Leonard, (eds J. Leonard and P. Leonard-Johnson) *The Fighting Padre: Letters from the Trenches, 1915-1918, of Pat Leonard, DSO* (Barnsley: Pen and Sword, 2010).
T.C. Livingstone and R. Scott (ed.), *Tommy's War: A First World War Diary 1913-18* (London: Harper, 2008).
J.G. Lockhart, *Cosmo Gordon Lang* (London: Hodder & Stoughton, 1949).
W.F. Lofthouse, *Altar Cross and Community* (London: Epworth, 1921).
A. G Mackinnon, *Malta, the Nurse of the Mediterranean* (London: Hodder & Stoughton, 1916).
F. MacNutt (ed.), *The Church in the Furnace*, (London: Macmillan, 1917).
A.A. Martin, *A Surgeon in Khaki: Through France and Flanders in World War I* (London: Arnold, 1916), re-printed with an introduction by G. Harper (Lincoln, NE: University of Nebraska Press, 2011).
B. Mathews (ed.), *Christ and the World at War* (London: James Clarke, 1917).
J. Moffat, "The Influence of the War upon the Religious Life and Thought of Great Britain" in *The American Journal of Theology*, vol. 20, no. 4, (Oct 1916), pp. 481-93.

C.E. Montague, *Disenchantment* (London: Chatto & Windus, 1922).
B.L. Montgomery, *Forward to Victory* (London: Hutchinson, 1946).
J.H. Moulton, "31. British and German Scholarship" in *Papers for Wartime* (London: OUP, 1915).
H.C.G. Moule, *Christus Consolator: Words for hearts in trouble* (London: SPCK, 1915).
J.K. Mozley, *The Impassibility of God – A Survey of Christian Thought* (Cambridge: CUP, 1926).
J.E.B. Munson, *Echoes of the Great War: The Diary of the Reverend Andrew Clark 1914–1919* (Oxford: OUP, 1985).
T.A.M. Nash (ed.), *The Diary of an Unprofessional Soldier* (Chippenham: Picton, 1992).
A. Nason (ed.), *For Love and Courage: The Letters of Lieutenant Colonel E.W. Hermon from the Western Front 1914-1917* (London: Preface Publishing, 2009).
G. Neville (ed.), *The Diaries of Edward Lee Hicks, Bishop of Lincoln, 1910-1919* (Woodbridge: Lincoln Record Society, 1991).
J. Oxenham, *'All's Well' Some Helpful Verse for These Dark Days of War* (London: Methuen, 1915).
—— *The King's Highway* (London: Methuen, 1916).
—— *'All Clear!' A Book of Verse Commemorative of the Great Peace* (London: Methuen, 1919).
J. Paterson-Smyth, *God and The War*, (London: Hodder & Stoughton, 1916).
G. Phizackerley (ed.), *The Diaries of Maria Gyte of Sheldon, Derbyshire 1913-1920* (Cromford: Scarthin Books, 1999).
G. L. Prestige, *The Life of Charles Gore – A Great Englishman* (London: Heinemann, 1935).
S. Price (ed.), *If you're reading this . . . Last letters from the Front Line* (London: Frontline Books, 2011).
T.W. Pym and G. Gordon, *Papers from Picardy by Two Chaplains* (London: Constable, 1917).
H. Rashdall, *The Idea of Atonement in Christian Theology* (London: Macmillan, 1920).
E. Raymond, *The Story of My Days: An Autobiography 1888–1922* (London: Cassell, 1968).
J.L. Rees (ed.), *Sermons and Hymns by Timothy Rees* (London: Mowbray, 1946).
A.C. Robinson and P.E.H. Hair (eds.), R. J. Rider, *Reflections on the Battlefield – from infantryman to chaplain 1914–1919* (Liverpool: Liverpool University Press, 2001).
G.T. Rogers, "Reunion: Defeat or a New Offensive" in *The Modern Churchman*, vol. XXX1 (Dec. 1941), pp. 361-368.
S. Rogerson, *Twelve Days on the Somme: A memoir of the trenches, November 1916* (London: Greenhill Books, 2006).
C. Rolt, *The World's Redemption* (London: Longmans, Green & Co., 1913).
G. Roynon (ed.), *Home Fires Burning: The Great War Diaries of Georgina Lee* (Stroud: The History Press, 2006).
—— *Ypres Diary 1914–1915; The Memoirs of Sir Morgan Crofton* (Stroud: The History Press, 2010).

—— *War Diaries. A Chaplain at Gallipoli: The Great War Diaries of Kenneth Best* (London: Simon & Schuster, 2011).

S. Sassoon, *Counter Attack and Other Poems* (London: Heinemann, 1918).

W. Sellers, *With Our Fighting Men at the Front* (London: The Religious Tract Society, 1915).

G. Slater (ed.), *My Warrior Sons – The Borton Family Diary, 1914-18* (London: P. Davies, 1973).

H. Maynard Smith, *Frank, Bishop of Zanzibar* (London: SPCK, 1926).

G.V. Smith, *The Bishop of London's Visit to the Front* (London: Longmans, Green & Co., 1915).

The Southwell Diocesan Calendar, Clergy List and General Almanac, 1914 (Nottingham: Southwell Diocese, 1914).

F.C. Spurr, *Some Chaplains in Khaki* (London: Allenson, 1916).

G. Stephenson, *Edward Stuart Talbot, 1844–1934* (London: SPCK, 1936).

B.H. Streeter, "The Suffering of God", *The Hibbert Journal* (April 1914), pp. 603–11.

G.A. Studdert Kennedy, *The Hardest Part* (London: Hodder & Stoughton, 1918).

—— *Rough Rhymes of a Padre* (London: Hodder & Stoughton, 1918).

—— *More Rough Rhymes of a Padre* (London: Hodder & Stoughton, 1920).

—— *Peace Rhymes of a Padre* (London: Hodder & Stoughton, 1920).

—— *I Believe; Sermons on the Apostles' Creed* (London: Hodder & Stoughton, 1921).

—— *The Sorrows of God and Other Poems* (London: Hodder & Stoughton, 1921).

—— *The Best of Studdert Kennedy* 'edited by a friend', (London: Hodder & Stoughton, 1947).

T. Sykes, "The Brotherhood Movement" in D.P. Thompson and H.L. Simpson, *Modern Evangelistic Movements* (Glasgow: Thomson & Cowan, 1924).

E.S. Talbot, *The War and the Duty of the Church* (London: Macmillan, 1915).

H. Tennyson, *Alfred Lord Tennyson – A Memoir – By his son*, vol. ii. (London: Macmillan, 1897).

J. Terraine (ed.) *General Jack's Diary* (London: Eyre & Spottiswoode, 1964).

T. Tiplady, *The Cross at the Front* (London: Revell, 1917).

—— *The Soul of the Soldier* (London: Revell, 1918).

R. Van Emden (ed.) *Sapper Martin: The Secret Great War Diary of Jack Martin* (London: Bloomsbury, 2009).

E.C. Vaughan, *Some Desperate Glory; The World War One Diary of a British Officer* (London: F. Warne, 1981).

C.S. Wallis, *Fifty Thousand Miles on a Hospital Ship* (London: Religious Tract Society, 1917).

A.G. West, with introduction by N. Jones, *Diary of a Dead Officer, Being the Posthumous Papers of Arthur Graeme West* (London: Greenhill Books, 2007). First published with an introduction by C.E.M. Joad, (London: Allen & Unwin, 1919).

T.L.B. Westerdale, *Messages from Mars* (London: C.H. Kelly, 1917).

F. Weston, *The Christ and His Critics: An Open Letter to The European Missionaries of his Diocese* (London: Mowbray, 1919).

J.J. Willis et. al., *Towards a United Church 1913 1947* (London: Edinburgh House Press, 1947).

Published Secondary Sources

L. Adey, *Class and Idol in the English Hymn* (Vancouver: University of British Columbia Press, 1988).
M. Austin, *Almost Like a Dream – A Parish at War* (Whitchurch: Merton Priory Press, 1999).
—— *Under the Heavy Clouds: The Church of England in Derbyshire and Nottinghamshire 1911-15* (Whitchurch: Merton Priory Press, 2004).
—— *Like a Swift Hurricane* (Chesterfield: Merton Priory Press, 2014).
R.H. Bainton, *Christian Attitudes to War and Peace* (New York: Abingdon Press, 1960).
R. Baukham, "'Only the Suffering God can Help': Divine Passibility in Modern Theology", *Themelios*, vol. 9, no. 3 (1984), pp. 6–12.
R. Beaken, *The Church of England and the Home Front 1914-1918: Civilians, Soldiers and Religion in Wartime Colchester* (Woodbridge: Boydell & Brewer, 2015).
G.K.A. Bell, *Randall Davidson, Archbishop of Canterbury* (London: OUP, 1952).
S. Bell, "The Church of England and the First World War" in S. Parker and T. Lawson (eds), *God and War* (Farnham: Ashgate, 2012), pp. 33-59.
—— 'The Theology of Woodbine Willie in Context' in M. Snape and E. Madigan (eds.), *The Clergy in Khaki: British Army Chaplains in the First World War* (Farnham: Ashgate, 2013), pp. 95-110.
—— 'Malign or Maligned? – Arthur Winnington-Ingram, Bishop of London, in the First World War' in *Journal for the History of Modern Theology / Zeitschrift für Neuere Theologiegeschichte*, vol. 20, no. 1 (Nov. 2013), pp. 117-133.
—— 'Collapsing Class Barriers – another Myth of the Trenches?' in *Crucible: The Christian Journal of Social Ethics* (Apr-Jun 2014), pp. 35-42.
—— '"Soldiers of Christ arise": Religious Nationalism in the East Midlands during World War I', *Midland History*, vol. 39, no. 2 (Autumn, 2014), pp. 219-35.
—— 'From Collusion to Condemnation – the evolving voice of "Woodbine Willie"' in A.K. Smith and K. Cowman (eds), *Landscapes and Voices of the Great War* (London: Routledge, 2017), pp. 151-172.
C. Beresford, *The Bath at War* (Bakewell: Country Books / Ashridge Press, 2007).
B. Bond, *The Unquiet Western Front: Britain's Role in Literature and History* (Cambridge: Cambridge University Press, 2002).
M.W. Brierley, "Introducing the Early British Passibilists", *Journal for the History of Modern Theology*, vol. 8 (2001), pp. 218-33.
—— 'Ripon Hall, Henry Major and the Shaping of English Liberal Theology' in M.D. Chapman (ed.), *Ambassadors of Christ: Commemorating 150 Years of Theological Education in Cuddesdon 1854–2004* (Aldershot: Ashgate, 2004), pp. 89-155.
M. Brown, *The Imperial War Museum Book of 1918: Year of Victory* (London: Pan Books, 1999).

S. J. Brown, *Providence and Empire, 1815-1914* (Harlow: Routledge, 2008).
Bob Bushaway, "Name upon Name: The Great War and Remembrance", in R. Porter (ed.), *The Myths of the English* (Cambridge: Polity Press, 1992), pp. 136-67.
G. Byrne, *Modern Spiritualism and the Church of England, 1850–1939* (Woodbridge: Boydell Press, 2010).
S.C. Carpenter, *Winnington-Ingram: The biography of Arthur Foley Winnington-Ingram, Bishop of London* (London: Hodder & Stoughton, 1949).
O. Chadwick, *Hensley Henson: a study in the friction between Church and State* (Norwich: Canterbury Press, 1983).
M.D. Chapman (ed.) *Ambassadors of Christ: Commemorating 150 Years of Theological Education in Cuddesdon 1854–2004* (Aldershot: Ashgate, 2004).
A. Clark, *The Donkeys* (London: Hutchinson, 1961).
C. Clark, *The Sleepwalkers: How Europe went to War in 1914* (London: Penguin, 2013).
G. Corrigan, *Mud, Blood and Poppycock* (London: Cassell, 2004).
J. Cox, *The English Churches in a Secular Society: Lambeth, 1870–1930* (Oxford: OUP, 1982).
R. Currie, A. Gilbert and L. Horsley, *Churches and Church-goers: Patterns of Church Growth in the British Isles since 1700* (Oxford: OUP, 1977).
S. Dark, *Archbishop Davidson and the English Church* (London: Phillip Allan, 1929).
R. Davies et. al. (eds), *A History of the Methodist Church in Great Britain, vol. 3* (London: Epworth Press, 1983).
R. Davies, *'A Student in Arms': Donald Hankey and Edwardian Society at War* (Farnham: Ashgate, 2013).
R. Ellis, 'Geoffrey Studdert Kennedy: The Pastor and the Suffering God', *Transformation*, 22/3, (2005), p. 166-75.
G. R. Evans, *Edward Hicks – Pacifist Bishop at War* (Oxford: Lion Books, 2014).
P. Fiddes, *The Creative Suffering of God* (Oxford: Clarendon Press, 1988).
C. Field, '"The Faith Society"? Quantifying Religious Belonging in Edwardian Britain, 1901–1914' in *Journal of Religious History*, vol. 37, no. 1 (March 2013), pp. 39-63.
—— 'Gradualist or Revolutionary Secularization? A Case Study of Religious Belonging in Inter-War Britain, 1918-1939' in *Church History and Religious Culture 93* (2013), pp. 57-93.
—— 'Keeping the Spiritual Home Fires Burning: Religious Belonging in Britain during the First World War' in *War and Society*, vol. 33, no. 4 (October 2014), pp. 244-68.
P. Fiennes, *To War With God: The Army Chaplain who Lost his Faith,* (Edinburgh: Mainstream Publishing, 2011).
S. Foreman, *From Palace to Power: an illustrated history of Whitehall* (Brighton: The Alpha Press, 1995).
D. Forrester, *Beliefs, Values and Policies: Conviction Politics in a Secular Age* (Oxford: Clarendon Press, 1989).

—— 'The Scope of Public Theology' in *Studies in Christian Ethics*, vol. 17, no. 5, 2004, pp. 5-19.

—— *Apocalypse Now: Reflections on Faith in a Time of Terror* (Farnham: Ashgate, 2005).

P. Fussell, *The Great War and Modern Memory* (London: OUP, 1975).

A. Gregory, *The Silence of Memory: Armistice Day 1919-1946* (London: Berg, 1994).

—— *The Last Great War: British Society and the First World War* (Cambridge: Cambridge University Press, 2008).

M. Grimley, 'The Church and the Bomb: Anglicans and the Campaign for Nuclear Disarmament, c. 1958–1984' in S. Parker and T. Lawson (eds.), *God and War* (Farnham: Ashgate, 2012), pp. 147-164.

A. Hastings, *A History of English Christianity, 1920-1985* (London: Fount, 1986).

J. Hayward, *Myths and Legends of the First World War* (Stroud: The History Press, 2010).

J. Hazelgrove, 'Spiritualism after the Great War' in *Twentieth Century British History*, vol. 10, no. 4 (London, 1999), pp. 404-430.

B. Hebblethwaite, *The Incarnation: Collected Essays in Christology* (Cambridge: Cambridge University Press, 1987).

R. Holman, *Woodbine Willie: An Unsung Hero of World War One* (Oxford: Lion Books, 2013).

F. House, 'The Barrier of Impassibility', *Theology*, 83 (1980), pp. 409–15.

P. Howson, *Muddling Through – The Organisation of British Army Chaplaincy in World War 1* (Solihull: Helion, 2013).

J. Hull, 'School Worship (England and Wales)' in Paul Bradshaw (ed.), *New SCM Dictionary of Liturgy and Worship* (London: SCM Press, 2002).

T. Johnstone and J. Hagerty, *The Cross on the Sword: Catholic Chaplains in The Forces* (London: Geoffrey Chapman, 1996).

T. Kennedy, *British Quakerism, 1860–1920* (London: OUP, 2001).

S. Koss, *Nonconformity in Modern British Politics* (London: Batsford, 1975).

P. Lee, 'Military Intervention in the Cold War Era' in S. Parker and T. Lawson (eds.), *God and War* (Farnham: Ashgate, 2012), pp. 187-205.

R. Lloyd, *The Church of England 1900-1965* (London: SCM Press, 1966).

D. Love, *Scottish Covenanter Stories: Tales from the Killing Times* (Glasgow: Neil Wilson, 2013).

R.H. MacDonald, *The Language of Empire: Myths and Metaphors of Popular Imperialism, 1880-1918* (Manchester: Manchester University Press, 1994).

E. Madigan, 'Hidden Courage: Post-War Literature and Anglican Army Chaplains on the Western Front', in H. Jones, J. O'Brien and C. Schmidt-Supprian (eds), *Untold War – New Perspectives in First World War Studies* (Leiden: Brill, 2008), pp. 63-94.

—— *Faith Under Fire: Anglican Chaplains and the Great War* (Basingstoke: Palgrave Macmillan, 2011).

B. Manning, *Essays in Orthodox Dissent* (London: Independent Press, 1939).

A. Marrin, *The Last Crusade: The Church of England in the First World War* (Durham, NC: Duke University Press, 1974).
M. Middlebrook, *First Day on the Somme, 1 July 1916* (London: Penguin Books, 1984).
J. Moltmann, *The Crucified God,* (London: SCM Press, 1974).
—— *The Trinity and the Kingdom of God* (London: SCM Press, 1981).
C. Moore-Bick, *Playing the Game: The British Junior Infantry Officer on the Western Front 1914-18* (Solihull: Helion, 2011).
E. Morris and E. Roberts, *Public Sculpture of Cheshire and Merseyside (excluding Liverpool)* (Liverpool: Liverpool University Press, 2012).
J.K. Mozley, (ed.), *G.A. Studdert Kennedy by his Friends* (London: Hodder & Stoughton, 1929).
J.K. Mozley, *Some Tendencies in British Theology from the Publication of Lux Mundi to the Present Day* (London: SPCK, 1952).
J. Munsey Turner, "Methodism in England 1900-1932" in R. Davies et. al. (eds), *A History of the Methodist Church in Great Britain, vol. 3* (London: Epworth Press, 1983), pp. 309–361.
J.E.B. Munson, "The Oxford Movement by the End of the Nineteenth Century: The Anglo-Catholic Clergy", *Church History,* vol. 44, no. 3 (Sept. 1975), pp. 382-395.
S. Neill, *A History of Christian Missions (revised edition)* (Harmondsworth: Penguin Books, 1986).
S. Orwell and I. Angus (eds.), *Essays, Journalism and Letters of George Orwell, Vol II, 1940-43* (London: Harcourt, 1993).
M. Osborne and S. Kingsley Kent, *Africans and Britons in the Age of Empires, 1660–1980* (Abingdon: Routledge, 2015).
L. Parker, *Shellshocked Prophets: Former Anglican Army Chaplains in Inter-War Britain* (Solihull: Helion, 2015).
P. Parker, *The Old Lie – The Great War and the Public School Ethos* (London: Bloomsbury, 1987).
C. Pennell, *A Kingdom United* (London: OUP, 2012).
A.W. Porter, *Religion versus Empire? British Protestant missionaries and overseas expansion, 1700-1914* (Manchester: Manchester University Press, 2004).
W. Purcell, *Woodbine Willie: a study of the life of Geoffrey Studdert Kennedy* (London: Mowbray, 1982, first published in 1962.)
J. Rae, *Conscience and politics: the British government and the conscientious objector to military service, 1916-1919* (London: OUP, 1970).
C. Royle, *Opened Doors* (London: Meat Trades' Journal Co., 1949).
R. Runcie, "The God of Battles and the Fight for Faith" in M. Gilbert (ed.), *The Straits of War: Gallipoli Remembered* (Stroud: The History Press, 2000), pp. 37-48.
R. Schweitzer, "The Cross and the Trenches: Religious Faith and Doubt Among Some British Soldiers on the Western Front", *War and Society,* vol. 16, no. 2 (October 1998), pp. 33-57.
—— *The Cross and the Trenches: Religious Faith and Doubt Among British and American Great War Soldiers* (Westport: Praeger, 2003).

R. Skirth and D. Barrett (ed.), *The Reluctant Tommy* (London: Pan Books, 2010).

M. F. Snape, *God and the British Soldier: Religion and the British Army in the First and Second World Wars* (Oxford: Routledge, 2005).

—— (ed.), *The Back Parts of War: The YMCA Memoirs and Letters of Barclay Baron, 1915-1919* (Woodbridge: Boydell Press, 2009).

—— "Civilians, Soldiers and Perceptions of the Afterlife in Britain during the First World War" in P. Clarke and T. Claydon (eds), *The Church, the Afterlife and the Fate of the Soul* in *Studies in Church History*, 45 (Woodbridge: Ecclesiastical History Society, 2009), pp. 371-403.

—— "Church of England Army Chaplains in the First World War: Goodbye to 'Goodbye to All That'", *Journal of Ecclesiastical History*, vol. 62, no. 2, (April 2011), pp. 318-45.

M.F. Snape and S.G. Parker, 'Keeping faith and coping: belief, popular religiosity and the British people' in P. Liddle and J. Bourne (eds), *The Great World War, 1914–45: Volume 2* (London: Collins, 2001), pp. 397–420.

M. Snape and E. Madigan (eds), *The Clergy in Khaki: New Perspectives on British Army Chaplaincy in the First World War* (Farnham: Ashgate, 2013).

M. Stephen, *The Price of Pity* (London: Pen and Sword Books, 1996).

K. Taylor and T. Brown, *A Derbyshire Parish at War* (Bakewell: Country Books, 2000).

W. Temple, *Life of Bishop Percival* (London: Macmillan, 1921).

D. Todman, *The Great War: Myth and Memory* (London: Continuum, 2005).

J.W. Tuffley, *Grain from Galilee* (London: Headley, 1935).

A. Turberfield, *John Scott Lidgett – Archbishop of British Methodism* (Peterborough: Epworth Press, 2003).

G.S. Wakefield, "God and Some English Poets: 9. Twentieth-Century Trends" in *Expository Times*, vol. 106, no. 5 (February 1995), pp. 138-42.

A. Watson and P. Porter, "Bereaved and aggrieved: combat motivation and the ideology of sacrifice in the First World War", *Historical Research*, vol. 83, no. 219 (February 2010), pp. 146-64.

R. Watson and K. Trickett (eds), *Companion to Hymns and Psalms* (Peterborough: Epworth Press, 1988).

T. Weinandy, *Does God Suffer?* (Notre Dame IN: University of Notre Dame Press, 2000).

A. Wilkinson, *The Church of England and the First World War* (London: SCM, 1978).

—— *Dissent or Conform? War, Peace and the English Churches, 1900–1945* (London: SCM, 1986).

S.C. Williams, *Religious Belief and Popular Culture in Southwark c.1880–1939* (Oxford: Clarendon Press, 1999).

C. Williamson, 'The Church of England and the Falklands War' in S. Parker and T. Lawson (eds), *God and War* (Farnham: Ashgate, 2012), pp. 165-186.

T.C. Worsley, *Flannelled Fool* (London: Hogarth Press, 1985)

Secondary on-line sources

Biographical information regarding the Revd. Samuel Parkes: http://www.dawley-heritage.co.uk/unpublished-articles/111/samuel-parkes-bio, retrieved 8 March 2015.

Information about the Westminster Dragoons: http://www.westminsterdragoons.co.uk/Westminster_Dragoons/Library.html, retrieved 19 May 2015.

www.britishnewspaperarchive.co.uk

D. Snow, 'Remembrance Sunday should not be dominated by religion' in *The Guardian* (on-line edition), 6 November 2014, http://www.theguardian.com/commentisfree/2014/nov/06/remembrance-sunday-lack-of-secular-presence retrieved 24 March 2015.

Radio programmes

God and the Great War, Radio 3, first broadcast 9 November 2014, 18:45. Recording available at http://www.bbc.co.uk/programmes/b04nql0m, retrieved 11 January 2016.

Beyond Belief: Battle of the Somme, Radio 4, first broadcast 27 June 2016, 16:30. Recording available at http://www.bbc.co.uk/programmes/b07h6n1q, retrieved 2 August 2016.

Theses

S. Mews, Religion and English Society in the First World War, unpublished Ph.D. thesis, University of Cambridge, 1973.

C. Winter, Pathways to Passibility: The Emergence of the 'Suffering God' in Twentieth Century Theology, unpublished M.C.S. thesis, Regent College Vancouver, 2005.

INDEX OF PEOPLE

INDEX OF PLACES

INDEX OF GENERAL & MISCELLANEOUS TERMS